REAL-WORLD CORPORATE GOVERNANCE

A Programme for Profit-Enhancing Stewardship

NIGEL KENDALL
and
ARTHUR KENDALL

London · Hong Kong · Johannesburg
Melbourne · Singapore · Washington DC

PITMAN PUBLISHING
128 Long Acre, London WC2E 9AN
Tel: +44 (0)171 447 2000
Fax: +44 (0)171 240 5771

A Division of Pearson Professional Limited

First published in Great Britain in 1998

© Pearson Professional Limited 1998

The right of Nigel Kendall and Arthur Kendall to be identified
as authors of this work has been asserted by them in accordance
with the Copyright, Design and Patents Act 1988.

ISBN 0 273 62826 7

British Library Cataloguing in Publication Data
A CIP catalogue record for this book can be obtained from
the British Library.

All rights reserved; no part of this publication may be reproduced,
stored in a retrieval system, or transmitted in any form or by any means,
electronic, mechanical, photocopying, recording, or otherwise without either
the prior written permission of the Publishers or a licence permitting restricted
copying in the United Kingdom issued by the Copyright Licensing Agency Ltd,
90 Tottenham Court Road, London W1P 9HE. This book may not be lent,
resold, hired out or otherwise disposed of by way of trade in any form
of binding or cover other than that in which it is published,
without the prior consent of the Publishers.

1 3 5 7 9 10 8 6 4 2

Typeset by Northern Phototypesetting Co Ltd, Bolton
Printed and bound in Great Britain by
Biddles Ltd, Guildford and King's Lynn

*The Publishers' policy is to use paper manufactured
from sustainable forests.*

ABOUT THE AUTHORS

Nigel Kendall is a Chartered Accountant, who trained with Peat Marwick Mitchell (KPMG). He has a wide-ranging career history including: a sales executive with IBM, Group Chief Accountant of SGB Group, the finance director of a venture capital organisation, plus 14 years with PA Consulting Group, finishing as a director of the Strategy Practice.

In 1991, he and colleagues established their own management consultancy, Knightsbridge Consulting Group. Out of this Nigel and a colleague formed Kenski Partners, which has specialised in recent years in advising the boards of fast growing businesses and organisations facing major change.

Their particular emphasis is on building value and advising companies contemplating trade sale or flotation. He regularly works with boards of companies on corporate governance issues and good boardroom practice. His experience covers a wide range of companies from very large to small-medium sized companies, including working with the boards of BP Chemicals, Agip Coal, United Friendly, CRS, Wolff Olins and Whittard of Chelsea.

With his wide spectrum of knowledge, Nigel is well placed as an authority on various issues and has published books on international financial management, corporate governance and non-executive directorship.

Arthur Kendall has lived in France and Spain. He is very much of the new European generation speaking six languages. He runs his own company, Tangley International, providing a personally crafted service for language and culture courses.

He played a major role in setting up a local newspaper, subsequently contributing regular features as deputy editor, including overseas articles during a spell as foreign correspondent.

His recent business experience has involved him in corporate strategy studies, business appraisals and market research.

CONTENTS

Preface	ix
Foreword by Richard Balding, Vice Chairman, United Assurance Group plc	xi
Foreword by Harry Moore, Chief Executive, Co-operative Retail Services Ltd	xiii
Acknowledgements	xiv
Introduction	xv

Part A
THE TRUTH ABOUT CORPORATE GOVERNANCE

1 Why do we have to take corporate governance seriously?   3
- The issue of integrity   5
- Topicality   6
- Lack of directors' training   9
- Review   10

2 What is corporate governance?   13
- Introduction   15
- Historical background   15
- Recent questions   16
- Definitions   18
- Development of corporate governance as an issue   21
- Duties in UK law   26
- What is good corporate governance and why?   29
- Conclusion   31

3 Corporate Governance is in the eye of the stakeholder   33
- Introduction   35
- Shareholders/investors   35
- Employees   39
- Customers   42
- Suppliers/trading partners   43
- Community and environment   45
- The State   47
- Conclusion   48

CONTENTS

4 Different countries, different models — 49
- Introduction — 51
- UK — 51
- Germany — 52
- France — 56
- Japan — 59
- The US — 61
- The European Union — 63
- Conclusion — 65

5 Impact of size — 69
- Introduction — 71
- The five stages of growth — 71
- Corporate governance and the smaller company — 74
- Conclusion — 82

6 Another type of organisation – the UK co-operative — 83
- Introduction — 85
- History of the UK co-operative movement — 85
- Corporate governance and the Co-op — 92
- How the co-operative movement works today — 95
- Conclusion — 96

7 Key people — 99
- Introduction — 101
- Chairman — 102
- Executives — 103
- Non-executive directors — 106
- Conclusion — 108

8 Future influences — 111
- Introduction — 113
- Parliament/DTI — 113
- Stock Exchange — 114
- Corporate sector pressure groups — 116
- The Green movement — 117
- Co-operatives and mutuals — 119

Part B
HOW TO PRACTISE GOOD CORPORATE GOVERNANCE

9 A new approach to corporate governance   123
The Five Golden Rules
Introduction   125
Corporate cultures and vision   125
Principles of good corporate governance   127
Five Golden Rules   128
Good corporate governance is good management   129
Corporate governance and the strategic management process   131
The whole picture   132

10 A question of ethics   137
Rule 1: The ethical approach

11 Towards a common goal   145
Rule 2: Congruence of goals
The right goals   147
Checking the goal   149

12 The whole picture   155
Rule 3: Corporate governance as an integral part of the strategy process
Internal analysis   159
External analysis   171
Stakeholder analysis   180
Confirm or change goal   191
Formulating strategy   195
Implementation   202

13 Shaping up   211
Rule 4: Organising to deliver good corporate governance
Principles of organisation   214
The board and corporate governance   215
Brief for the board   215
Board structure   217
Appointment and removal of directors   221
Induction and training   223
Board effectiveness   224
Accountability   224

14	**'It's good to talk'**	227
	Rule 5: Accountability and reporting to deliver good corporate governance	
	Customers	232
	Owners	235
	Employees	238
	Suppliers and trading partners	240
	Community	242
15	**What does business think?**	245
	Introduction	247
	Responses to Hampel	247
	The popular view	248
	Usefulness of the non-executive director	251
	Corporate governance at its best	252
	Conclusion	253

Part C
CORPORATE GOVERNANCE IN PRACTICE

16	**A large insurer**	257
	History of the company	259
	Current goals	262
	Stakeholder analysis	262
	Conclusions regarding corporate governance	272
17	**A smaller, fast-growth company**	275
	History of the company	277
	Current goals	278
	Stakeholder analysis	279
	Conclusions regarding corporate governance	282
	Appendix A: A Stakeholder Model – measuring stakeholder views	285
	Appendix B: Extract from Preliminary Report from the Committee on Corporate Governance (the Hampel Committee)	296
	Index	301

PREFACE

'No one pretends that democracy is perfect or all-wise. Indeed it has been said that democracy is the worst form of government except all those other forms that have been tried from time to time.'

WINSTON CHURCHILL to the House of Commons

This new approach to the issue of corporate governance reflects two needs: one, a fresh look at an issue which has, in the opinion of the authors, become caught up in itself as a topic of debate and second, the need for a practical guide for those who are responsible for implementing the increasingly prolific guidelines, and help in solving the problems that exist in defining the director's role. As Sir John Harvey-Jones, one-time chief executive of ICI, said:

> Management consultants are there for every conceivable part of the manager's job. But you try getting advice, guidance, a course, or a specialist book on the skills of being a good director of a company and you will find almost nothing except a great deal of mystique.[1]

The reason for this is, of course, that different people have different beliefs and there is no one right answer, given that each of the world's strongest economies has a different model. The authors, therefore, do not claim to be God's Gift to directors, or Provider of All Unanswered Questions (though we hope to answer a few!), nor do we favour one model over another. After all, each model has its proven flaws. Most people would agree, however, that in the perfect world, everybody would share in the rights as well as the responsibilities of business. And there are already a number of generally agreed principles on what is good practice and *seen* to be good practice.

What is more vague, and what the authors hope to clarify in this volume, is how to reach these goals of best practice, and more than that, *why* we need to reach them, and what consequences – and benefits – there will be of actions taken to reach them.

The result is a step-by-step guide on what needs to be done and how, including explanations and consequences of each action, in plain, easy to read English. It starts by redefining corporate governance somewhat, as we believe that it has become too much of an issue in itself (as outlined above). The endless volumes which continue to pour fourth from the rich pool of 'expertise' is proof of this, and the danger is that people are becoming – or already have become – obsessed with corporate governance *per se*, when really they should be looking at the macro impact on business and performance. As interested parties, we are, after all, after the same thing – the health and prosperity of the company.

[1] Quoted in *Corporate Governance*, by Robert Monks and Nell Minow, Blackwell Business, 1995

FOREWORD

RICHARD BALDING
Vice Chairman, United Assurance Group plc

This topical book makes a fresh and original contribution to the corporate governance debate which concerns all those who are responsible for the running of a company.

The concept developed by the authors is that, by definition, success in business flows from the operation of good corporate governance, which in itself requires not only a healthy measure of business acumen but also an ethical approach to the task. There are a number of companies which are household names and have achieved widespread public recognition because they exemplify these twin virtues.

As businesses grow and become larger, their earlier formative influences, which were instrumental in their success, become less pervasive. In this book, the authors expand on previous work to propose a powerful methodology which builds an ethical approach into the heart of corporate strategy development. They describe a way of ensuring that as businesses grow larger and more impersonal, the benign philosophy of the founding fathers which once imbued the organisation, is replaced by a systematic approach to the way the company behaves. This approach ensures that the valid interest, concerns and welfare of all those who have a stake in the business are taken into account.

The authors have flattered me by including a case study of the company of which I was Chief Executive for ten years. I am not sure we really deserve to be held out as a model, but I do like to think that, at our best, we exemplified some of the characteristics of a well run family business, even as we grew in size. Indeed our staff – and sometimes too our suppliers and advisers – frequently said that "It felt like being part of a family," implying, I think, a degree of mutual trust and common purpose. I am sure this contributed to the fact that we were so often rewarded with dedication which exceeded by far anything we had a right to expect.

We are at a stage in the development of ideas where the free enterprise system increasingly is seen by the majority of people in democratic countries as the best way forward. And yet, the same people have a growing worry about globalisation and the use of power in business by "faceless executives" for purposes which may seem to promote their own interests. The general good often requires commercial decisions to be taken that will sometimes have unpalatable effects on individual lives. Acceptance of change will be much more easily obtained if those who must take such decisions are seen to include proper consideration for all those that are affected.

It is always the task of leadership to demonstrate those particular qualities of integrity and commitment which will win the hearts and minds of those involved in an enterprise and encourage them to give of their best. The approach to corporate governance promoted in this book will greatly assist in that process.

FOREWORD

HARRY MOORE
Chief Executive, Co-operative Retail Services Ltd

If timing is everything, then this book has everything, but that should be no surprise considering that this is a book about corporate governance and, to use the authors' own words, 'We believe therefore that, for all the endless discussions and academic theories about corporate governance, in reality there is nothing new or radical in it and it really boils down to good sound business management.' This is indeed a book about good sound business management, written in a good sound business sense, and good sound business sense will always be topical. Whilst there may well be 'nothing new under the sun', the authors examine exhaustively the whole subject of corporate governance in a way that is always practical and eminently readable.

Chapter 6 of this book deals with the United Kingdom Co-operative Movement, in which I have worked for the last quarter of a century or so. At the end of Chapter 6, the authors ask, 'Are the [Co-operative] Societies fighting the right battle?' They may be relieved to know that the writer of this foreword believes the Movement is, perhaps belatedly, beginning to fight the right battle and in a way which gives it a good chance of success.

The lessons on corporate governance learned from a careful reading of this book will assist enormously in fighting that particular good fight.

ACKNOWLEDGEMENTS

The authors would like to thank all those who contributed to their thinking in producing this book, though of course the thoughts expressed and the judgements are entirely their own.

Among those who kindly gave of their opinions and experience we would like to pay particular tribute to Harry Moore and Peter Rowbotham and their colleagues at CRS, especially our friend David Boardman; Richard Balding and George Mack and their colleagues at United Friendly, and Eddie Marchbanks at Photobition. Among a long list of others who have most helpfully given of their time we would particularly thank Richard Bagley, late of the IOD and now Secretary and Clerk to the Commonwealth Development Corporation, David Saltmarsh, Secretary of Reckitt and Colman, Michael Hart, formerly Chairman of Foreign and Colonial Management, Nick Fox Director of Equitable Life, George Bain, Principal, London Business School, Lloyd Wilkinson, Chief Executive and General Secretary, the Co-operative Union, Clive Lewis, Head of the business bureau at the Board for Chartered Accountants in Business, and Dawn Hands and her colleagues at bmg research – and we extend our grateful thanks to the many others too numerous to list by name here who have contributed to our thinking and experience.

We also thank our friends at Pitman, especially Richard Stagg, Amelia Lakin and Linda Dhondy for their help, advice and encouragement.

Finally, our thanks to Sandy, precious wife and mother, for putting up with nearly 18 months of debate about a topic far removed from her artistic interests, and inputting regular dashes of common sense into arcane discussions.

INTRODUCTION

Corporate governance, it seems, is suffering from the same syndrome as marketing did in the '50s and '60s (some would argue it still is in the '90s). No one in the real world can agree exactly what it means, or how, if at all, it should be incorporated into a company's strategy.

Different people have different definitions of it, some more practical than others. Certainly, everyone knows about Cadbury and Greenbury, and knows that as a result they have to give away more information than they used to – supposedly for the benefit of shareholders and society. But ask more detailed and searching questions about what purpose it serves, what the goals of corporate governance should be and what they are doing specifically towards reaching these goals, and the answers will be less defined and will vary widely from individual to individual, as will the very response to corporate governance.

> **No one in the real world can agree exactly what corporate governance means**

Some people think of it as a new and important concept which aims to assure shareholders that their money is in safe hands. Others think of it more as another name for *organisation* – in other words good corporate governance is already, or should already be, practised in a well run corporation – a few in this group take the view, therefore, that it should not be given so much importance. As the chairman of a leading merchant bank said, 'A board is either competent or not'.[1]

> **Corporate governance is both a new effort to ensure accountability and responsibility and a set of principles**

All these views are valid in some way. Many companies have always made an effort to be socially responsible, allocating resources (both capital and human) to assure that, as far as possible, all interested parties are satisfied. What is also true is that it is only fairly recently, due to extreme and well-publicised cases of large-scale abuse of power, that it has become a matter of widespread public concern and debate. The truth is therefore somewhere in the middle. Corporate governance is both a new effort to ensure accountability and responsibility and a set of principles which should be incorporated into every part of the organisation, whether it be relations with suppliers, capital investment or decisions affecting the environment or the community.

INTRODUCTION

Like marketing, it is not just a concept, but (should be) a function. Marketing was born of a reaction to the era of product-orientation, and is the concept of putting the consumer first – it should not, therefore, be separated from the rest of the company as the sales department used to be. But at the same time, it is clearly a function in that it is the mechanism which physically puts you in touch with the consumers of your products.

We can apply the same theory to corporate governance. We have established that in principle it is a good thing – and one that will not go away – which aims to make companies responsible and accountable. But this is not sufficient. While it appears to take in every facet of the complex world of business, it is still largely one-dimensional and theoretical. And what much discussion on the subject, at least in the public domain still fails to accept that it is only looking at responsibility on the part of the *company*. The generally accepted position still seems to be that it is the *company* which should be wholly responsible for all the actions it takes, and it is the shareholders who are always the victims. What is also true is that many (all-too-often inaccurate) assumptions are made about the views held by each of the interested parties.

> What is therefore needed is a *practical* approach to corporate governance

What is therefore needed is a *practical* approach to corporate governance, and one that brings us closer to all interested parties, just as marketing brings us closer to our customers. In taking this approach, we need to take into account, among other things, two fundamental principles:

- the need to look from all points of view in all directions – asking each party interested in the fortunes of the company what it thinks and wants from the company;
- the need to involve the other parties, especially the three key groups: customers, shareholders, and staff, in the formulation and implementation of the company's strategy.

In the following chapters we have set out our approach to corporate governance, following these principles. It is not merely theoretical, but has been used by the authors in their work with clients to achieve an improvement in the standard of corporate governance, closer and better relations between all the interested parties, and a congruence of expectations and goals between the stakeholders, as we shall often refer to them.

The book is divided into four parts:

- Part A: a background to the debate on corporate governance

- Part B: a methodology for implementing a regime of good corporate governance, which we have called the 'Five Golden Rules of Good Corporate Governance'
- Part C: in which we give two case studies to illustrate our views on corporate governance in action, one large company and one smaller but rapidly growing
- Appendices: in which we include a stakeholder model which has been designed to open and maintain proper channels of communication with the key stakeholding groups, and thus create better relations with them.

The book has been designed to encourage the adoption of good corporate governance as a natural part of corporate management, and to discourage its further development as a specialist area, providing fees for accountants, lawyers and lobby groups. To this end, we have given enough of a general background for those not familiar with the subject of corporate governance, and with insufficient time to read the growing wealth of academic writings on the subject, to become acquainted with the issues. More critically, we have then set out a methodology for incorporating the whole subject into general management theory and practice.

> **The book has been designed to encourage the adoption of good corporate governance as a natural part of corporate management**

The approach sets out to incorporate the aims behind both Cadbury and Greenbury, and the Hampel Committee, which at the time of writing has published only a preliminary report, and to get away from the lip-service approach to corporate governance exemplified by strictly-regulated box-ticking.

[1] Quoted from a survey conducted by the authors; see Chapter 15

Part A

THE TRUTH ABOUT CORPORATE GOVERNANCE

The empty debate versus the serious reality

Chapter 1

WHY DO WE HAVE TO TAKE CORPORATE GOVERNANCE SERIOUSLY?

The issue of integrity 5

Topicality 6

Lack of directors' training 9

Review 10

'I'm a strong believer in the free enterprise system. The way we're trying to do it is the capitalist system on the moral high ground. If a warehouseman can retire and buy his cottage or put his kids through higher education, that's what we're trying to do.'

JOHN NEILL,
Chief Executive of Unipart[1]

This first section of this book sets out to put the subject of corporate governance in perspective, and the above quotation shows why, despite concerns about bureaucracy getting in the way of enterprise, it deserves to be treated seriously. It should not be seen simply as a counterproductive interference with the proper exercise of good management but rather as an integral part of good management.

The issue of integrity

The underlying conduct of business has probably been improving steadily if gently for the past 50 years, but with a generally wider level of education, particularly at the highest, tertiary level of education, there is a greater awareness of the existence and importance of business. Hence not only is the remuneration of top businesspeople now a newsworthy topic, but even more so is their conduct.

The fundamental issue to be addressed, therefore, is whether the boards of companies, both large and small, and through them the managements of these organisations, are carrying out their duties in a manner which is in the mainstream of what society as a whole would consider ethical and proper behaviour.

In these days of moral relativism, it is very important that the directors recognise that the general public has its own broad view on these issues, and if the directors depart too far from that view they will invite trouble, no matter how much they may feel that they are in the mainstream of their own industry culture. This trouble will be expressed through exposure in the popular and serious press with potentially severe short-term consequences for the organisation concerned. More dangerously for commerce and industry as a whole, behaviour by senior figures which is seen, however unfairly, by the general public as unacceptable, will increase the longer term threat of extended regulation and control to remedy supposed flaws in the free market economy.

There is little difference between the various political parties in most of the advanced economies in terms of their approach to what are seen as business ethics, since the current attraction of populist approaches leaves little room for the advocates of big business, large organisations, and the highly paid individuals who run them to explain calmly and rationally why they behave the way they do.

Perception is in the eye of the beholder, and corporate governance, while a technical term to accountants, lawyers and the like, is known by the readers of the popular newspapers by names such as honesty, decency, fairness. Similarly, what the professional would call questionable practice in this arena is criticised by the general public using words such as 'rip-off', 'cheating' and 'crooked'.

The central issue today, therefore, in the field of corporate governance is not whether most listed companies comply with the various provisions of the Cadbury Code and its successors. The key point is whether the top management of large organisations especially, but actually of that of business in general, is seen as possessed of integrity in the eyes of the general public. This is the spirit that gave support to the principle of setting up the Cadbury Committee, not simply a desire to lay down some rules on the financial aspects of corporate governance to prevent innocent fund managers being misled by greedy directors.

Topicality

The introduction of the new concept of privatisation by the Conservative Government in the UK in the 1980s gave rise to the opportunity for rapid, and in some cases substantial financial gains by various parts of the community. These were in some cases clearly undeserved and in other cases plainly unfair to other parts of the community, and focused attention on the way in which some large organisations were being run.

Example

The award of large increases in salaries and granting of share options to the management of the utilities were seen as unfair by a general public which perceived the management to be, by and large, the same people as before privatisation, with the same jobs. The fact that the jobs had changed and were arguably more demanding was not seen as an adequate reason for their remuneration to be raised by a multiple, and for many of them to be given the opportunity to become millionaires. No effective action was ever taken to remedy these supposed injustices, though New Labour's idea of retribution, to inflict a windfall tax many years later, can be seen in Christopher Booker's words about the growth of regulation generally, as 'using a sledgehammer to miss the nut'.

This coincided with the occurrence of several substantial business frauds or other forms of scandalous business behaviour, of the type which happen at regular intervals, and have done since the early days of modern industrial and commercial history.

Example

In the Guinness affair the management of a leading brewer was found to have organised an operation covertly to support the price of its shares while attempting a major takeover of an industry competitor, with the full knowledge and involvement of its merchant bank. This was recognised to have gone well beyond the bounds of acceptable behaviour. In this case, unlike with the utilities, heads did roll, though arguably the Bank of England was more effective than the Department of Trade and Industry in effecting punishment of those for whom it was responsible.

In recent times, however, the media publicity which these events occasion, and the view of elected Members of Parliament that they must be seen to be doing something, gave rise to a new focus on what became popularly known as corporate governance, though this term has been in use for several decades, and much legislation has been passed over the years which would rank as addressing deemed failures of corporate governance, though not described in these terms.

Example

A major and far-reaching piece of legislation aimed at protecting the consumer was the Financial Services Act of 1986 – not generally thought of as addressing corporate governance. Undoubtedly though, this Act was framed to attack the failings in ethical management which caused unsuitable financial products to be sold to insufficiently informed and supposedly defenceless members of the public. Pre-dating Cadbury by several years, this particular Act has had far-reaching consequences with huge attendant costs, which, of course, have been borne ultimately by the consumer.

If it was expected by MPs in the 1980s that the extra public attention on these matters would cure the perceived problems identified in this field, this has not appeared to be the outcome in practice. Indeed, there are perhaps parallels with the way in which Nye Bevan predicted in the 1950s that the introduction of a free National Health Service in the UK would give rise to an initial cost, but that this would fall away to nearly zero as the nation became healthier, whereas in practice the cost has grown steadily ever since to its current level approaching 10 per cent of government expenditure. Similarly, the introduction of rules and regulations specifically focused on the subject of corporate governance has led to demands for more and more intervention by those who have taken a particular interest in the subject and express their views regularly and very publicly on the supposed rights and wrongs of corporate behaviour. We can observe the growth of more and more rules and guidance on the subject, with a marked lack of focus on the relationship between cost and benefit.

However, the facts of life are that we are where we are now, and for the foreseeable future corporate governance is going to be a topic of interest to the media and their readers and viewers, at least in terms of populist attacks on perceived fat cats and excessive remuneration. These perceived excesses will be played against the minimal pay increases which they have granted to worthy junior staff, and their use of brutal reorganisations following takeovers, coupled with uncaring redundancies for armies of breadwinners in disadvantaged regions who will therefore never be able to work again, with all the knock-on effect on those who depend on the existence of a big local employer in these deprived areas.

The unions may not have the power they once had to make life difficult for management, but the press may become an equally significant constraint on tough but rational decision-making.

Example

The attempt by Richard Giordano as chairman of British Gas to give a rational remuneration package to his chief executive Cedric Brown gave insufficient consideration to the public impact of what was seen as a massive increase in pay. Coming so soon after the recession which had cost so many jobs, this move caused attention to be focused on the perceived deficiencies in British Gas's operational performance, which were played against the pay of its top management. The media assault did lasting damage to British Gas's reputation, together with that of its previously highly regarded chairman, and apparently led to Brown's early retirement.

Lack of directors' training

A corollary to the focus on corporate behaviour and the behaviour of senior corporate employees is the attention increasingly being paid to the qualification of these senior people to carry out their responsibilities. There has never been any formal qualification required to run an organisation, and none to be a director. In practice, of course, most large and well run organisations will look for suitable professional qualifications in their senior staff, and the organisation PRONED was created in the 1980s with the intention of providing a pool of suitable experienced people from which quoted companies could reliably select non-executive directors. However, the specific role of direction has not to date been regarded as a profession or even a discipline.

We can perhaps summarise the position as follows:

- the role of director has been legally defined in the Companies Acts, but ...
- ... though there has been much attention paid over the years to what is properly the concern of a director, and what is generally accepted to be proper behaviour and where the bounds of ethical practice should be drawn, there has been no generally agreed syllabus or qualification which can be tackled by aspiring directors
- hence there is no professional certificate of training and achievement which can be sought by those who wish to appoint such people.

An attempt is being made to address this specifically by the Institute of Directors through its director training programme, which appears to be attracting a good take up of directors who wish to broaden their knowledge and experience of good directorial practice. This programme provides the opportunity to earn a Diploma in Corporate Direction, and a link-up with a business school has been designed to integrate parts of this programme into the MBA course.

In the particular area of what is generally perceived as corporate governance, there is a clear and growing need for directors to be aware of:

- their statutory and regulatory obligations
- their ethical obligations
- what constitutes good operational practice.

This need will not go away in the foreseeable future, and arguably should never go away, since it is part of the requirements of good managerial practice and not simply an esoteric niche in the framework of regulations covering the running of limited companies. This is perhaps particularly so since this niche has its own vocal professional practitioners whose mission in life is to draw attention to failings and shortfalls from best practice in this field. These practitioners, ranging from the small specialist consultancy, Pensions & Investment Research Consultants (PIRC) in the UK, to the giant California Public Employees Retirement System (CalPERS) in the USA, and their continuing focus on the performance of boards of directors, will not go away in the near future either.

Review

The previous paragraphs summarise why good corporate governance is of major importance to the people who run large and small organisations at the present time. The following seven chapters are intended to provide a background in the subject for those many readers who, as busy managers, have had little time to go beyond headlines or auditors' checklists. These chapters are written to provide a perspective on the subject by:

- tracing the development of current received wisdom
- showing how different elements are affected by the exercise of good corporate governance
- illustrating the need for caution in translating an Anglo-Saxon model into different countries and cultures
- showing how the need to consider corporate governance develops as an organisation grows
- considering different types of organisation and their different needs
- looking at the managers and staff and the different parts they play in a system of good corporate governance
- summing up the potential future influences in the corporate governance debate.

This part of the book is used to express and justify the authors' belief that good corporate governance is part and parcel of good management and is properly considered in this way. It is not simply about compliance with the letter of the latest guidelines. That way lies legislation, an avoidance industry and anti-avoidance legislation, with a growing army of bureaucrats to police it. Moreover, these days the Treasury has discovered off-balance-sheet finance, and all this will be done through self-financing regulation, paid for of course ultimately by the customer.

To avoid this horror, and to halt if not reverse the advancing regulatory forces, management must be whiter than white in the public perception. Moreover, it must be skilled at presenting itself in a way which shows its ethical approach to full advantage. This is achieved by good corporate governance running through the bones of the organisation and emanating from its every pore. It is not achieved by technical compliance with professionally complex standards which the general public neither understands nor cares about.

NOTE

[1] In the *Financial Times*, 6 February 1997.

Chapter 2

WHAT IS CORPORATE GOVERNANCE?

Introduction *15*

Historical background *15*

Recent questions *16*

Definitions *18*

Development of corporate governance as an issue *21*

Duties in UK law *26*

What is good corporate governance and why? *29*

Conclusion *31*

'Top management is a "trustee" responsible for managing the enterprise in the best balanced interest of shareholders, customers, employees, suppliers and plant community cities.'

RALPH CORDINER,
CEO of General Electric Company[1]

Introduction

The corporation, in contrast, for example, to a partnership, separates ownership from control. This is fundamental to the question of corporate governance because it means that without monitoring and control, the system is open to abuse of the corporation by often 'self-interested' managers, who may have other objectives than shareholder value.

On the one hand we need to look at directors' fiduciary responsibility in regard to other people's money. They need to take these shareholders and all other interested parties into account when formulating goals and objectives.

However, there is a small question mark over the matter of ownership itself. Are shareholders really owners? In the original sense of the word, certainly not, because the corporation is not a physical entity and thus many of the characteristics of ownership cannot be truly applied and because they do not have many of the normal responsibilities of ownership. Many shareholders, thanks to limited liability (which can be considered to be a concession granted to make up for loss of control), are interested solely in making money from activities of the corporation, when perhaps they should also be concerned as to how this money is earned; (we examine shareholder responsibilities in detail in Chapter 3).

On the other hand we should also be aware of shareholders' responsibility, not just in insisting on controls of management in relation to their own holdings, but also in ensuring that management takes decisions which reflect good corporate governance in other fields, for example employees, social responsibility – the community, and – an especially sensitive matter these days – the environment.

Historical background

While corporate governance is a fairly recent *issue*, there is, in fact, nothing new about the *concept*. It has been in existence as long as the corporation itself – really as long as there has been large-scale trade, reflecting the need for responsibility in the handling of money and the conduct of commercial activities. A merchant of old necessarily had to ensure that any venture for which he provided capital was being planned responsibly, and that he was kept informed.

The basis for British company law, which grew up in the nineteenth century, was to offer business the protection of limited liability by separating personal liability from that of corporate organisations. Personal liability could therefore be limited to the amount of the shareholding in an incorporated company, limited by shares. This worked well when the shareholders were truly proprietors, and it still obtains today, of course, in medium and small businesses. Major companies, on the other hand, do not usually function like that any more.

The size of companies began to change towards the end of the last century as a result of the new technologies of the Industrial Revolution, which required much larger firms to create economies of scale. Shareholders ceased to manage them directly and hired professional managers – below board level – to run them instead. As time went on the managers began to graduate to board level, and gradually came to form the majority of board members. The process of completely separating ownership and control was accelerated after the Second World War when financial institutions started to build up their industrial investment portfolios. The fund managers who handled these investments had no interest in individual shares as such. By definition their job was to balance their portfolios which they did by diversifying them. They were content to leave the management of the companies to the professional managers. The formal division between boards of directors and the business management lasted longest in the financial services sector, where it was for a long time customary to separate the board, the gentlemen, from the executive management, the players. The chief general manager was often the only member of management to sit on the board. Banks began to change their structures in the 1970s and building societies and insurance/assurance companies followed suit in the 1980s, though there are still many examples left of this former structure, especially in the smaller organisation.

Recent questions

The corporate governance debate in the UK has focused on the relationship between management and shareholders (see next section), and the system is based on maximising profits (supposedly for the shareholders). The legal background on which this is set is a tripartite system of directors, shareholders and auditors:

Whereas the directors are regarded as leaders for a company's management, directed towards maximisation of the company's profits, the role of the shareholders is to ensure, *inter alia,* that their directors will maximise profits on their behalf. The company's auditors will wish to ensure that there are no financial irregularities in the company and that the directors provide a 'true and fair view' of the company's performance.[2]

The view that the purpose of an organisation is solely for making profit is, in this day and age, very limited and in many ways idealistic. The corporation has other obligations besides those to its shareholders. Indeed the shareholders must share in the responsibilities the company has towards its other stakeholders. 'Corporate Social Responsibility' is now the keyword. This means not just abiding by the local laws and regulations and so on, but active support and involvement in the individual communities in which the company is an important wealth and employment generator. Social responsibility has been given particular importance in recent years in the US, largely due to pressure from lobbyists. Various groups, from consumer rights groups to trade unions have insisted that the company realises that every action it takes has consequences for the community and that therefore it should take the affected parties into account at all levels of the company.

The law often regards the corporation as having similar rights and responsibilities as a person. Indeed in 1886 the Supreme Court in the US declared that 'corporations would henceforth be considered "persons"' as part of the 14th Amendment to the constitution. If considered in this way, duties to the stakeholders become still clearer. The corporation, like a person, must have ethics, morals and values. Monks and Minow in their comprehensive textbook *Corporate Governance,* present us with Thomas Donaldson's analytical structure within which this question of the company being a 'moral person' can be addressed:

> In order to qualify as a moral agent, a corporation would need to embody a process of moral decision-making. This process seems to require at a minimum:
>
> - The capacity to use moral reasons in decision-making.
> - The capacity of the decision-making process to control not only overt corporate acts, but also the structure of policies and rules.
>
> [The first] is necessary to raise the corporation above the level of a mere machine. To be a moral agent, something must have reasons for what it does, not simply causes for what it does and for something to be a moral agent, some of those reasons must be moral ones. Obviously, corporations

are unable to think as humans, but they can be morally accountable. That is, with the proper internal structure, corporations, like humans, can be liable to give an account of their behavior where the account stipulates which moral reasons prompted their behavior.[3]

The ethical question is a key one and will be examined in detail in Part B. Suffice it to say here that the corporate governance debate clearly needs to be widened to examine the relationships between the company (*with* its shareholders) and its employees, customers, suppliers, creditors, the environment and the public at large. An increasing number of people are calling for changes in corporate structure, which at present fails to ensure the accountability and responsibility of the company towards all interested parties. Of course it is impossible to guarantee complete ethical behaviour and avoid abuses of power, and, as we discussed in the last chapter, attempts to do so by following the path of legislation will only lead to more problems without achieving their original goal and will only serve progressively and insidiously to stifle the commercial organisation.

What *can* be done, however, is to use preventive in place of prescriptive medicine. That is, put the principles of good corporate governance (particularly ethics) back into the company's very culture (see below). Proponents of change do not come up with any concrete propositions for change or a practical system of evaluation and implementation of the necessary checks and controls. But it is to this end that this book is driving, based on a model which is not just workable in theory, but is actually *being* used in the real world.

Definitions

What is corporate governance?

Before we look at a proper definition of 'corporate governance', it is important to realise that it means different things to different people. On one level, as we pointed out in the last chapter, the consequence is that the general public, unfamiliar with the term and informed of such issues by the press, is aware of (and sometimes makes noises about) concepts such as honesty, responsibility and environmental friendliness, and gets upset about bosses being awarded seemingly excessively high salaries. While this often represents a lack of knowledge and understanding of business, and certainly of the specific corporation (of which even the City analysts are periodically guilty), heads of these companies ignore public

WHAT IS CORPORATE GOVERNANCE?

opinion at their peril. Part of corporate governance is to be *seen* to be acting responsibly, and informing all interested parties, or stakeholders, of decisions which will affect them.

On another level, we must remember that the great deal of discussion and debate on corporate governance that we have seen in recent times has taken place almost exclusively in the UK and US. The continental Europeans and the Japanese, even today, barely know the expression below the level of the multinational corporation. One of the reasons for this is simply terminology, and the fact that, as we repeatedly comment in this book, the discussion has lost touch with the reality of managing the corporation effectively. This latter point is what these other nations have still been primarily concerned with.

In the Anglophone world, corporate governance is usually discussed in terms of a struggle between greedy and self-serving boards of management and non-involved and vulnerable shareholders. Indeed it has been said, rather ponderously, that corporate governance consists of two elements:

1. **The long-term relationship** which has to deal with checks and balances, incentives for managers and communications between management and investors.
2. **The transactional relationship** which involves dealing with disclosure and authority.

This implies an adversarial relationship between management and investors, and an attitude of mutual suspicion. This is the basis for much of the rationale of the Cadbury Report, and is one of the reasons why it prescribes in some detail the way in which the board should conduct itself: consistency and transparency towards shareholders are its watchwords. The Code of Practice sets out guidelines for:

- constitution and procedures for the board of directors
- attributes and appointment procedures for non-executive directors
- executive directors' contracts and emoluments
- reporting and controls.

We prefer to take a rather broader view, as the reader will have noticed, which places the Cadbury Code in a wider context and shows its recommendations emerging naturally in the course of a company's evolution. In an earlier book on corporate governance,[4] one of the authors defined good corporate governance as consisting of five elements which the board must consider:

- long-term strategic goals
- employees: past, present and future
- environment/community
- customers/suppliers
- compliance (legal/regulatory).

This definition is explained in more detail below. It was endorsed by Sir Adrian Cadbury in his foreword to another of the authors' books on the subject, directed at the smaller company.[5]

In Part B of this book we extend and update the above definition by describing five rules by which a system of good corporate governance should be operated.

Other considerations

The separation of ownership and control (explained in an earlier section) created freedom to take much bigger risks than previously possible in order to expand. It was this freedom which prevented for so long the permission of such organisations to exist, with the potential dangers it implied.[6] And it is this freedom which has required mechanisms to be constructed to try and prevent it being abused.

This has led to different systems in different countries, depending on which constituent or interested party in the company's operations has been given the most importance. For example, in Germany's business culture there is extensive employee representation, and in Japan, the shareholder has traditionally been given virtually no say at all in company affairs. So the concept is not just about shareholder protection and director responsibility, as in the Anglo-Saxon model. Each model has a different style of corporate governance. What is meant here is that the term corporate governance could equally be called *organisation*. Or perhaps it is the other way round – that governance is another way of saying organisation. In this way we can refer to corporate governance as being different styles of organisation, and how a company should be run *well*.

The ideal scenario, of course, would be that all parties are given an equal share of corporate decision-making. This would require an effective, democratic system capable of finding a balance between often conflicting interests, but if this can be achieved it will prevent any one party abusing the company. This is possible because with this sharing of company planning and direction, comes shared responsibility and accountability. In this ideal scenario, everyone is accountable to each other.

Although this may at first sight seem a hopeless task, the indications are that, as investment is becoming more and more globally liquid, corporate governance will seek to combine the best of all models in place in different parts of the world. What is certain is that the idea of corporate governance should affect every part of the organisation of the company, and therefore, every part of the organisation should reflect good corporate governance. If we try and implement this concept, we are inevitably heading towards the ideal scenario.

Development of corporate governance as an issue

The debate

As we have already commented upon, corporate governance in this country has always traditionally, though not exclusively, been based on profit maximisation and generation of shareholder wealth. The director is a fiduciary of other people's money, and as Adam Smith observed, it cannot be expected that directors will be as vigilant and careful with other people's money as they will be with their own.

Various committees have been set up over the years to try and address this problem of lack of control. As early as 1945, the Cohen Committee noted that while the tripartite system with its delegation of management was necessary, there were cases of abuse of power by company directors. This, the committee declared, made it 'desirable to devise provisions which will make it difficult for directors to secure the hurried passage of controversial measures'.[7] The committee's terms of reference were 'to consider and report what major amendments were desirable in the Companies Act, 1929, and, in particular, to review the requirements prescribed in regard to the formation and affairs of companies and the safeguards afforded for investors and for the public interest.'

The Jenkins Committee (1962) was also set up to investigate company law reform, and attempted to clarify the duties of directors and the rights of shareholders. It recommended wider disclosure of information to make abuse of power more difficult, but did feel that it was impossible to define exhaustively the duties of directors. The committee remarked that shareholders still had a reasonable control of company direction, but only exercised it when things went badly wrong. Sheikh and Chatterjee deduce from this that corporate governance seems to have been primarily about keeping shareholders happy in monetary terms, which, they point out, was what the committee argued should be avoided.

> The fact remains that it is the shareholders who may need directions from directors as to how the company's image and future profitability might be secured by being conscious of corporate social responsibilities.[8]

The debate, then, is about whether shareholders should become involved in the management of the business. Clearly, directors need to be given a reasonable amount of freedom to do their jobs. What is also clearly true is that as the situation still stands today, there needs to be more accountability, not just to shareholders, but to the other stakeholders.

It was Robert Maxwell and his ilk who sparked off the modern corporate governance debate, however, culminating in the formation of the Cadbury Committee, which published its report in May 1992. The committee, chaired by Sir Adrian Cadbury, was set up by the Financial Reporting Council, the Stock Exchange, and the accountancy profession to report on 'The Financial Aspects of Corporate Governance'. The report set out fairly the safe, established view of best practice in governance and gave a nudge to the non-executive director movement, but no more. It was criticised by the business press for not being radical enough.

The report accepted the current unitary board structure and responsibilities of directors. It stated that listed, or to-be-listed companies, must have non-executives and that these were to fill the audit committees and be a majority on the remuneration committees. There were also recommendations for strengthening Annual General Meetings (regarding directors' contracts) and for improvement in the reporting of accounting information.

As a previous book by one of the authors pointed out at the time of the report,[9] what should be remembered is the fact that the committee was reporting not on corporate governance in general, but on 'good financial corporate governance', focusing on 'the control and reporting functions of boards, and on the role of auditors'. The committee's report therefore centred on the negative and inward aspects of accounting, reporting and control. However, it did miss the opportunity to broaden out the remit of the committee to cover the outward looking, business and profit-generating aspects of governance.

In 1994, after continued media hype about the allegedly huge salaries of some senior executives, the Greenbury Committee was set up to investigate this very sensitive issue. Its report:

- requested that compliance with the Code of Practice be made mandatory for listed companies
- reinforced the Remuneration Committee and made it accountable to shareholders
- insisted on formal and complete disclosure of remuneration details with shareholder approval required
- advised that remuneration policy should 'attract, retain and motivate' directors of the necessary quality without being excessive, and
- pressed for constraint in deciding compensation packages for outgoing executives, taking into account performance and reasons for departure.

The feeling among *shareholders*, however, seems to be that the issue is not so much about how much executives are paid (except in cases of clear excess) but that there should be a clear link between remuneration and performance. Gill Nott, Chief Executive of Proshare, has commented,

> Most of the individual shareholders are not concerned about high pay *per se*. They want to see directors rewarded for being effective. Shareholders are concerned about how well the company has done and how this is reflected in shareholder return.[10]

The Codes of Practice produced by the Cadbury and Greenbury committees are, as they stand, voluntary, not mandatory, which partly explains the timidity of some of the recommendations. The hope is that companies will use the recommendations to create a more transparent corporate structure without the need for legal enforcement. The Jenkins Committee agreed on the undesirability of regulations, which, it said, would 'seriously hamper the activities of honest men in order to defeat an occasional wrongdoer'.[11] It is arguable, however, that the need for more concrete controls are more pressing these days and that a certain amount of legislation is inevitable, at least regarding disclosure (and auditing) and directors' remuneration, if not from the UK Government then from Brussels.

In 1997 the task of deciding the best way forward in corporate governance lies with Sir Ronnie Hampel and his committee. It was set up in November 1995 to examine issues arising out of the Cadbury and Greenbury reports. Its line, which the reader will realise is the same as that of the authors, has been to try to calm the situation down. Emotions have been running high in the last few years since Cadbury, brought to fever-pitch during Greenbury with the bloodbath over remuneration disclosure, particularly in regard to directors' pensions. In October 1996, when a consultation document was launched, Sir Ronnie warned against over-regulation, saying 'We must not stifle, we must stimulate. Without prospering business we have no corporate governance'. An extract from the Preliminary Report of the Hampel Committee is included in Appendix B.

Government attitude

Despite this abundance of debate, committee formation and report writing, very little of the recommendations which it produced has actually been incorporated into company law. This is partly due to changes of government, but also because, despite overwhelming evidence to support certain legislation, governments have been unwilling or unable to force through unpopular bills, no matter how attractive in theory they are.

The 1970s saw various attempts to reform company law, starting with the *Company Law Reform* paper (1973), in which the Conservative Government aimed to make directors generally more socially responsible and recommended the appointing of non-executives to the board. This was attacked as inadequate by the Labour Party in 1977, which produced a Green Paper, *The Community and the Company*, giving its recommendations for legislation to protect public interest. In the same year the Conservative Government produced a White Paper entitled *The Conduct of Company Directors*, which called for a Bill to define the duties of directors, and the Companies Bill 1978, which proposed *inter alia* a statutory code of conduct. The result of all these documents was absolutely nothing, as far as new laws were concerned, demonstrating the difficulty in imposing legislation.

Business response

In 1973 the CBI published a report, *The Responsibilities of the British Public Company*, in which it affirmed the business community's view that self-regulation was the most desirable way forward to deal with the demands of a changing society. The report said that companies should improve relations with shareholders, but also that these should join the board in ensuring the interests of the other stakeholders are duly represented.

The Institute of Directors published a similar document (*Guidelines for Directors*) in 1985 stating once again that the way to avoid an increase in laws was to have effective self-regulation, and that the company was the link between customers and 'all the parties which contributed to the customer's satisfaction. These parties include the "stakeholders" such as suppliers, employees, creditors and the community.'[12]

It will be obvious from this and the summary of the CBI report below, that the desirability of the stakeholder concept and the business community's countervailing attitude towards corporate control and governance have both been recognised for many years now. Yet just as nothing concrete has come out of the various committees and parliamentary Bills over the years, it seems nothing has really been achieved from this angle, either. We must be conscious of this when we look at the pressure exerted on Sir Ronnie Hampel's committee by businesses large and small to stem the flow of regulation and calm down the corporate governance debate. On a more positive note, it is true that the tide of corporate governance that has swept the country in recent years (and which continues to sweep other nations) has changed the landscape for ever, and we can be more optimistic that there will be an inevitable improvement which will lead to a better image for business.

Sheikh and Chatterjee summarised the contents of the CBI report:

> The CBI's response to the challenges of corporate governance was largely limited to formulating Principles of Corporate Conduct. Their principles required, *inter alia*, that the company board should be required to develop a closer relationship with the company's shareholders. It must provide all shareholders with full information about its progress. The principles also acknowledged that shareholders, as owners of the business, had a responsibility that extended beyond the buying and selling of shares. In order to allow them to exercise their responsibility, they should be provided with proper information on which they could form their own judgements. Institutional shareholders had expertise which was not usually available to private shareholders. It was essential that institutions should fulfil their full role as shareholders in the interest of all shareholders. The principles also recognised that directors' duties extend to other constituencies. These principles required that the board develop closer relationships with its employees towards a common purpose. The main purpose would be to secure a wider participation in the decision-making process which would include some participation of employees. Further, a company should be responsive to informed public opinion, such as that on the protection of the environment and the social consequences of its business activities.

The Emperor has no clothes

Corporate governance, then, is not – or should not be – about debate and discussion on executive compensation, shareholder protection, legislation and so on. In recent times, the issue has become not only a subject of fierce debate and public outcry, but also, as a result of this and arising regulation, a subject which wearies many company directors. Put in other words, there is very little substance to modern corporate governance, in the view of the authors – the emperor has no clothes. What is behind all the fracas is to a great extent common sense, like many principles in business. Directors, for example, should naturally be responsible in their role as fiduciaries of other people's money.

To use another metaphor, there is so much smoke, that we have lost sight of the fire. This fire is the real message of corporate governance, which is undoubtedly beneficial to all, that we should be *good* directors. As the previous chapter mentioned, Cadbury and Greenbury did not arise simply to produce legislation, but to encourage self-regulation, with the ultimate goal that in applying the recommendations, the company will become more efficient, gain shareholder value, and hopefully increase market value as a result.

This is the bottom line. We all want to increase our value, and 'corporate governance' is often seen as cost ineffective, bringing little or no benefits – the smoke gets in our eyes, as it were. What we need to do is to apply the principles of good governance to the whole corporation.

This could be described as: 'looking at management through corporate governance-tinted glasses' *ie taking a fresh look at management structure taking into account all interested parties and ensuring all the necessary monitoring and controls are in place to ensure that shareholder value is always at the forefront.*

Compare this with the definition in *Director's Monthly*:

> Effective corporate governance ensures that long-term strategic objectives and plans are established, and that the proper management and management structure are in place to achieve those objectives, while at the same time making sure that the structure functions **to maintain the corporation's integrity, reputation, and accountability to its relevant constituencies.**

Duties in UK law

The legal framework

Companies

There are about 3.5 million registered companies in the UK, of which 1 million have employees and some 7,000 are plcs. The law implicitly assumes growth and survival, but the key aim of companies is to make a profit, both for the providers of capital and as a source of investment for future growth.

The shareholders have the main interest in the company. Their interest is a property right which is limited by the extent of their shareholding, hence the term 'limited liability'. The other stakeholders, such as creditors and providers of finance, have a contract with the company which defines their interest. The company is managed by shareholders in general meeting who may (and usually do) delegate their powers to the directors. The directors are appointed by the shareholders, though, in practice, the shareholders usually confirm the appointments made by the board between public shareholders' meetings. The function of the board, which is a collective function and responsibility, is to:

- determine the company's purpose and 'ethics'
- decide the direction, that is, the strategy
- plan
- delegate to managers or committees of the board and control them
- report and make recommendations to shareholders.

Directors

The directors are elected by shareholders in general meeting and while the law in the UK provides for them to have regard to the interests of employees and to those who have legal contracts with the company, there is no legal requirement for any specific party or interest group to be represented on the board. It is up to the Annual General Meeting of the shareholders. No employee consents are required for company actions such as takeovers or mergers.

The directors' duty is to the company and to those to whom the company has a legal liability. Directors have a duty to ensure compliance with the Companies Acts 1985 and 1989 in relation to the preparation of company accounts, and though only one director need actually sign them, there is implied approval by all the directors unless they have taken steps to show otherwise. Directors – all directors – have personal liability if the company can be shown to have been trading 'wrongfully', that is, continuing to trade when there was no reasonable prospect of its being able to pay its debts.

The law does not recognise any separate class of director, such as executive and non-executive. We shall look at this more closely in Chapter 13, and also consider it in Chapter 15. All directors are equally responsible, and furthermore the decisions that are taken are of the whole board, even if a director has voted against it. Authorities are increasingly taking action for breaches of statutory or other duties by directors.

Directors' duties

Sheikh and Chatterjee identify three main categories of duty in UK company law:

- duty of care and skill
- fiduciary duties
- statutory duties.

Under the duty of care and skill, Sheikh and Chatterjee draw attention to the limitations of common law, which are lax to say the least. A director is only obliged under common law to have the minimum qualifications and show only minimal care and attention to company affairs. Examples of his duties include attending board meetings 'when he is reasonably able to do so', and the allowance of delegation of duties to 'officials in whom he has placed trust'. These are both statements which can be interpreted to suit the individual, and do not paint a terribly reassuring picture of how the director is expected to behave.

It is argued that the Insolvency Act 1986 has raised the standards of performance of these duties. Under the Act, a director who fails to take every step he or she ought to have taken to prevent the company going into insolvent liquidation if he or she knew or ought to have concluded that there was no reasonable prospect of avoiding the outcome, may be required by the court to contribute personally to the company's assets for the benefit of the creditors. The main purpose of the recent legislation is to protect company creditors and shareholders, and this is being achieved by making directors personally liable. Resignation will not relieve a director of this liability.

UK company law imposes additional, fiduciary duties on the director. These include:

- a duty to act in good faith
- a duty not to act for improper purposes
- a duty not to engage in 'corporate opportunities'
- a duty not to fetter future discretion.

Sheikh and Chatterjee argue, quite reasonably, that these fiduciary duties set a higher standard of conduct than the rather less defined common law duties of care and skill: 'They are a means of monitoring directors' actions to ensure that they do not abuse their powers or possess uncontrollable powers to the detriment of their shareholders.'[13]

What is good corporate governance and why?

Corporate governance, then, should be recognised as a set of standards which aims to improve the company's image, efficiency and effectiveness and social responsibility. Compliance with the likes of Cadbury and Greenbury are a good way of displaying to interested parties, or stakeholders, that the company takes the issue seriously, and if companies participate in the spirit of the recommendations, and show efforts in self-regulation, then the need for legislation – obviously undesirable – will be reduced or eliminated.

Particularly important these days are environmental and community issues. It is no longer enough to comply with legal requirements. Companies need to be 'socially responsible' when making decisions, for example, about locations for waste disposal or those affecting manufacturing plants. Of course, many companies have always held this philosophy and made positive efforts in the areas in which they operate to be good members of the local community.

But there are always those who don't. Legislation usually arises because of the bad behaviour of a minority which, therefore, affects the majority. But rather than look upon this as an unnecessary annoyance, it can be used to the advantage of the company by publicising the fact that they have always operated in a responsible way and speaking out in favour of cleaning up the bad practices of this minority of offenders. Indeed it can be part of corporate identity – the brand image, a vitally important marketing tool – to create a good perception of the company among all stakeholders.

This sums up the approach which should be taken to the issue of corporate governance as a whole. It has been difficult to identify benefits which are directly related to corporate governance *per se* (although some people to whom we have spoken say they can), and therefore there is little empirical evidence to suggest that there is a positive correlation between resources spent on corporate governance and improved results. But rather than fight it – which would be a futile task – far better to use the limelight created by debate on the subject to show how well the company is run, while simultaneously using the opportunity to fine-tune the company's practices, however sound they might be.

Of course this exercise could reveal – and aims to do so – flaws in corporate structure, which may have lain unnoticed due to having insufficient independent representation. In this case it is the chance to act and be seen to act. This is not admitting weakness, especially given the marketing techniques which can be used to influence public opinion, it is merely displaying the constant search for perfection.

Our definition

The discussion so far has illustrated that corporate governance is not just about directors' obligations towards shareholders, as other models demonstrate. And we have mentioned that different countries have different ideas as to what constitutes good corporate governance (we will examine different models in Chapter 4). Therefore any satisfactory definition, to be applicable to a modern, global company, must synthesise best practice from the biggest economic powers into something which can be applied across all major countries. In essence we believe that good corporate governance consists of a system of structuring, operating and controlling a company such as to achieve the following:

- a fundamental ethical basis to the operation, running through the pores
- fulfilling the long-term strategic goal of the owners, which, after survival may consist of building shareholder value, establishing a dominant market share or maintaining a technical lead in a chosen sphere. It will certainly not be the same for all organisations, but will take into account the expectations of all the key stakeholders, in particular:
  - considering and caring for the interests of employees, past, present and future, which we take to comprise the whole life-cycle including planning future needs, recruitment, training, working environment, severance and retirement procedures, through to looking after pensioners
  - working to maintain excellent relations with both customers and suppliers, in terms of such matters as quality of service provided, considerate ordering and account settlement procedures, etc
  - taking account of the needs of the environment and the local community, both in terms of the physical effects of the company's operations and the economic and cultural interaction with the local population
- maintaining proper compliance with all the applicable legal and regulatory requirements under which the company is carrying out its activities.

We believe that a well-run organisation must be structured in such a way that all the above requirements are catered for and can be seen to be operating effectively by all the interest groups concerned. There must be sufficient transparency for this to be readily observable by them without their having to rely on extensive and expensive independent monitoring procedures. A company achieving its owners' goals under such an organisational structure will, we believe, have a good and effective form of corporate governance.

We develop these principles into our Five Golden Rules of good corporate governance in Part B.

Conclusion

The evidence so far produced, and that which appears every day in the press, leads us to suggest that maybe the importance now attached to the issue is the result of actions by self-seeking lobbyists, rather than proven grounds for a radical change in the way corporations should operate. This is proved at least partially by the fact that most top companies have not needed to make major structural or operational changes to comply with Cadbury and Greenbury (if they haven't chosen to oppose them – often for perfectly valid reasons) except in the area of disclosure. In any event they generally find they have nothing to fear from being more transparent.

We believe, therefore, that for all the endless discussions and academic theories about corporate governance, in reality, there is nothing new or radical in it and it really boils down to good, sound business management.

It is, however, clearly beneficial that the issue has been brought to a head, as it has exposed (thanks to 'classic' cases like that of the Maxwell corporation and its raid on pensioners' savings) the flaws in corporate structure, and recent efforts at reform attempt to address these difficulties by making everyone more accountable and socially responsible.

Finally, we believe that by putting pressure on corporations to adhere to the guidelines set out, by declaring universally that it is a good thing, good corporate governance should be promoted and encouraged through self-regulation rather than enforcing laws, turning to this method only as a last resort. Throughout the book we talk of 'corporate ethics': if the company incorporates into its very culture the principles of good corporate governance we suggest – especially the stakeholder-in-strategy approach – this will be much more effective than any law or regulation could ever be. There is always a way round rules and no matter how much regulation, or even legislation is produced, it will not prevent scandal, as has been repeatedly proved over the years.[14] But if you believe in the concepts *behind* the rules, they become not so much rules, but rather statements of your own corporate philosophy.

NOTES

[1] *Corporate Governance* by Monks and Minow, Blackwell Business, 1995.

[2] *Corporate Governance & Corporate Control*, edited by Dr Saleem Sheikh & Pr William Rees. Quote from *Perspectives on corporate governance*, Dr Sheikh and Pr Chatterjee. This book was a very useful reference, especially for the legal points.

[3] Thomas Donaldson, *Corporations & Morality*, Prentice-Hall, 1982. *Corporate Governance*, by Robert Monks and Nell Minow (Blackwell Business, 1995) was a most useful guide in writing this part of the book.

[4] *Corporate Governance*, Sheridan and Kendall (FT Pitman Publishing, 1992).

[5] *Good Corporate Governance – An Aid to Growth for the Smaller Company*, Nigel Kendall, Accountancy Books, 1994.

[6] Monks and Minnow reflect on the subject: 'Adam Smith and Karl Marx did not agree on much, but they both thought that the corporate form of organisation was unworkable, and for remarkably similar reasons. They questioned whether it is possible to create a structure that will operate efficiently and fairly, despite the fact that there is a separation between ownership and control.'

[7] Board of Trade, *Report of the Committee on Company Law Amendment*, 1943 ('Cohen Committee'). op. cit. 2.

[8] Op. cit. 2.

[9] Op. cit. 4.

[10] Interviewed by Neville Bain & David Band in *Winning Ways through corporate governance* (MacMillan Business, 1996).

[11] Board of Trade, *Report of the Company Law Committee*, 1962 ('Jenkins Committee'). Op. cit. 2.

[12] Op. cit. 1. Further, an article in *Accountancy* magazine, February 1997, pointed out that this idea is not a new one: 'Since the 1930s economists such as Coase and Galbraith have expounded the idea that companies operate by balancing the competing claims of shareholders, workers, creditors and the local community. Leading UK companies, such as Marks & Spencer, have recognised these claims for a long time.' It also cites another report by the Accounting Standard Steering Committee in 1975, *The Corporate Report*, which acknowledged the existence of multiple business constituencies.

[13] Op. cit. 2.

[14] Most recently the Companies Act and the Financial Services Act of the 1980s failed to prevent the scandals of the 1990s, and the Codes of Best Practice have even less clout.

Chapter 3

CORPORATE GOVERNANCE IS IN THE EYE OF THE STAKEHOLDER

Introduction 35

Shareholders/investors 35

Employees 39

Customers 42

Suppliers/trading partners 43

Community and environment 45

The State 47

Conclusion 48

'To my mind there is no such thing as an innocent purchaser of stocks ... Stockholders cannot be innocent merely by reason of the fact that they have not personally had anything to do with the decision of questions arising in the conduct of the business.'
SUPREME COURT JUSTICE LOUIS BRANDEIS (1911)[1]

Introduction

Having established that we believe good corporate governance involves taking all stakeholders into account, we will now examine more closely their expectations, rights and responsibilities. Since previous debate has been largely concerned with making boards responsible towards shareholders, we will concentrate here on the shareholders' responsibility towards the other stakeholders, as touched upon in the last chapter. The other sections focus on responding to the needs of each of the stakeholder groups and incorporating them into the business culture. We help explain these points with three illustrations: Hermes' Code of Conduct, Hewlett Packard's people philosophy, and Shell's ethical complacency.

Shareholders/investors

If shareholders are considered to be 'owners' of a company, then they should also be recognised as having certain responsibilities, which ownership of any type entails. We discussed in Chapter 2 how the corporation is like a 'person'. This brings about the problem that there is no direct link between offender and victim, meaning directors can use the company to take actions without personally suffering the consequences. Shareholders feel they have every right to react if these actions are detrimental to their financial stake, but usually refuse to accept the responsibility for intervening to try to prevent it, a power which they do in fact possess. And often, particularly institutions with portfolios to balance, they are interested more in short-term gain than in longer term performance. There is also the increasingly important question of acting against the best interests of the wider community, another responsibility they must recognise more and more.

Then there is the very question of ownership to consider. Does the shareholder really 'own' the company? With separation of ownership and control, can the term 'property' still be appropriate? A share of stock is certainly not a physical asset of the company. Monks and Minow point out that ownership in a modern corporation is 'fractionated', and identify other respects in which share ownership differs from traditional notions of ownership, in *numerical*, *legal*, *functional* and *personal* terms.

Bearle and Means commented: 'It has often been said that the owner of a horse is responsible. If the horse lives he must feed it. If the horse dies he must bury it. No such responsibility attaches itself to a share of stock.'

There are, then, two options open to shareholders. Either they accept a lack of control over their investment and the company's activities, which is clearly undesirable, both from their point of view and considering that to avoid abuses of power by directors an effective system of checks (of which they are an important part) is needed; or they change their attitude to investment and use their existing rights the better to control the company and protect the interests of the other stakeholders. And while there has been talk of a 'shareholder revolution', there has been very little actual action taken. Anne Simpson of PIRC says there is no such revolution and accuses institutional investors of 'masterful inactivity'. Wanting to encourage individuals and institutions to become more involved with their investments, she says 'Protesting at an AGM is one thing. Getting more constructively involved with their companies is another thing.'

Rights of shareholders
1. The right to sell the stock.
2. The right to vote by proxy.
3. The right to bring suit for damages if the company's directors or managers fail to meet their obligations.
4. The right to certain information from the company.
5. Certain residual rights following the company's liquidation (or its filing for reorganisation under bankruptcy laws), once creditors and other claimants are paid off.

Institutional investors

Case study: Institutional shareholder activism

HERMES' CODE OF CORPORATE GOVERNANCE

Hermes, the £32bn BT and Post Office pension fund, has been making quite a lot of noise in the last few years epitomising the active role which should be played by investors. In March 1997 it sent its own code of corporate governance and voting policies to all the companies in which it invests. Among its most radical demands is that non-executives should receive half their remuneration in shares instead of cash, and that the chief executive should not move on to become chairman without a break.[2]

This is an exception to the inactivity criticised by PIRC and other groups, although a couple of observations should be made here. Firstly, shareholder involvement in corporate affairs should not just be to restrain the investee company (although control is obviously crucial) but to be constructive and work *with* the company, not against it – after all it is clearly in their best interests that the company is not burdened with excessive rules and regulations which inhibit efficiency and effectiveness and thus performance. Secondly, it should be pointed out that Hermes is in itself an organisation with 'shareholders' – the pension fund holders. Have these shareholders had a say in these matters, and is the board practising good corporate governance itself?

Hermes is one of the few to challenge their investee companies. The truth is, the institutions do have power over their investments only most have not understood (or accepted?) their responsibilities. They are agitating for more recognition and information, but it is legitimate to ask what they bring to the companies which they have invested in, in return. They still act as if the small shareholder rules, and that everything can be solved through share transfers. But to whom? Only to another institution, of course. One fund manager's ex-growth fund is another's recovery share. The big funds are locked in: why sell to Glaxo to get more BP paper which they already had? The situation has been worsening for a number of years now, as more and more of the largest British companies disappear, often into foreign ownership. The fewer companies in existence, the fewer opportunities exist to balance their risks.

> With the liberalisation of world stock exchanges, many companies are seeking listings in countries where this was previously difficult or undesirable. There is now competition between stock exchanges, and as discussed in Chapter 8, the London Stock Exchange is losing market share as more commercially-minded (often the recently liberalised) exchanges attract business away from the too tradition-set City-owned market.

The institutions employ only two sanctions against bad management: action to remove management, or at least the chairman, which has been growing in popularity in recent years; and an assent to a takeover. But though these catch the headlines, they still reflect the minority of cases. In general, as long as things go reasonably well, there is no shareholder control at all. The shareholders are free riders and management has it all its own way, though to be sure the published accounts will be full of references to working on behalf of the shareholders.

To understand the apparent lack of control, it is important to realise that the institutions are investors, and see themselves as such, not as owners. Their interest is in their funds and the performance of the funds, rather than the companies they have invested in, and they are judged, publicly, on their funds' performances. Their aim is to maximise returns on their own shareholdings by constantly adjusting their investment portfolios. Underperformance to them means underperforming shares, while to a German or Japanese bank, it means underperforming companies. The two may not necessarily be the same thing. UK institutions still take a financial view of the company, German and Japanese ones still generally take an industrial view. The answer to the problem shares in the UK has for long been to sell them in the same way as companies seek to sell underperforming assets, or at worst, to hold them in the hope of a bid. On the continent the preference is much more to get rid of underperforming managers rather than selling or breaking up businesses, a practice which is regarded as almost obscene, witness the recent translation of a hostile bid by the German steel giant Krupp for its underperforming rival, Thyssen, into an agreed merger as a result of public and political pressure.

Private shareholders

By accepting the benefits of limited liability – not losing more than he invested – and transferability – being free to sell out whenever he likes, the shareholder is also accepting that he can claim very little moral influence as an individual on corporate direction.

The average small shareholder is, like the institution, only really interested in whether the company is performing well and that he is getting good returns on his investment. If misfortune befalls the company, the natural thing to do, therefore, is to sell. But this caution often goes beyond simply avoiding misfortune. It is symbolic of the fickle attitude which causes such huge fluctuations at the hands of speculators. The appointing of a popular figure as chief executive, for example, often causes dramatic rises in the price of shares, and the opposite is equally true; also trading prices and volumes are often unstable around the time of the Annual General Meeting, especially if there is any hint of scandal.

While one of the key characteristics of shares is transferability, we must ask ourselves whether it is such a good thing having such free movement of capital. Is it really appropriate that one man's arrival can have a more dramatic effect on short-term share performance than the company's own trading performance? Surely the latter is more important. It should *not* be 'who you know, not what you know'.

It shouldn't matter who you are, as long as you do the job well. Obviously the fluctuations reflect reputation, but if the company wishing to appoint a particular individual has the confidence in its man, it should be able to do so without fear of negative market reactions. After all it is in a far better position to judge, at least if it is applying good corporate governance and hence has a good level of control, responsibility and independent representation.

Indeed there is a strong argument for *not* appointing members of the 'Great and Good': often these people are appointed as a backscratching exercise and/or to enhance the company's reputation with the City, when really they may be completely unsuitable for the job. And there are plenty of candidates who, whilst often never given the opportunity or reputation, are very capable. Michael Ost had not been considered one of these 'Great and Good' while transforming McKechnie over the last 10 years. He was finally given recognition earlier this year, by being appointed chief executive of Coats Viyella, Europe's largest clothing and textiles company. On this occasion, the share price rose modestly by six pence to 136½p.

It is true, then, that most of the time shareholders show their disapproval of company policy simply by selling their shares, rather than taking action to try and change the situation. In a large public company, this action by the private shareholder is totally ineffective in influencing policy. Of course someone investing in a private company, may do so for control rather than for short-term equity gains, and the smaller size and limited number of participants make the individual investor much more powerful in this type of company. Corporate governance – equally important in the smaller firm, especially during growth – is potentially much more workable as a great deal more attention can be paid to individual stakeholders. But private shareholders in large public companies still have an important role to play; at a minimum they should recognise the responsibilities they have. However, unless this group is well-organised enough to stand together against strong management (or equally, big institutional investors) very little can be achieved.

Employees

It has been usual for a long time for chairmen and directors to thank their workforce in their annual accounts. Would it be cynical to suggest that perhaps now they are beginning to mean it?

Corporate managers, busy with their calculations of shareholder value and portfolio analysis, often forget that a company is only as good as its people, and that the staff have a much greater stake in the company than most of the shareholders. They depend on it for their careers, their livelihood, and eventually, their pensions.

Americans are continually surprised at the difficulty in dismissing employees in continental Europe (we exclude the UK quite specifically). On the continent the company is often seen not as a piece of financial real estate, as it were, but from the industrial point of view, as a living organism, of concern to the community (or communities) that houses it and the employees that work in it, one of the main objectives being to ensure that it gives those employees the scope and space to develop and to live useful, fulfilling and rewarding lives.

Northern European companies have always emphasised their concern to involve the staff in the company. This is much more than just having employees on the board, though that is very important. Deutsche Bank takes great care to co-operate with employee representatives in staff councils both at local and group level, though it did run into problems in the Krupp-Thyssen affair of March 1997 (see Chapter 4). Works councils such as these serve as a very useful communications channel to ensure that staff are informed and that their views are at least heard. It is very important to remember, however, that employee representation on supervisory councils in Germany and The Netherlands and the workers' councils of Belgium and France does not constitute an involvement in management. Supervision and consultation are not management.

What has been the focus of a great deal of public attention and debate about corporate governance since the Mirror Group Newspapers affair is that companies need to have concern not just for their present employees, but for past employees as well. German companies take care to honour their retired staff but they do not have the same legal relationships with them through the pension funds that UK companies do. Past employees are greatly dependent on the company and are therefore very vunerable, as the above affair graphically and catastrophically demonstrated. Caring for pensioners (including deferred pensioners) and ensuring there is a solid system of checks and controls of the pension funds is a fundamental part of corporate governance. Furthermore, if the company is seen to have good provisions for pensioners with secure and responsibly managed pension funds, this will also appeal to future employees. This is the final area, which is often forgotten, and it is clearly beneficial to the company to have a reputation for responsibility all round, including caring about the future.

There are shining examples, however, of organisations of long standing which have always recognised that fair treatment and active involvement of the workforce produces great benefits from loyalty to efficiency.

We quote three in this book: the John Lewis Partnership (see Chapter 15) operates as a mutual under a trust scheme where employees are regarded as (and called) partners; the PA Charter (see Chapter 9), established by Ernest Butten in 1944, planned to create a world leader out of the organisation, with a unique system based entirely on people and their individual expertise; finally, it was Hewlett Packard's vision (see also Chapter 9) which almost single-handedly created Silicon Valley and therefore the computer industry. Let us look briefly at how this vision placed people at the forefront of the organisation.

Case study: Employees as stakeholders

'THE HP WAY'

When they started the company in 1939, Bill Hewlett and David Packard wanted more than profits revenue and a constant stream of new, happy customers. For them, business success also included:

- a focus on fields of interest in which innovative, meaningful contributions were possible
- a dedicated, fairly compensated workforce and a working environment that fostered intense individual creativity
- a companywide commitment to community involvement.

These, and other factors, such as openness to change and the virtue of sustained hard work, have made their approach to business famous the world over: *The HP Way*. In his book telling the story of the company, David Packard says:

> From the beginning, Bill Hewlett and I have had a strong belief in people. We believe that people *want* to do a good job and that it is important for them to enjoy their work at Hewlett Packard. We try to make it possible for our people to feel a real sense of accomplishment in their work.
>
> Closely coupled with this is our strong belief that individuals be treated with consideration and respect and that achievements be recognised. It has always been important to Bill and me to create an environment in which people have a chance to be their best, to realise their potential, and to be recognised for their achievements.

He goes on to explain:

> The underlying principle of HP's personnel policies became the concept of sharing – sharing the responsibilities for defining and meeting goals, sharing in company ownership through stock purchase plans, sharing in profits, sharing the opportunities for personal and professional development, and even sharing the burdens created by occasional downturns in business.

Customers

There is no pecking order when it comes to stakeholders. By placing customers third in this discussion, we are not alluding to any lower priority. On the contrary, they are the lifeblood of any organisation. This may seem an obvious thing to say, but as with many basic principles similarly highlighted in this book, a surprising number of organisations seem to forget this. At best, what frequently occurs is that customer surveys and analyses are carried out, but with a preset idea of results, thus biasing the whole process and simply serving to confirm the directors' views. What is called for is a complete transformation in how these sovereigns interact with the company. While a marketing revolution has been going on since the 1950s and especially 1960s, many still do not really know their customers.

This applies both to the end-user – the 'consumer' – and the business customer who contributes to the fabrication of a product in the value chain. As far as the latter is concerned, the company has a smaller number of customers (who purchase in larger quantities) than, say, the commercial retailer. The importance of this relationship is therefore more obvious and in many ways easier to develop and maintain, as contact will be personal. However there is rarely 100 per cent satisfaction, and often there is dissatisfaction (especially among smaller accounts), due to neglect or maybe because other operational practices, not directly related to the customer, are disapproved of.

Complacency in customer relations is the first nail in the coffin as has been proved so many times. Frequent contact with *all* customers (depending on size) is what is needed to keep existing clients from deserting, through asking them if they feel happy with the level of service, quality and price they are receiving, and just as importantly how they feel about the company's other corporate governance practices.

Contact with end-consumers is more complicated and expensive, but the same applies. Marketing techniques are sufficiently developed – and improving all the time – to maintain a similar level of knowledge of customer expectations as with a single, larger customer. As far as corporate governance is concerned, consumer-orientation goes beyond the realm of using geo-demographical information to arouse needs and affect purchasing behaviour. It means that you become, and remain, aware of the consumers' feelings, not just about your product but about you as an institution, your ethical practices and the contribution you make to the community.

We will deal with this in Part B in the *Stakeholder Analysis*.

Suppliers/trading partners

The company and its corporate partners

Very few multinationals are so big and powerful that they can exist alone, outside a business network of alliances and partners, and even those that are big enough find that it pays them to work within such networks. Partnership is very different from the old-fashioned relationship with suppliers and dealers or agents: it means working together rather than each one trying to get the upper hand over the other.[3]

Renault talks about its partnership with suppliers who account for half the cost of its vehicles and the Japanese car industry and its relationship with its component suppliers and its agents has provided any number of examples. Britain's very efficient retail industry also demonstrates how companies can work together for their common good.

Marks & Spencer prides itself on working with its suppliers, but it also imposes stringent quality and cost controls on them empowered by its huge buying power. The company uses electronic data exchange and other such devices to manage its supply chain more effectively. But the link between M & S and its suppliers exists on another level, too. The huge importance of their customer means that these companies' investment programmes have to take account of M & S and its requirements. Marks & Spencer may not have its executives on the boards of supplier companies but no one can deny that it has an influence over their governance, using that term in its widest sense.

Increasing in importance at present are telecommunications alliances, hardly surprising considering the constant advances in technology and the enormous potential in this market as the year 2000 approaches. These alliances, born of a competitive need to share technology, tend to be quite unstable, though – as well as immensely complex, as the following example demonstrates (we hope the reader is able to follow the twists to the plot!). In 1997 Endesa, the dominant Spanish electricity group, broke off its relationship with Banco Central Hispano (BCH), the large commercial bank, over a rival bid for Retevisión, the country's second planned telecoms operator. BCH headed a consortium called Opera, backed by France Telecom and Sprint of the US. Deutsche Telecom, the third member of the Global One alliance, decided to stay out of the bid, apparently due to balance sheet restrictions, although it kept its options open to step into the attractive Spanish market in case its Global One partners won. AT&T somewhat surprisingly followed suit, despite a planned joint bid with Germany's Mannesman, which, also fairly surprisingly, presented a bid on its own despite its links with Unisource, another telecoms alliance consisting of the Dutch, Swedish and Swiss operators. Meanwhile, Endesa joined forces with Stet, saying the Italian operator valued its fibre-optic network more highly than France Telecom, BCH's main partner. Finally, in July 1997, the first 60 per cent of the newly-formed Retevisión was sold to Endesa[4] and Stet, plus Unión Fenosa and Euskaltel, raising Pta 116.4bn (around £465.6m).

Also in 1997, Telefónica, Spain's big national operator against which Retevisión was to compete, broke off its links with Unisource to join another alliance, Concert, which seemed to be faring better – and looked to benefit from Telefónica's substantial presence in South America. Concert is driven by British Telecom and MCI of the US, which had been given the all clear by the European Commission to go ahead with a planned $20bn merger. It was definitely the stronger of the three global alliances, despite the fact that Unisource was linked to the larger American operator, AT&T, and was continuing to expand. The situation is bound to have changed several times by the time this book hits the shelves.

More extravagant was the project dubbed the 'Internet-in-the-sky', a $9bn venture to launch more than 300 communications satellites to blanket the globe with Internet, business and interactive media services. Billionaires Craig McCaw, the telecoms entrepreneur and Bill Gates, founder of Microsoft, were joined by Boeing, which invested $100m in a 10 per cent stake in Teledesic, a company dreamt up by McCaw.[5]

Purchasing links

There is a growing trend in certain industries for products to be purchased within the framework of such partnerships. Close customer and supplier relationships are being developed, helped by the strong independence between companies as a result of processes like just-in-time (JIT). Buyers are organising networks of contractors and subcontractors among their suppliers, like the pyramid-shaped organisations of Japanese automobile producers. These relationships extend to collaboration in distribution and even the siting of warehouses and plants. Such relationships also have to involve the greater circulation of information among the partners and more openness in information between them. Renault's *Information Achat* programme, for instance, periodically brings together the CEOs of some 80 of the company's best suppliers. One of the objectives is to develop control procedures with the intention of reducing costs for everyone. The toughness is still there but the old adversarial buyer–seller relationship has changed. The goal is a perfect fit between supplier and customer.

Other types of links

British Aerospace (BAe) quite openly states that its future will have to lie in global alliances. Its competitor across the Channel, Aerospatiale, says its policy is to encourage alliances so as to give the company strategic advantage in each of the sectors and for each of the programmes in which it is engaged. A network of partnerships is seen as enabling it to broaden its market access and make it possible for R & D to be shared.

French and Italian groupings have traditionally worked on an extended family basis, where whole empires were constructed through cross-shareholdings and directorships between friends and allies, known as *noyaux durs* in France and the infamous *salotto buono* (good living room) in Italy. This is an extreme situation, however, and one which is under pressure. France, for example, has seen the end to a number of such relationships, examples being the merger of insurers Axa and UAP, and the unwinding of cross-participation by Société Générale, Alcatel Alsthom and Crédit Lyonnais.

Community and environment

Social impact

Multinational companies, as we have shown, have an interest in marking themselves as good citizens of every country and every community in which they operate. There is another side to this too. There is intense competition between countries, provinces and localities to attract strong, reputable companies because they bring employment, whether Disneyland to Paris, Nissan to Tyneside, or Volkswagen to the Czech Republic. Countries and communities have a strong interest in the success of the companies they play host to, and are only too aware of how they are affected by the companies' corporate decisions. They are affected at all levels, from entire countries such as Brunei, virtually depending on a single company, Shell Oil, to towns such as Seattle, which is synonymous with Boeing, or Eindhoven with Philips. Works closures affect much more than the direct employment; there are also the knock-on effects on indirect employment as evidenced by the closure of the steel mills around

PART A · THE TRUTH ABOUT CORPORATE GOVERNANCE

Corby or the coal mines in South Wales. When British Steel closed its plants in Lanarkshire in 1991, some 1,200 jobs were lost.

Environmental impact

The impact of social and environmental issues is one of the most influential forces in the world today – we will examine how we believe it will affect the state of corporate governance in Chapter 8. Here we will as a case in point look briefly at a group which has faced pressure over its environmental and human rights record in the months preceding the publication of this book: Royal Dutch/Shell.

Case study: Ignoring public opinion

SHELL: 'A STATE WITHIN A STATE'

In 1995, Shell, the largest international oil company, received widespread condemnation for its activities in Nigeria following the execution of minority rights activist Ken Saro Wiwa and an outcry in Europe over its plan – later dropped – to dump the obsolete Brent Spar oil storage installation in the Atlantic Ocean. In early 1997, John Jennings, chairman (until the AGM) of Shell Transport & Trading, the UK arm of the group, admitted that 'we had not been listening enough'. He said that environmental and human rights groups would now be invited to participate in some of its more sensitive projects, especially in Africa and Latin America. 'We should use the increased scrutiny of NGOs [non-governmental organisations] as a tool to strengthen our performance.' The company also published a Statement of General Business Principles, covering environmental issues. This came at a time when a shareholder resolution criticising Shell's environmental and social track record was launched. The company denied this was the reason for producing the new document, which, however, failed to stem the flow of criticism. The resolution was supported by 18 public and private pension funds, five religious institutions, an academic fund and individuals from a pressure group called the Ecumenical Committee on Corporate Responsibility, and was also backed by PIRC, whose members accounted for 12 per cent of the company's shares.

It was put to the AGM, but due to heavy campaigning – including personal visits to its top 50 shareholders – it was comfortably defeated. Supporters of the resolution and groups such as Friends of the Earth and the World Development Movement, which had been trying to take a more business-like approach to campaigning, criticised the board for refusing to allow external auditing of the company's environmental and social policies. Jennings, speaking at the AGM, said 'I have a problem with the concept of auditing policy. We have to leave the policy responsibility to the board.' But he also said the board shared the objectives of the resolution and admitted that the external 'verification in principle was desirable'. This admission, and the fact that the issue has had such an impact not just on the company in at least waking it from complacency, but on corporate ethics in general, has been claimed as a breakthrough by Anne Simpson of PIRC. Certainly it is true that this episode marks the beginning of new tactics by shareholders, taking the lead from the US; protests which give NGOs new power – an arrow in their quiver, as one group described it – which boards cannot ignore.

Shell has been the most secretive of the big international oil companies with a reputation for being arrogant. But the group's senior executives, including Cor Herkströter, the group's senior managing director believe it should become more transparent and accountable. In 1996, he acknowledged that Shell had 'become inward looking, isolated and consequently some have seen us as a "state within a state"'. It remains to be seen whether the company will deal with the criticism in a way which will satisfy its stakeholders – that is how it will become more ethical in its whole approach to governance.[6]

The State

As with all stakeholders, the company must have a two-way relationship with the State. From the company's point of view this means superficially being a good citizen and abiding by all applicable laws, which clearly affect all stakeholders, anyway. But again, good corporate governance is about more than that. It is difficult, however, to maintain a completely positive attitude towards the *spirit* of the law, due to the often burdensome legislation, the *letter* of the law. This is especially true when the State (or rather the resident government) does not fulfil its side of the stakeholder relationship. There will always be problems if a stakeholder demands too much of a company, for example, if shareholders want an unrealistically high dividend. It is the same for the State. If, for example, the rate of tax is very high, it will be worthwhile paying an avoidance industry – thus resulting in a fall in receipts, as demonstrated by the increase in receipts in the 1980s as a result of a reduction in the sky-high rates of tax in the 1970s, and the recent shortfall in UK VAT receipts as a result of continuous increases in this tax. A balance needs to be struck which benefits all parties. In the case of tax this means finding the level which will bring maximum revenue – not too low, but low enough to make an avoidance industry unnecessary.

We will look at future influences of and effects on Parliament and the DTI, and the Stock Exchange in Chapter 8.

Conclusion

In a well-run organisation, good stakeholder relationships should naturally and equally form as much a part of the management function as other, perhaps more tangible, factors. Having assessed and analysed the relative positions of all stakeholders towards the company – and each other, and obtained complete information on each group, this knowledge can be used as a highly effective tool in gaining competitive advantage. We have looked here at some of the most important features of each group (this chapter – indeed this book – is not, we reiterate, designed to go into extensive and deep discussion, which would contradict our own statement that there is too much debate). We have addressed the main issues surrounding them, and hopefully demonstrated to the reader our conviction that corporate governance is about the wider issues and shown how it concerns everybody, everywhere, not just finance directors who struggle with Cadbury and his successors. Simply by opening the mind to the opportunities presented in this approach will lift the weight of corporate governance from the shoulders of the weary director.

NOTES

[1] Quoted by Monks and Minow in *Corporate Governance*, Blackwell Business, 1995.
[2] From an article in the *Daily Telegraph*, 24 March 1997.
[3] There are lessons to be learnt here from the co-operative movement's philosophy – see Chapter 6.
[4] Endesa itself went under public offer in September 1997, following the privatisation trend that has been transforming Spanish business culture in recent years. Major privatisation in the 20 or so months up to that of Endesa, has involved the sale of some of the remaining stakes in Repsol, the petroleum giant, Téléfonica and Argentaria, the fast-growing bank, which alone have raised over Pta 1.1tr (£4.6bn). Information courtesy of Privatisation International, London.
[5] Information from the *Financial Times'* web site *FT.com* (http://www.FT.com).
[6] Based on articles in the *Financial Times* by Robert Corzine and William Lewis.

Chapter 4

DIFFERENT COUNTRIES, DIFFERENT MODELS

Introduction *51*

UK *51*

Germany *52*

France *56*

Japan *59*

The US *61*

The European Union *63*

Conclusion *65*

'You must understand that giving the Président Directeur-Général almost absolute power in a French company is in accordance with the French tradition of strong centralised leadership which goes back through de Gaulle and Napoleon to Louis XIV.'

A leading French industrialist[1]

Introduction

The aim of this chapter is not to provide an exhaustive study of the different models of corporate governance around the world, as this has already been done in other volumes, and is not within the scope of this one. The chapters in this first part serve to give the reader a background to corporate governance and the debate which surrounds it – with a global perspective appropriate to the growing number of global businesses. The purpose behind writing this book was to create a complete but usable guide to the subject. Thus a fairly brief background and comment was needed to accompany our practical model for implementing *good* corporate governance, which, together with declaring our dissatisfaction at the all-talk-and-no-action state of the debate, is the *raison d'être* of this book.

Here, then, we summarise the system of corporate governance in operation in the UK, the US, Germany, France and Japan, and examine the current debate within the European Union. The situation in the UK, particularly its legal background, was discussed in some depth in Chapter 2. Here, we simply summarise the basis for the current system. The other countries are explained on both a legal and cultural level.

UK

The key aim of business in the UK is held to be profit maximisation and wealth generation, particularly for shareholders. The debate on corporate governance has focused, as we have seen, on the relationship between management and shareholders. It starts from the simple premise that a company is a piece of property owned by its shareholders, and they get together once a year at least, to exercise their proprietal rights in annual general meetings, when, *inter alia*, they approve the accounts, appoint the auditors and elect the directors. If they disapprove of what the company is doing they can vote the directors out of office, or if they cannot do that, they always have the option of selling their shares. At the extreme, if enough people with enough shares do so, this can result in the sale of the company itself and such sales, or the threat of them, the theory goes, act to promote efficiency in a market economy by facing inefficient and badly performing managements with the prospect of being taken over.

Only shareholdings give such rights. Bankers and other lenders of money are not seen as playing any significant part in the governance of companies. Their role is regarded as strictly limited to lending money on the basis of commercial criteria. Their relationship with the company is a contractual one.

The company itself is run by a board of directors, some of whom will be executive managers and others, non-executives, that is, directors without portfolios. These outside, or independent directors are elected for their wisdom, experience and contacts. They are independent of the detailed operations of the company and they can bring a disinterested but expert viewpoint to bear on its affairs. In particular their role is to participate in, or run two key committees, the audit committee,[2] which oversees the financial probity of the company, and the emoluments or remuneration committee,[3] which fixes the chairman's and the executive directors' remuneration. Above all their job is to ensure that the chairman does not overstep the mark. On occasion they have to be instrumental in getting rid of him or her.

The non-executive director is regarded as quite essential in maintaining a balance in a company. If the problem is one of balance, or so goes the theory, then it can be solved by recruiting the right non-executive. Mr A or Mrs B or Ms C, or even Lord D, will solve everything. Though a recent survey[4] has indicated that more than half of all UK directors are non-executive, we would question the efficacy of this as the main route to good corporate governance, and we discuss this in Chapters 13 and 15.

Germany

Legal background

There are basically two types of company in Germany:

- **GmbH**, limited liability company: private – cf ltd
  Gesellschaft mit beschranker Haftung

- **AG**, stock corporation: public – cf plc
  Aktiengesellschaft

GmbH

These are private companies. Those with less than 500 employees do not need to have a supervisory council, one of the key features of the

German system of governance. There are about 434,000 GmbHs which account for nearly half of GNP.

AG

These are the larger companies. The total capital of these 3,000 or so public companies in Germany is smaller than the total capital of the private companies, and less than 700 of these AGs are quoted on the German stock exchanges, compared with 3,000 in the UK. The AG can issue bearer or registered shares and it is common for the articles to provide (as in many UK private companies) that any transfer of shares must be subject to the approval of the company ('vinculation'). It is estimated that about one third of all AGs have made use of this provision. Often there are also voting restrictions, such as limiting voting powers to 5 per cent or 10 per cent of capital no matter how many shares are actually owned. Often minority shareholders are virtually ignored. A significant size of cross-holdings between companies is permitted.

Two-tier structure

German companies have a two-tier structure: a management board (*Vorstand*) and a supervisory council (*Aufsichtsrat*). The phrase 'two-tier', however, gives the wrong impression: it is not that one is superior to the other. The two bodies function side-by-side, with different and very specific duties. The management board has total responsibility for managing the company, both its day-to-day operations as well as questions of policy. It must be emphasised that the supervisory council plays no part in management, as commented upon in the last chapter. Its role is to appoint and control members of the management board. In practice, a company's articles frequently provide that major matters require the approval of the supervisory council, which is made up of representatives of shareholders and employees. The members of the management board, however, are in a strong position with their five-year tenure of office. Basically the supervisory council can be likened in many ways to a UK board of directors, and the management board to its executive committee.

Labour law

Labour law in Germany is based on employee representation and co-determination, at shopfloor and supervisory council level. As a result of the Co-determination Act, 1976, half of the supervisory councils of AGs and GmbHs of more than 2,000 employees must be employee representatives. In practice, the chairman of the council, who has a casting vote, is invariably a representative of the shareholders. The employees, however, are protected by a provision that a 75 per cent vote is required for changes to the articles, including any changes in share capital, mergers and liquidations.

Cultural background

The German business culture is like the Japanese in that it does not regard the company as a piece of property, owned by its shareholders to do with what they will, but as a community, with obligations to its employees, customers and the surrounding communities, as well as to those who have provided it with finance. Profit is of course necessary and essential if the company is to survive and grow, but it is not an end in itself. Investors and employees can take a long view because in their different ways they are locked in, and they have a structure of governance that separates the long from the short term. The shareholders understand why dividends should be kept low in less than good times (let alone bad times) and money retained in the business. It has been reckoned that the UK's top 100 companies pay at least twice as much and sometimes three times as much out of their profits as their German counterparts. Corporate Germany takes a long-term view, epitomised by the ambitions of the *Mittelstand* companies, to provide for 'life beyond the grave'.

Another, important advantage of the German system is that it creates a structure that, through the supervisory council, makes accountability to its employees, owners and financiers easier. That, after all, is what governance is all about. UK and American companies could take some lessons from German governance, despite criticism that it is bureaucratic and rigid.

Set against that, it also lacks transparency, partly through an unwillingness of German business to admit the perhaps overly-strong role the banks play, and this is worsened by the fact that the Germans as a race can be very reluctant advocates of change. Both these factors were highlighted by the saga of the aborted hostile takeover of Thyssen by Krupp Hoesch (see below). Deutsche Bank, particularly, was in the uncomfortably contradictory position of being both the major backer of a hostile (albeit sound) takeover bid, a practice virtually unknown and certainly unwanted in Germany, and also a social icon. Its latter image suffered considerable damage as a result. However, a lot of the problems are more attributable to political and social factors than the corporate governance system which has no control over these. The power of the unions, which played a key role in the episode, is an example.

Case study: Germany needs to change

KRUPP AND THYSSEN: SIGNS OF TROUBLE?

On Tuesday 25 March 1997, 20,000 angry steel workers invaded Frankfurt to protest against the role of the banks. This was in reaction to the hostile bid by Krupp Hoesch for its bigger steel building rival, Thyssen. The bid had been called off the previous day, but this made no difference to Klaus Zwickel, head of the powerful IG Metall trade union, who addressed its members outside Deutsche Bank's headquarters. The bank, with Dresdner Bank and Goldman Sachs had backed the takeover with a DM15bn line of credit. With this revelation (prematurely leaked), Deutsche's image as a 'pillar of society' had been knocked for six, although it denied acting outside the unwritten German code of good behaviour. The result of the episode was an agreed friendly merger of the two companies' carbon steel interests, Thyssen owning 60 per cent of a new company, Thyssen Krupp Stahl, with an estimated loss of 6,000 jobs.

What was somewhat surprising about the episode – particularly to Gerhard Cromme, chief executive of Krupp – were the actions of Dieter Vogel, head of Thyssen, to obtain political support (he even telephoned Chancellor Kohl to ask for help) and mobilise so many workers so quickly (using Thyssen's own logistics division) against what Zwickel was allowed to brand 'Wild West tactics'. Many saw this as the death of the hostile takeover in Germany, although one Thyssen adviser believed there was a future for soundly financed hostile bids.

However, all this does mean that investment will be moved away from Germany, particularly to Eastern Europe, where wage costs are infinitely lower.[5] Germany has two main problems. For one, the Kohl administration seems to be incapable of, or unwilling to implement promised reforms and the unions have stepped into the political arena to defend the status quo – ordinary Germans are accustomed to some of the highest living standards in Europe. The second is that of transparency. Much of the negative publicity which caused the uproar may have been avoided if everything was discussed in public, involving the affected parties in negotiations[6] – this has to be the way forward for Germany, away from the rather secretive dealings which have characterised stakeholder relations until now. As one of Cromme's advisers said,

> German business has a choice. It can go on doing deals in the back rooms with banks and unions pandering to each other's self-interest, or it can do things in public under the transparent disciplines of the marketplace.

HOESCHT: A SIGN OF HOPE?

In December 1996, Hoescht, the German chemical group, announced the purchase of the minority shareholdings in France's Roussel-Uclaf. It was part of a strategic process to enhance shareholder value. During 1996, the group, led by chairman Jürgen Dormann, split itself into six parts, promised to float stakes in some of its divisions, and off-loaded its underperforming speciality chemicals businesses. It also promised to adopt US accounting standards and to gain a New York listing. All these moves were designed to make the group more transparent and increase its value; they were not in vain – the group's shares outperformed the Dax 100 by 44 per cent that year.

The move follows the example of other chemicals groups, such as the UK's ICI, Switzerland's Sandoz and Dow Chemical of the US, which have all, in recent years, split their chemicals from the pharmaceutical businesses. Further, Hoescht made no secret of the fact that it had been in talks with the French Government – which owned 4.3 per cent of Roussel – to ensure that it would take up any offer.

The power of the banks is undeniable. They sit on the supervisory councils, from where they can analyse and scutinise management performance. They also own large amounts of equity in a variety of companies including blue chip companies. But the banks do have a good understanding of the businesses in which they are involved. They have a mechanism for evaluating companies that is virtually unknown in the anglophone world's banks, the Sekretariat, invented in 1870 by Deutsche Bank, which consciously modelled it on the Prussian general staff. Thus the company is accountable to a body which doesn't contain non-executives brought in for general reasons, *one* of which is to represent the shareholders, but which actually contains some of the shareholders' own people.

France

Legal Background

There are various types of company in France. The most important ones are:

- **SARL**, limited liability company: private – cf ltd
  Sociétés à responsabilité limitée

- SA, public company: public – cf plc
  Société Anonyme

SARL, or SRL

This is the most common form of company, as is the GmbH in Germany and the Ltd in the UK. It requires a minimum of two shareholders (maximum 50) and a share capital of FF50,000. SARLs do not have boards of directors, instead they are run by one or more managers (*gérant*). Statutory auditing requirements vary depending on the size of the company.

SA

About 650 SAs are listed on the French stock exchanges and, as in Germany, shareholders' rights can be restricted by limiting the number of votes each shareholder has at general meetings. An SA's articles may go as far as to grant two votes per share, especially in takeover situations, for those shares which have been held by the same shareholder in registered form for anything from two to four years. SAs require a minimum of seven founder shareholders and a share capital of FF250,000. There is also a legal obligation to consult workers' committees, although employees do not have representatives on the board.

There are two systems of governance open to the SA. The first has a unitary board and is based on the formidable power of the *Président Directeur Général* (PDG), and the other has a supervisory council.

The first is the traditional and preferred system. The PDG is elected by the board (*Conseil d'Administration*) which in turn is elected by the shareholders. Most of the day-to-day running of the business is left to the PDG, with the board usually stepping in only in times of trouble. Jonathan Charkham, in his study of international corporate governance, notes:

> If a business is running well the board tends to remain entirely passive and to defer to the PDG, even on major decisions. If, however, problems arise it will accept and exercise power even to the extent of dismissing the PDG – though it tends to do this late in the day.[7]

The second, introduced in 1966, consists of a directorate (*Directoire*) with two to five members, which manages the company, and a supervisory council (*Conseil de Surveillance*). Though it resembles the German two-tier system, and has the seeming attraction of an apparently balanced nature, in reality it lacks any significant differences from the alternative. It provides limited improvement in curbing the power of the senior executive, who in both company forms, rarely shares much of this power with the other directors. Hence it is used only by a very small proportion of French companies.

Cultural background

The State and the private sector are very close in France, and there is still a high level of intervention, despite the various privatisation programmes initiated in the last 10 years (especially since 1993, when a programme of 21 privatisations was launched). The country's long tradition of centralisation, hierarchical rigidity, and respect is reflected in its attitude to governance, with the PDG at the helm of companies, and virtually not answerable to anyone, as noted above. If matters are put to the vote, it is tantamount to a vote of no confidence in the PDG.

France's unique business culture stems from the importance of the education system which dominates the country, in both sectors. France is still run by its star pupils, the so-called *élite* – graduates of the *grandes écoles*. These institutions of higher education, which cream off the best in the country, were originally set up to produce engineers and administrators to implement State policies. And because of the centralised, *dirigiste* method of running the economy, it used to be a requirement to have a career in the civil service before moving into the private sector. Certainly it helps having this experience to understand how the economy works and therefore how to manoeuvre your company within this system. Unlike in the UK and the US, where senior executives may have worked their way up from the bottom, French companies are generally run by ex-senior civil servants, who may move freely from public to private sector. Of course there are exceptions, companies which are run by their founders and/or non-*élite* entrepreneurs, some fine examples of which are Carrefour, Moulinex, and Leclerc which is run by a priest.

The old boys' network goes far beyond similar traditions in other countries, as all the *élite* have had exactly the same education and background, and thus are all like-minded in their approach. But there has been a weakening of this stronghold in recent times, with an increasing amount of people not from the *élite* class in business. The last few years have been a period of transition. There have been various changes in the law, such as a strengthening of the board's powers, and a shift away from, or rather a dilution of, the hard line *dirigiste* system of governance. It seems that no one really knows which direction to go in – towards the freer anglophone model, or the more balanced German model. And the situation does not look as if it will resolve itself quickly. It may take EU harmonisation measures to bring things back down to earth again.

What is certain, and what may influence the outcome, is that the shareholder movement has been picking up momentum and has brought about a number of significant changes. In Chapter 3 we saw how the *noyaux durs*, the systems of cross-shareholdings and directorship among companies was dissolving, and this was to a great extent due to the protestations of shareholders – more significantly, the small shareholders. These have been getting together to try and block decisions which they disapprove of – often the institutions are not so dedicated in their good corporate governance objectives as they claim to be. In June 1996, for example, the boards of Eurotunnel and Crédit Foncier de France were given a scolding when their 1995 accounts were approved by just 62.5 per cent and 52.7 per cent respectively of those voting.

While these are dramatic examples, it is symptomatic of the trend towards shareholder militancy. Unfortunately the AGM is still a fairly ineffective platform for the private shareholder to bring about changes, when shares are usually owned mainly by the institutions. There are signs of increased activism among institutions, however: '... a drive for a better return on equity – still low in many French quoted companies – may prove the most important destabilising influence on entrenched Gallic boardroom attitudes', says Andrew Jack,[8] who goes on to remark how, thanks to new legislation institutions are beginning to invest large new sums, traditionally the case in Anglo-Saxon and Dutch pension funds. 'There is still a long way to go', he said, 'but shareholder value is likely to increasingly shift from a marketing tool or a talking point to a necessity for a growing number of boards.'

Japan

Legal structure

Kabushiki Kaisha

Businesses in Japan which seek the benefit of limited liability with public subscription for their shares, have to register as *Kabushiki Kaisha*. These must have a minimum of three directors, elected by the shareholders, but most major companies have many more. There is little place for non-executive directors in the UK or US sense of the word, though there are directors appointed to the board through the links the company has with its business partners. In some cases, too, retired executives could be appointed to the board. The Commercial Code also calls for 'representative directors' (*daihyo torishimariyaku*) to be elected to the board. Their role is to represent the company in its dealings with third parties such as government, the authorities, banks and other companies in the industry. The chairman and president will usually be among the most senior of the representative directors.

The symbolic role of the bank is crucial in providing the focus for reflecting the vision and values of the leadership to the members of the organisation, but a key part in the management of the corporation is also played by the meetings of the top management group (*jomukai*) and the meetings of the general managers (*keiei kaigi*).

Cultural background

It is well known that Japan has a business culture all of its own. Corporate governance takes place behind the scenes between the senior corporate officials and the major institutional shareholders in whose hands ownership is concentrated. The background to the company will be the *kairetsu*, or grouping of cross-shareholdings, into which the company fits. Many of the shareholding institutions will be banks, which will also be substantial lenders to the company. The company itself is very much regarded as a social unit with a unity between management and labour, and the managers (who will have risen through the ranks) will see themselves as representatives of the employees as much as of the shareholders. There is a virtual separation of operation from supervision, and the management changes that take place tend to occur as a result of discussions behind the scenes between the financial interests and senior management.

Government's involvement in the private sector is even stronger than in France, often bordering on corruption – indeed the last few years have seen a number of incidents of such behaviour, for example that which led to the collapse of the Liberal Democratic Party. This, and the weakening of the Japanese economy in recent years, may be signs of an imminent collapse of a system which has hitherto proved highly successful, as demonstrated by Japan's incredible trading performance in the world market. The faults in the system are clearly that it is far too inward-looking and closed up in its tight network of companies and banks. But partly in response to the economic slow-down and a sudden drop in profitability, some far reaching changes have been taking place in the 1990s, both short term, such as legal reforms on shareholders' rights, independent auditors and corporate independence from main bank financing, and long-term changes in Japanese society and attitudes.

The recession in Japan has led to a severe decline in the number of small businesses. The survivors are those which have created new ways of doing business; for example, there is a growing trend in the manufacturing sector to cut operating costs in the battle with larger competitors by outsourcing to the large firms themselves. The Government itself has instigated a programme to investigate entrepreneurialism and determine whether it can be encouraged by education.

The US

Legal background

Governance is a matter of serious concern in the US. It is now a stock exchange requirement that companies should have audit committees as a condition of quotation. This also means that company boards must have a proportion of outside directors.

In the US, companies incorporate under the laws of various different states which differ from each other and, indeed, compete in a sense with each other. The US has no national corporate law, allowing every state to develop its own. Particular states have developed anti-takeover laws to entice companies to their state. In 1990 there was a rash of anti-takeover legislation at state level, most notably in Pennsylvania and Massachusetts. In Pennsylvania, and in several other states, for instance, a company has to take account of other parties, such as the suppliers, when making takeovers. The state of Delaware is famous for being a 'corporate haven' and is the market leader in this type of legislation and the rulings of its courts are therefore carefully watched. As long ago as 1989 there was a landmark decision by a Delaware court over the proposed Time-Warner merger which upheld the right of management to reject one takeover bid in favour of a lower-priced deal which the board considered was better in view of its long-term strategy.

There is a growing tendency in the US courts to look at the process of decision-making to see whether it is reasonable, coupled with a rise in shareholder activism and lawsuits.

Cultural background

The US and the UK have very similar systems of corporate governance, as noted in previous chapters. There are differences in emphasis and attitude, though, just as there are differences between the two societies. Three important differences are:

- **NEDs** – In major US companies, the board contains a high proportion of non-executive directors; in the UK, typically less than half are non-executives
- **CE–Chairman** – At least three-quarters of US companies have the same person in the posts of chairman and chief executive officer; in UK public companies, the chairman is usually a non-executive
- **Equity** – About 60 per cent of equity in US companies is held by foreign investors; in the UK the percentage is roughly reversed, with UK institutions holding nearly 70 per cent.

While boards of US companies are heavily dominated by non-executives, the ruling management is still usually extremely strong. This is partly due to the tendency to combine the positions of chairman and chief executive which puts the person concerned in a position of enormous strength. Monks and Minow point out that 'it makes management accountable to a body led by management'. The situation is compounded by the fact that the majority of these non-executives are usually executive officers (often chairmen and CEOs) of other companies.

There is also a sprinkling of academics and political worthies on the board of directors, but this does not necessarily ensure 'independence', as the mere fact of having NEDs also fails to do so. There is a feeling that the system is too comfortable for executive management. Graef Crystal has described the composition of a typical US board as 'ten friends of management, a woman and a black'.[9]

This has, of course, been under attack for some time, spurred by the excesses of the 1980s' takeover wave with its examples of corporate greed. There have been growing signs of shareholder restlessness, especially from institutions, some of which have been pressing for reforms in governance rules.

> CalPERS [California Public Employees Retirement System] has not only prodded individual companies to some effect, but also initiated the movement to persuade the SEC [Securities and Exchange Commission] to change some of its rules, in which it was able to muster some significant support.[10]

Other institutions, such as CALSTRS, another pension fund, have also been making loud noises about having more power to intervene when management is underperforming. Reform rests in the hands of politicians, of course, and, as seen in the failed attempts at legislation in the 1970s in the UK, change is often impaired by conflicting political interests. However, the snowball has been set rolling, and the likelihood is that institutions will make louder noises rather than back down.[11] And if it is true that what happens first in the US is bound to happen later in the UK, then we can expect a similar wave of activism in this country. Already institutional investors have been putting pressure on companies to make directors' compensation more stock-orientated, thus ensuring an interest in good performance. What is also important (some would argue more important) is that shareholder activism is directed not just to their own investment, but to the protection of other stakeholders' interests, as discussed in Chapter 3.

The European Union

In 1969, Dennis Thompson[12] remarked on the urgency felt by many people for the formation of a European (limited) company. Nearly 30 years later, despite the nine directives passed in the '70s and '80s, of which the Fifth Directive (1983) is well known, the EU statute is still being negotiated. The statute provides a uniform but optional regime for the formation of *Societas Europeas* (SE). It excludes certain areas such as social security and employment law, taxation and competition, which it leaves to the member states' own laws. The Fifth Directive sets out the structure of such an organisation, with a choice between one or two tiers:

- **Two tier:** This contains a management board and a supervisory board. The latter would have wide-ranging powers from electing the management board to receiving timely information, especially regarding the annual accounts.
- **One tier:** The company would be managed by an administration board, which would be controlled by non-executives. The number of non-executives on the board should be divisible by three and be greater than the number of executives.

The Directive also requires member states to enable employees to participate in the supervision and strategic development of an SE, but not with uniform legislation. Indeed, the Directive allows a choice between various alternatives; all must, however, have employee representation, whether it be on the board (administration or supervisory) or in a separate body (eg a works council).

Response to the EU statute

Ramón Tamames, an authority on the European Union, argues that it is compulsory employee participation and the auditing obligations which seem to have caused the Fifth Directive to be rejected up to now.[13] Certainly it shows the German domination of European issues since the 1950s, Germany being the only country which has a significant amount of employee participation; the French system, whilst including employee consultation, has no board representation or participation to any great extent; the Dutch system limits employees' representation to a supervisory role; southern European systems have even less enthusiasm for employee representation, although they are keen (at least in theory) on employee rights.

But the UK has been most opposed to employee participation, rejecting the Social Chapter of the Maastricht Treaty (as a result of which, in 1994, it became compulsory for companies with more than 1,000 workers to have a workers' committee to represent all its European employees). It is easy to criticise the actions and attitudes of the UK in Europe since the War, when there was a stubborn and ill-founded belief that Britain could do without the rest of Europe. Failure to realise the necessity of participating in the European Community from the beginning, compounded by indecision and inertia, has kept the UK out of the forum of European decision-making. However, not all its complaints are unjustified. There are strong arguments to support the British fear of over-prescription and over-definition:[14]

> [The UK] does not see any overriding need for European uniformity: if the Americans can have variety between States in the same country, why should not EC countries with their vastly differing histories and traditions have variety too.[15]

At the time of writing, the UK's 'New Labour' Government has expresssed its intention to incorporate the Social Chapter into UK legislation, a move which has been welcomed by the other EU members, though the precise implications of this remain to be clarified.

Conclusion

To judge one system as being better than another is not really justifiable. Each system discussed has its strengths and weaknesses, and each country has had its share of success using its chosen system. This debate also depends on what is considered to be 'best': are we talking, for example, in terms of economic success, competitiveness, balance of interests? In the latter terms, which is the most appropriate in terms of corporate governance, the German system is probably the best. But having balance just for the sake of balance is not a complete response. The German, (and Japanese, to which many of these arguments also apply) system has been criticised for concentating too much on *running* the company – albeit well – and ignoring market forces, especially on the global scale. The success of the two economies has been based on great but rather introverted efficiency and effectiveness, rather than dynamic, extrovert commercialisation (although there are exceptions, of course, such as Sony, which has been making big noises everywhere for years). This is seen by some as the reason for both countries' sudden weakening, as globalisation, especially of marketing and investment capitalism, takes off in the approach to the trilennium. As discussed, though, far-reaching changes, especially in Japan, are taking place which will open up these markets to global investment hunters.

What the UK and US have in freedom of markets and dynamic business activity, they lack in balance of power. This illustrates the apparent dichotomy in corporate governance between freedom and control. While other systems are perhaps too constrained, the anglophone model is perhaps *too* free, and lacks some of the checks and controls, which should be there firstly to stop offenders, and secondly to reassure stakeholders of their good intentions. These additional controls would probably be deemed unnecessary for those companies who already behave responsibly, and the companies themselves would certainly feel that they needed no such extra impositions.

As we have already seen, the debate has historically focused on shareholders, and other stakeholders are not given – except in a few cases – any say in corporate direction. Some of these, such as employees, who rely on the company for survival, not for profit, have perhaps more right to such involvement than shareholders. The argument then arises that if employee representation is such a good idea, how is it that the UK has a far better strike record in recent years than her European neighbours, who have such systems? The answer, of course lies in the macroeconomic perspective, of the political system and governmental decisions affecting the whole country (and the temperament of the society!), not in the microeconomic[16] issues of commercial practices and what are effectively individual situations within markets and industries. This may also help explain why Japan and Germany have been suffering from apparently weakening economies. While some would argue that the crises threatening Germany are symptoms of a failing system, it is arguable that the political quagmire is a greater influence here than any breakdown in the corporate governance system. The latter may be in itself very effective, despite the somewhat inward-looking nature of its protagonists.

NOTES

[1] Quotation drawn from *Keeping Good Company*, Jonathan Charkham, Oxford University Press, 1995.
[2] See The Cadbury Code of Practice: 'The board should establish an audit committee of at least 3 non-executive directors with written terms of reference which deal clearly with its authority and duties.' (Section 4.3).
[3] See the Greenbury Code of Practice: 'Remuneration committees should consist exclusively of Non-Executive Directors with no personal financial interest other than as shareholders in the matters to be decided, no potential conflicts of interest arising from cross-directorships and no day-to-day involvement in running the business.' (Section A4)
[4] Institute of Chartered Accountants and PRONED, May 1997.
[5] Wage costs in the Czech Republic, for example, are 95 per cent lower than in Western Germany. The German Trade and Industry Federation calculates that companies will create 300,000 new jobs, mostly in Eastern Europe, over the next three years.
[6] A proud embodiment of this can be found in Photobition (see Chapter 17), whose entrepreneurial boss, Eddie Marchbanks, finds it only to everyone's benefit to have everything out in the open.
[7] *Keeping Good Company*, Jonathan Charkham, Oxford University Press 1995.
[8] Quote and other information from an article in the *Financial Times*, 10 December 1996.
[9] *Financial Times*, 13 April 1992
[10] Op. cit. 7.
[11] See Chapter 8, Future Influences.
[12] La Unión Europea, Ramón Tamames.
[13] Ibid.
[14] By no means the least of these is the fact that Britain has the only unwritten constitution in the Western world, and it is also the oldest; this compares with, for example, the 10 political regimes experienced in France between 1789 and 1958

(birth date of the present constitution, the Fifth Republic), all of which came to a sticky end, mainly because the detail in which the constitution was written (and rewritten) offended one group of people or another. There are many similarities, and indeed lessons, to be drawn from this when looking at the goal of European political and economic union. And with regions such as the Basque Country, Catalonia (though less so these days), and regions in the Eastern Block wanting independence, we may well see a Europe of provinces, more than nation states – and far less one European Nation.

15 Op. cit. 7.
16 This does not mean that we are not referring to the whole country. Economics is, as John Kay reminds us, not just about forecasting inflation, growth and interest rates; microeconomics is about the study of markets, industries and firms: 'Most people – including many economists – still think that macro relates to big issues, micro to the small'.

Chapter 5

IMPACT OF SIZE

Introduction 71

The five stages of growth 71

Corporate governance and the smaller company 74

Conclusion 82

'The framework of governance has continually to evolve ... not simply to develop in parallel with the development of a business, but to keep one step ahead.'

SIR ADRIAN CADBURY,
talking from his own experience about the transition from a family firm to a publicly-quoted company[1]

Introduction

Corporate governance is seen to affect the larger organisation. This is not a view with which we would strictly agree, but rather that good corporate governance becomes more important ethically as a company grows because the interests of owners and managers start to separate. The purpose of this chapter, therefore, is to examine the implications for the smaller company as it expands, and both the case studies later in the book have been chosen to illustrate companies progressing from owner-manager to listed company status.

We start by identifying and summarising five stages of growth from a small private company to a global corporation. We then look at the first two stages in detail, that is up to the point where the company puts its head above the water and moves into public view. It is at this point – probably around getting a listing – that the company needs to have all the checks and controls in place to be beyond reproach when its procedures come under public scrutiny. It makes sense, therefore, to start thinking about corporate governance very early on, at the very least for planning purposes. This section sets out the sorts of things the board should be thinking about to plan for this entry into the public domain.

The five stages of growth

Companies can conveniently be grouped into five categories:

- small private company
- small/medium-sized enterprises (SMEs)
- medium-sized listed UK-focused company
- large public company operating in UK, EU, US
- global corporation operating in UK, EU, North America, Far East, etc.

Small private company

The characteristics of a small private company are likely to be:

- private shareholders
- usually owner-managed
- board represents owners and possibly personal advisers

- information available may be limited, but such as it is, is accessible to all
- public face is of limited relevance: under threshold of public view.

Its needs and appropriate solutions regarding good corporate governance are likely to include:

- professional management which can handle growth and related changes.

Small/medium-sized enterprises (SMEs)

The characteristics of SMEs are likely to be:

- mainly private shareholders
- often owner-managed
- information available:
  - often relatively limited
  - but accessible to shareholder-directors
  - so knowledge of the business is open to active owners
- *all* shareholders may not be treated the same as active ones
- arrangements may prejudice interests of some minority shareholders.

An SME's needs and appropriate solutions regarding good corporate governance are likely to include:

- non-executive directors with a specially defined role to safeguard *all* shareholders' interests:
  - to ensure that the board keeps on the straight and narrow.

Medium-sized listed UK-focused company

The characteristics of a medium-sized listed company are likely to be:

- a range of shareholders
- limited institutional ownership
- run by professional management
- may be residual family involvement in management
- needs to comply publicly/visibly with regulatory regimes
- little need to consider other countries' regimes/cultures
- management motivation and shareholders' interests now some way apart and need monitoring.

A medium-sized company's needs and appropriate solutions regarding good corporate governance are likely to include:

- a minimum of three non-executive directors (per Cadbury) with specific briefs.

Large public company operating in UK, EU, US

The characteristics of a large international public company are likely to be:

- mainly institutional shareholders
- board of professional managers plus NEDs; shareholders kept informed by:
  - management briefings
  - market analysts' assessments
- public face now a significant factor:
  - need to be seen as a good citizen in several countries/cultures
  - need for compliance with several different regulatory regimes
- top class management, ambitious, mobile:
  - more than capable of running rings round remote shareholders
- stakeholder concept now becomes more pressing.

A large international public company's needs/solutions regarding good corporate governance are likely to include:

- top class non-executive directors with carefully defined brief to consider/protect *all* interests

Global corporation operating in UK, EU, North America, Far East, etc

The characteristics of a global company are likely to be:

- almost entirely owned by large and small institutions, possibly drawn from several different countries
- needing to comply with several countries':
  - trading regulatory regimes and different trading cultures
  - stock exchange quotation rules
  - employment practices
- high public profile *re* all aspects of good corporate governance.

A global company's needs/solutions regarding good corporate governance are likely to include:

- top class, internationally experienced non-executive directors with clear briefs to represent all interests
- executives and non-executive directors need to know what constitutes good corporate governance and:
  - set objectives accordingly
  - establish appropriate monitoring/reporting systems to advise
  - manage accordingly:

Corporate governance and the smaller company

The other chapters in Part A are mainly descriptive, giving the reader a summary of – and our opinions on – the current state of the corporate governance debate. Here, for ease of reading and clarity of meaning, we use a fictional company to demonstrate the development and growth from a small private business to a SME. It represents in more detail how a typical business might look at these stages of growth, including the effects of particular actions, such as acquisitions. At each stage we state the issues the board should be considering, using the elements of good corporate governance discussed in Chapter 2.

Let us remind ourselves of these elements:

- *ensure a fundamental ethical basis*
- *fulfil the long-term strategic goal of the owners, taking into account the expectations of all the key stakeholders, and in particular:*
  - *consider and care for the interests of employees, past, present and future*
  - *work to maintain excellent relations with both customers and suppliers*
  - *take account of the needs of the environment and the local community*
- *maintain proper compliance with all applicable legal and regulatory requirements.*

A number of the issues of corporate governance which apply to large companies often do not apply or at least are not as important to smaller companies, such as concern over major environmental impact of operations. The emphasis is on good business management, and the directors will not normally be thinking along the lines of corporate governance at all. It will probably take them a long time to do so (though this chapter shows that they should, at least for planning purposes, as we advised at the beginning). In the example below, we will therefore expand the goal element so as better to reflect the development of the company, particularly regarding the change in the approach to corporate governance as the company grows, and to show how the issue relates to smaller companies. We shall consider the goal under the two headings of:

A. **Good business management**
   Fulfilling the agreed long-term strategic goals via successful implementation of the strategic plan, hence complying with annual operating plans and budgets.

B. **Good relations with shareholders**
   At a certain point in its development a company needs to establish special mechanisms to deal properly with the interests of remote shareholders.

Small private company

Nameless Ltd is a recently established business. It has two main directors who own most of the shares, except for a small stake belonging to a third director, who is acting as book-keeper. The company operates from a small office and employs a part-time secretary to ease administration problems.

Corporate governance and the small private company

Corporate governance to Nameless is currently all about ensuring the survival of the business, and earning enough profits to provide a living for the directors and their families and to generate sufficient of a surplus to invest in the business with a view to expansion. Let us look at the five elements of good corporate governance in relation to the company's role at this stage:

1. Fulfil the long-term strategic goal of the owners

At this stage the owners are also the managers, so the problem of conflicts of interests between management and remote shareholders is not present. As explained, therefore, we will divide this point to show that the principal need of the company at present is for good management capable of handling growth.

A. **Good business management**
We see that the directors' main concerns are:

(i) Marketing/image
- How to determine price levels for their products and whether the company is competitive enough to achieve a level of sales which will enable

them both to make a profit after costs and to have sufficient to keep their families.
- Whether the premises are in a suitable location for the business in terms of transport links, concentration of local business, etc.
- How to market the company more widely and establish a reputation.
- Putting as much as possible of their available time into selling.
- Getting the best price for their products.

(ii) Production/operating efficiency/comparative performance
- The initial capital cost of process-related equipment they buy: what is the ability of the company to afford it in relation to their expected level of sales?
- Materials the company uses, the quantity they think they need to buy, and the price offered by the various suppliers.
- The rent they pay.
- Spending as little as possible on items other than those directly relating to the production of goods/services which can be sold.

(iii) Financial structure
- The finance they have arranged with the bank: is it enough, and are the charges and interest acceptable and affordable?

(iv) Personnel/organisation
- Division of duties: are they clear about the role each has to play, and are they comfortable with the particular duties/jobs they have agreed?
- Leadership: does one of them have a stronger personality and better business sense, and if so does he use it constructively? Do the others accept his leadership?

B. Good relations with shareholders
The responsibility of each director towards his co-shareholders probably represents this dimension at least as effectively as it would to the board of a large company, especially regarding behaviour of the two larger majority shareholders towards the third, minority, shareholder.

2. Consider and care for the interests of employees, past, present and future

With the only outside employee being the part-time secretary, this clearly has limited significance at this stage, although it should be kept always in mind so as to create an immediate positive image when they start taking on staff.

3. Take account of the needs of the environment and the local community

Apart from such actions as using unleaded petrol and recycled paper, the environment is not an important part of the directors' considerations at present, and their actions will not affect the community to any great extent, either.

4. Work to maintain excellent relations with both customers and suppliers

(i) Customers
- Attracting the customers: how to keep their existing customers and build a relationship with them; how to attract new ones, and entice customers away from competitors.

(ii) Suppliers
- Getting credit from important suppliers and building a reputation for reliability.

5. Maintain proper compliance with all applicable legal and regulatory equirements

The directors need to remember the requirements of the Inland Revenue, Customs & Excise, and Companies House, and the importance of meticulous record-keeping to future peace of mind should be at the forefront of everyday business. In particular, they must be prepared for visits by the VAT inspector. As the company grows, their current auditing arrangements may be insufficient, and they will need to appoint auditors capable of handling payment of VAT and PAYE, compliance with the Health and Safety at Work Act, and ensuring that all necessary insurances are paid up.

> We would point out here, that while corporate governance is usually referred to in the context of large companies, it is still an important consideration for the smaller company, even though many aspects do not apply directly. In particular, we would make these observations relating to issues which a forward-looking board with its sights set on growth (a company which is not growing is probably dying), should be considering:
> - **Good business management** – if the company is thinking about

the elements of good corporate governance set out in our definition, the chances of something going wrong will be much reduced and the goals for growth will be easier to fulfil.

- **Compliance** – (planning for the future by) ensuring that the business is being run in a way that will make compliance to the various codes more or less automatic when they become applicable (e.g. applying for listing on the Stock Exchange).

- **Trading partners** – establishing good relationships with customers and suppliers early on and building an excellent reputation.

- **Staff** – maintaining good, close relationship with staff when the business expands.

Growth

Nameless grows quickly and acquires a small company in its sector, issuing shares to the venture capitalist who funds the deal. It quickly needs to formalise the business and establish a structure capable of meeting the needs of the various constituencies. The appearance of the first outside shareholder as a result of the merger is significant and will need to be handled carefully. In particular the expanded board needs to:

(i) Strive to achieve the business objectives
- turnover for the combined business: set targets – £n for Year 2
- profit growth: eg trebled by end of Year 2
- sort out the amalgamation process, which involves: redundancies, rationalising assets, production, selling and marketing, premises and national networks of outlets, offices, etc disposing of surplus space.

(ii) Tighten up the board procedures and reporting
- regular monthly meetings with a strict agenda
- board papers prepared and circulated
- regular monthly management accounts
- proper budgets.

Small/medium-sized companies (SMEs)

Nameless Works Ltd, as it is now called, is rapidly growing into a sizeable business, with a turnover of some £35m; it employs about 500 people, and has a board of six consisting of the original three, two who have worked their way up through the ranks, and one non-executive appointed by the venture capitalists who funded the acquisition.

Corporate governance and the SME

It will be obvious that corporate governance has become a significant factor to Nameless Works (NW, as we shall now refer to it) and if the directors have not done so already, they should conduct some sort of corporate governance audit to make sure that all the issues are given due consideration. While the directors may think they are building a soundly based and properly run business, how is NW's management style evolving to match the requirements of good practice?

1. Fulfil the long-term strategic goal of the owners

A. Good business management

Developing as it is into a major company, the board needs to install in NW the systems and procedures necessary to run such a business effectively. The key tasks are to:

(i) formulate a properly developed strategy covering the next three years to achieve a listing (assuming this complies with the goal of the shareholders).

(ii) turn this into a business plan with clear programmes for:
- market development
- product range development
- best practice in operational standards of performance
- organisational development and human resource planning
- information systems to monitor and control progress
- an appropriate financial structure to support the plans.

(iii) create a financial plan and budgets reflecting these targets.

Board meetings should be increasingly professional, with the agenda and papers circulated in advance of the meetings, and the monthly accounts pack arriving with capital expenditure authorisation requests and explanations of all the significant budget/actual variances.

B. Good relations with shareholders

While the original shareholders are still on the board, their stakes have been diluted by an increasing, albeit still minority, outside body of shareholders. There are thus two levels of consideration here:

(i) relations between the founder directors, who represent the majority, and the other executive directors, who also have stakes.

(ii) relations between the board/company and outside shareholders.

The original owners may well have different objectives from the other directors. They may, for example, be looking to realise a part of the value of their shareholding, and will probably, therefore, be more cautious than the newer members, who are likely to be ambitious and keen to pursue strategies which involve more risk. Similarly, the outside shareholders will want a certain amount of security. They need to be handled carefully and kept on-side, which means in particular:

- regular consultation, which at this stage can – and should – be done in person
- complete information, especially regarding possible investments/acquisitions, etc
- ensuring through the above that the shareholders are fully aware of the risks as well as the opportunities involved with new ventures.

2. Consider and care for the interests of employees, past, present and future

By now it has become apparent to the board that they must have a professional personnel function that knows how these matters are handled in large and well-run organisations. An experienced personnel manager should therefore be appointed with the brief to set out a programme covering most importantly:

- a three-year resource plan, indicating skill needs
- job descriptions, grading and remuneration scales
- recruitment (and severance) procedures
- training and development requirements
- health and life assurance and pension arrangements
- internal communications.

While the programme will incur a significant new overhead, it should secure the effectiveness and morale of the staff side of the business in a way which has not been hitherto addressed, and is essential as a sound base for future development.

3. Take account of the needs of the environment and the local community

This will now become an important issue for NW for future planning, and should be formally incorporated into board discussion and strategy. Consideration should be given at two levels:

- *in general terms* – eg the effects of this and other mergers/acquisitions – the company is now a substantial employer; use of enlarged resources – clean operating systems, waste disposal, etc
- *in specific terms* – eg planning of particular projects.

4. Work to maintain excellent relations with both customers and suppliers

By now, Nameless Works should have established a good, positive corporate identity, from the point of view of both customers and suppliers.

(i) Customers: the sales director has been focusing on trawling the enlarged customer base. Issues have arisen which might better be thought of as marketing, such as:
- building a brand image for some of the key offerings
- establishing an industry reputation, possibly through setting up a new trade association.

(ii) Suppliers: attention should be focused on building trusting relationships with a few suppliers, in particular maintaining a reputation as a good payer of bills. Internal issues include:
- maximising discounts
- ensuring that the tightening of financial control resulting from the merger does not negatively affect this reputation.

5. Maintain proper compliance with all applicable legal and regulatory requirements

Progressive tightening in procedures is starting to ensure that all the main legislation is being broadly complied with, though as the company is now well above the threshold of public view, it needs to pay more attention to the detail in particular legislation. The company should have:

- an experienced professional to handle compliance with employment law

- a health and safety manager to cover the plethora of legislation in this area
- auditors of the calibre and size able to give the best professional advice for the company's specific needs and uncover any major problems.

Conclusion

By ensuring that from the start the company is run using a system of good corporate governance, stronger growth is possible and ethical behaviour and responsibility will automatically be part of the corporate philosophy – this will give substantial competitive advantage and an excellent corporate identity which will make it very attractive to shareholders. Above all, transparency is key, and this obviously will come naturally if the company has always been run in an open, honest way.

All this needs constant monitoring, though, and it is very easy to stray from the path, especially when the original owner-managers begin to cede control of the company.

In Part B we will look at how a system of good corporate governance can be achieved and maintained; while it is directed at the larger company, with the view to correcting possible current imbalances, the principles are universally applicable – and how much better (and easier) it would be for the smaller company to set this system up early on before the mould sets.

NOTES

[1] From Sir Adrian Cadbury's foreword to *Good Corporate Governance – An Aid to Growth for the Smaller Company*, by Nigel Kendall, Accountancy Books, 1994. This book is recommended to the reader for a fuller treatment of the needs of a smaller, growing company.

Chapter 6

ANOTHER TYPE OF ORGANISATION – THE UK CO-OPERATIVE

Introduction 85

History of the UK co-operative movement 85

Corporate governance and the Co-op 92

How the co-operative movement works today 95

Conclusion 96

'A Co-operative society ... is a voluntary organisation set up by consumers or producers to serve their own needs ... Clearly it accepts responsibilities towards its employees, the public at large, and the State. But its distinctive obligation is to its members as consumers or producers, and not, as with a capitalist enterprise, to the owners of capital.'

From the Gaitskell Report, 1958.[1]

Introduction

Corporate governance is not just an important issue for major listed companies. We saw in Chapter 5 how it affects smaller companies. In this chapter we will look at what it means for another type of organisation, the co-operative. Worker co-operatives, producer co-operatives, credit unions, and to a lesser extent consumer co-operatives exist all over the globe. In terms of governance, there can be as many as three levels:

- *primary co-operatives:* where members of the society elect the board
- *secondary co-operatives:* where societies set up and own a society
- *tertiary societies:* where a society is set up and owned by secondary societies

As an example of co-operative principles in action, we will look here at the development of the co-operative movement in the UK, which has come under the spotlight with the formulation and defeat of a hostile external bid for the largest society, the Co-operative Wholesale Society.

History of the UK co-operative movement

The majority of successful co-operatives in the world today exist for the benefit of producers, and are widely found in the fields of agriculture and related fields, where the co-operative organisation provides superior services to those that the producers individually would be able to afford. For example, 70 per cent of the wine made in the Dão region of Portugal is still produced by local co-operatives which provide local growers with a ready outlet for their grapes and prompt payment to cover their costs.[2]

Interestingly, the first successful co-operative venture in the UK was a consumer co-operative set up in Rochdale in 1844, where it was common for mill workers to be paid in 'mill money', a form of currency which was only usable at stores which had an arrangement with local mill owners, and where adulteration of food was a widespead practice. The 28 working men who established the retail society which they called the Rochdale Equitable Pioneers Society, with capital of £28, founded what amounted to a buyers' club which guaranteed the quality of the food and offered affordable prices. More unusually, it also offered a rebate of a share of the surplus to members in proportion to the volume of their purchases –

the famous 'dividend'. Another of its early principles was that the society should be controlled by its members, who should each have a single vote, and that the membership of the society should be open and free of religious or political affiliation.

Early influences from people like Robert Owen, Welsh manufacturer and social reformer, gave the co-operative movement a strong concern for social improvement, but the vision of a self-sufficient co-operative community never proved viable over the long term. Rather, it was the retail form of co-operative society that flourished, to the extent that there were some 1,400 co-operative societies in existence by the end of the nineteenth century.

> **The Rochdale Principles**[3]
> 1. Voluntary and open membership.
> 2. Democratic control – one member, one vote.
> 3. Payment of limited interest on capital.
> 4. Surplus allocated for co-operative development, the common good or in proportion to members' purchases (the dividend).
> 5. Education facilities for members and workers.
> 6. Co-operation of all societies at all levels.
> 7. Cash trading.
> 8. Political and religious neutrality.

To supply these growing retail co-operatives with a wide range of food and other products, the Co-operative Wholesale Society (CWS) was formed in 1863, to combine the buying power of the individual societies. The CWS was run on similar principles to the other societies, but whereas the retail societies' members were the buying consumers, the CWS's membership consisted of the various retail societies themselves. In due course, as this highly successful mass purchasing operation grew, it became a major importer with business interests round the world, and developed huge farming and manufacturing concerns in the UK.

In 1867 the societies founded the Co-operative Insurance Company to provide insurances for the retail societies, being prevented by the current law from engaging in insurance themselves. In due course the law changed and the company was converted to a society, and in 1912–13 the shareholding societies sold their shares to the CWS and the Scottish CWS. When these two merged in 1973, the Co-operative Insurance Society became wholly owned by the CWS.

In 1872 the Co-operative Bank was formed as the Loan and Deposits Department of the CWS, initially serving the financial requirements of the retail societies. It became a clearing bank in 1975, and is a company owned by the CWS rather than a co-operative society, though it promotes itself as an exponent of what it describes as co-operative values.

In 1934 the decision was taken to set up the CWS Retail Co-operative

Society, which in 1956 became the Co-operative Retail Services (CRS). The purpose was to open co-operative shops in areas where there were no local societies. At that stage, there were no individual members and control lay with the CWS. Its first significant development was two years later when the Cardiff Co-operative Society, which had got into financial difficulties, was transferred into its ownership in 1936, and over the years other large and small societies followed, usually for similar reasons. As a result, CRS acquired a growing number of individual consumer members, and control gradually passed from the CWS into the hands of the individual members.

A seminal event in the Movement's history was the independent review commissioned following the Edinburgh Congress of the Co-operative Union in 1955 and chaired by Hugh Gaitskell,[4] leader of the Labour Party at that time, which reported in 1958. Around that time, in 1955, there were 932 societies, with a membership of 11.9 million, combined sales of £897 million, representing 6.8 per cent of all sales of goods and services, 11 per cent of total retail trade, 14.5 per cent of sales of food and household stores, and a surplus of 6.3 per cent on sales. The Movement owned over 30,000 shops, 250 factories and the largest wholesaling organisation in the UK, and had pioneered the introduction of self-service in the UK. The review was undertaken because of concern at the marked slowing down of expansion of the co-operatives whose share of retail trade had scarcely grown since before the war, compared with multiple shops, whose share had doubled. The report particularly pointed to loss of market share in non-food.

Its findings are interesting in the light of the business and governance challenges facing the Movement today, and are summarised below.

Framework of principles

Regarding governance in the Movement, the commission assumed the continuation of application of the following four basic principles:

- *democratic principle:* that is, one member one vote. However, it acknowledged that the degree of member participation was much less than in the early days, and consequently the reality of democratic control clearly depended on the fraction of members who did participate (estimated at <1 per cent attending business meetings and <2 per cent voting in elections) being representative of the whole. Moreover, the elected board no longer could or should take part in day to day management, but should focus on supervision and control

- *distributable surplus belongs to the consumer*, or more accurately to the member, by way of rebate on purchases, rather than to the capital holder
- *fixed return on capital*, eliminating the possibility of capital gains
- *consumer protection* selling at prices which were never consistently undercut, never selling shoddy or untested goods, maintaining highest standards of shop location, lay-out and service.

Recommendations to the retail societies

The report made detailed recommendations to the retail societies:

- sell at the market prices of the most successful private competitors and treat the 'dividend' as a residual, choosing additional allocation of surpluses to reserve rather than increasing dividends
- a serious under-investment needed to be remedied – some £200m capital expenditure being thought necessary to achieve the next 10 years' expansion targets (over £2bn in today's money); the report was not confident about the means of finding the money, citing higher rates of interest on deposits, increased depreciation and greater allocations to reserve generally as possible answers
- changed and improved methods of management, separating the policy-making and supervisory roles of the board from the executive roles of managers, and introducing modern methods of management
- amalgamating smaller societies into larger ones to produce an 'ideal' number of around 200–300 to achieve essential economies of scale.

Recommendations to the Co-operative Union

Various recommendations were made, including the role of the Union in the proposed amalgamation, setting up machinery for dealing with labour relations matters, organisational changes within the structure of the Union, and a big increase in societies' contributions to the Union funds.

Recommendations to the CWS

The report considered the CWS and its position as a supplier to the retail societies. Its recommendations were under the headings of:

- *production policy*, regarding which it challenged traditional arguments for a vertically integrated Movement with 'monopoly' production, and recommended focusing the Movement's limited available capital on

expansion in retail rather than production, with a narrowing of ranges and decisions based on return on capital
- *merchandising and wholesaling policy*, where it urged the wholesale societies to be more commercial, and to drop the secrecy in their invoicing-through agreements with retail societies which made them the object of suspicion by those societies
- *merchandising of co-operative productions*, where the report came down clearly on the side of retail societies *not* being obliged to keep the factories full through moral pressure to be 'loyal'
- *financial policy* to include greater effort to increase allocations to reserve, and introduce new loan instruments to increase the external capital.

Reorganisation of the wholesale societies

It was recommended that a lay supervisory council be set up, elected, but part-time, whose role would be essentially a trustee and supervisory one, exercised on behalf of member societies, sanctioning policy and avoiding interference in detailed management.

It was further recommended that each council should appoint a full-time central management board, to be managerially responsible for the organisation as a whole.

A Co-operative Retail Development Society

Recognising the limitations of the Movement's responses to market forces, the report suggested the setting up of a new federal society to carry out the creation of a number of chains of specialised shops, particularly in clothing and footwear, to compete with the rapidly expanding private specialised chains. These would operate across society boundaries, hence the need for central planning and establishment. However, it would not own its own capital but be funded by the Union and the wholesale societies.

Regular constitutional reviews

Finally, the commission recommended that the Movement should formally examine both major constitutional issues, and also its basic trading policies, at least once in every decade.

Looking at the Gaitskell Report 40 years on, several things stand out:

- the loss of market share highlighted in 1958 has continued to this day, dropping to 7.1 per cent for food and 3.7 per cent for food and non-food
- the gross under-investment in the infrastructure which they identified was not subsequently adequately addressed, and with a few outstanding exceptions, co-op stores are generally suffering from a dowdy image as a result
- the famed 'divi' was under pressure at the time, being criticised for diverting resources away from investment, and was abandoned in the 1970s
- the introversion of management was illustrated by pressure to keep ordering from the CWS factories regardless of customers' lack of desire for their products
- there was a parallel lack of market awareness, with a 'me-too' reply to the great advances of competitors, shown by the 'big is beautiful' response to competitive pressure, rather than addressing the real needs and desires of customers. This compares most unfavourably with the genuine innovation which characterised the first 80 years of the Movement's development
- the big constitutional issue – that only 1–2 per cent of members took any interest in the democratic process of running the business – was kicked into touch by suggesting that this was not currently seen as a problem, though it had to be watched, and these matters should be subsequently reviewed every 10 years.

At the time of writing, there are some 50 large retail consumer co-operative societies in the UK, with a nominal membership of 9.1 million people in 1996 – less than one million of whom are thought to be active, or for that matter, traceable. They still account for a large section of the economy, though, with a turnover of around £7.9bn in 1996, (see Figure 6.2) and 75,000 employees.

However, the Movement's market share relative to the competition has been declining for the best part of 70 years, and questions are increasingly being asked as to what actions need to be taken to counter this seemingly inexorable trend. Furthermore, there has been a tradition of tight control and discipline exercised by management in the largest societies, coupled with a lack of involvement of the vast majority of members in the democratic process which is supposed to approve policy and supervise management. Add to this the fact that the membership in these consumer co-operatives by and large no longer equates to the customers, and one would have to say that a reconsideration of the issue of corporate governance in this sector is becoming increasingly urgent.

ANOTHER TYPE OF ORGANISATION – THE UK CO-OPERATIVE

Fig 6.1 The UK consumer co-operative movement today

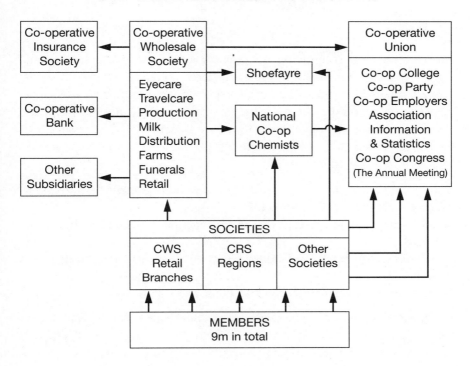

Fig 6.2 Statistics Review 1996–7[5]

£million	1996	1995	% change
Turnover	7,949	7,782	+2.1
Trading surplus	136	160	–14.7
% sales	1.9	2.2	
Retentions	52	77	–31.7
% sales	0.7	1.1	
Share capital	271	224	+21.0
Reserves	1,205	1,175	+2.6
Societies	52	53	–1.0
Membership	9,132	8,996	+1.5

91

Corporate governance and the Co-op

Cadbury

In fact, there has recently been a governance debate, and it has focused on control of management by society boards and members. The Co-operative Union's Working Group on Corporate Governance was set up in 1993 to report on the direction and control of co-operative societies and 'make recommendations on good practice to achieve the necessary high standards of reporting and accountability'. It saw its commission as making an important contribution to:

- improving the quality of direction and management in pursuit of improved business performance
- achieving the highest standards in management's accountability to the board
- promoting openness and transparency in relations between directors and members
- reinvigorating membership recruitment and involvement.

Its considerations were not really, then, about the wider aspects of corporate governance. This is not surprising since it followed Cadbury's agenda. Many of its recommendations, for example the establishment of a remuneration committee and inclusion of senior management remuneration in reports, clearly stem from discussions of the Cadbury Committee. Professor Brian Harvey, chairman of the working group, insists, however, that its role 'was not simply that of "good housekeeper", tidily furnishing the co-operative retail sector with its own "me too", version of the Cadbury Report.'[6] Further, it does not prescribe a rigid, sector-wide code of conduct, but asks individual societies to form their own code.

This is made easier by the fact that co-operative societies are subject to Industrial & Provident Societies legislation rather than Companies Acts, so do not have many of the constraints that companies do. While this may be considered a problem, it is also an opportunity for the co-operative movement itself to formulate rules which are more constructive and relevant to its widely varied nature.

This is why the Governance Working Group pressed for individual societies to form their own codes of conduct:

> It was not appropriate ... for the working group to offer an 'off the peg' code of business ethics for 'Anytown Co-operative Society'. However, any

code is likely to be based on an initial 'credo' statement setting out the society's overall commitment to certain values (such as democracy and mutuality), business objectives and stakeholder groups. The subsequent obligations and standards in the society's relations with particular stakeholders would then be expressed in directive statements which gave guidance on, or prohibited, specific conduct.[7]

Lanica bid approach to CWS

The governance of the co-operative movement was brought into sharper focus in February 1997, when newspapers reported that Andrew Regan, a young entrepreneur, was planning to make a bid for the CWS, or some part of it. Mr Regan and his company, Lanica, had set up a bid vehicle, Galileo, and after the leaking of his plans, he then wrote to CWS expressing his wish to discuss the sale to him of the non-food business. After several weeks the approach was turned down, the chief executive expressing his unwillingness to enter into any kind of talks with Mr Regan.

During this period, and subsequently, all kinds of speculation grew as to what Mr Regan's objectives really were, the consensus being that he intended to try to acquire the whole of CWS and break it up, realising a significant gain in the process. The word in the City was that, in addition to the 300 corporate members of CWS, there were around half a million members of CWS and he planned to offer each of them £1,000, valuing the bid at up to £1bn. He was then reputed to have obtained preliminary agreement to sell on various parts of the portfolio, in particular the Co-op Bank to Allied Irish Banks for £400m, a number of prime stores to Sainsbury, again worth several hundred million pounds, and to have drawn up plans for Co-operative Insurance Society (CIS) to be distributed between its members and policyholders, and other businesses to be sold off.

Graham Melmoth, chief executive of CWS and Alan Prescott, deputy chief executive and chairman of the Co-op Bank, hired a top Warburg corporate finance man, Brian Keelan, and fought a totally successful action to defeat Mr Regan. Their tactics entailed the use of private detectives to tail key executives, resulting in the dismissal of Allan Green, head of retailing, and his deputy for alleged theft of confidential documents, frightening off Lanica's financial backers and getting apologies for improper behaviour from various City institutions which had supported Mr Regan.

However, in the process, several important issues of corporate governance arose. In particular:

- the chief executive refused to submit details of Galileo's approach to his board or members, reportedly returning the bid document unopened; that is the members of the society were not permitted to see the content of an approach to them
- the remainder of the co-operative movement was put under severe moral pressure by the CWS management to support its refusal to talk to Mr Regan; that is, most of the key shareholders were pressured to accept a situation where they were not being allowed to read a potential offer to them
- the CWS board, which had taken the high moral ground about the co-operative democratic principles and 150 years of ethical behaviour, not only thus appeared to disenfranchise its members, but also made use of covert surveillance; surely laying itself open to charges of hypocrisy
- at no point in the process was there any material discussion of how the management of CWS proposed to take credible action to reverse the long-term decline in the society's market position which was attacked by the prospective bidder, other than to propose unification of the whole Movement, a suggestion dismissed in 1958 and a grand and final version of the failed merger solution adopted by societies over the decades; so the real concerns of that key stakeholder group, the members, about management's performance were not discussed, and this goes for the other two chief stakeholder groups too: the customers and staff
- despite the City and other commentators drawing attention to these points, there was no observable comment about the third group. This group, the staff, would of course provide much of the value that was released, and their interests do not seem to have figured much in the calculations of the financiers.

Co-operative Bank and ethics – banning tobacco sales

At the 1997 Congress, Terry Thomas, managing director of the Co-operative Bank was quoted as proposing that the retail societies should contemplate taking a marketing advantage by adopting the ethical trading position of banning cigarette sales.

Apart from the fact that the bank sells no tobacco and would not itself be affected by the adverse consequences of misreading the commercial costs of such a decision, the corporate governance issues arising out of this remark include the following significant points:

- the retail societies are members' consumer co-operatives, and should

therefore sell to the members/customers those goods which the members/customers want
- there is no evidence that the members/customers want to stop smoking, or to buy all their cigarettes solely from non-co-operative retailers
- Mr Thomas was not reported as suggesting that the members be consulted about such a decision, though this must surely be the proper course before embarking on a course involving both significant self-denial and commercial risk.

How the co-operative movement works today

Looking at the Movement as a set of consumer co-operatives, which need to find a role for themselves in the fiercely competitive retailing world of today, a number of issues arise.

- *Stakeholder interests:* to what extent are the interests of *all* stakeholder groups being taken into account by the managements of the societies, ie, what do the customers/members really want, and are there needs for which the privately owned retailers are not providing?
- *Pressure to conform:* CWS is the largest society and regards itself as the 'keeper of the flame'; in this role, and being the giant, it has for many years tended to dominate the smaller societies, often to its own advantage, a point criticised by the 1958 report.
- *Ownership and voting:* the number of members who attend meetings and who vote in elections in the democratic process remains at the low level of 1–2 per cent of the total as identified by the Gaitskell report, and probably not more than 10 per cent of active members; the Gaitskell report discussed the obvious dangers resulting from control by such a small proportion of members.
- *Dead members' rights:* the societies all carry a long list of members who could only be reached via a medium; the current legal position prevents them from being removed without the consent of themselves or the next of kin; at this time, in principle, their consent would have to be obtained to a liquidation or buy-out, though in reality a majority of those present and voting has been the accepted practice; however, in the event of a bid for a profitable society, presumably they would be entitled to an equal share of the proceeds.
- *Members v consumers:* what is the difference between a mutual and a co-operative? The key point is the 'working together', rather than sim-

ply sharing of surpluses; one of the most serious concerns of all in a consumer co-operative is the progressive separation of customers and members who are the two stakeholder groups who are 'working together'; it seems likely that in most large retail societies only a very small proportion of members are actually customers, and vice versa; to the extent that this is true, this makes a mockery of the claim that the societies are being run as consumer co-operatives, and indeed, would raise questions as to the extent to which they complied with the provisions of the 1965 Industrial and Provident Societies Act.

- *Co-operation – fact v myth:* one of the original Rochdale Principles was that the societies should co-operate with each other at all levels; sadly, the problems in achieving this were referred to in the 1958 report and continue to this day; the inclination of the major societies to paddle their own canoes has not diminished over the past 40 years, and amalgamations have generally been made from a position of weakness or bankruptcy; after all these years it seems misguided to plan on any other basis.
- *Politics:* the Movement was set up on a non-religious, non-political basis, but inevitably, being involved in the relief of social problems, it got involved in the social reform movement and became progressively politicised and associated with one political party; it is questionable whether this bias is appropriate in this day and age, and it would be interesting to know the views of the totality of members; to the best of our knowledge there has been no recent survey to ascertain this.

Conclusion

From the point of view of good corporate governance, there ought to be a number of lessons to be learnt from the experience of the co-operative business culture. Among the advantages of the system, at least in principle, are:

- *structure* – a dual-board system[8] allows the opportunity for greater independence from executive objectives and therefore more meaningful representation of stakeholder interests, employees' in addition to members'
- *trust* – the result of the above should mean that there is a greater degree of mutual trust between direction (*and* management) and the three key groups: members, customers and employees

- *mutuality* – there is an increasing trend among large multinational companies to form alliances, work together and share resources (see Chapter 3). This has always been a fundamental concept of the co-operative movement – the very name means 'working together'!

The co-operative movement in the UK has a long and honourable history. Since World War I, however, its well of innovation seems to have been gradually drying up, and it has progressively lost market share in an expanding and increasingly wealthy society. It has also developed autocratic management traditions over the years, and a command and control approach will always inhibit an organisation's ability to adapt in a changing world. Furthermore, the labours involved in establishing the movement have created deeply held, visceral sets of beliefs, and there has been a reluctance to question whether the form of governance devised for a society of 28 people in Rochdale in 1844 should be modified in any significant way to meet the needs of today's billion pound businesses employing tens of thousands of staff and having hundreds of thousands of members. Finally, there seems to be almost an unwillingness to accept that the objectives of the founders: good quality food at reasonable prices, available to the poorest sections of society, have been largely achieved by a combination of top quality retailing, growing wealth in society and the underpinning of the welfare state.

The Movement has won its war; the world has moved on, and there are new challenges in a world that seems likely to be progressively 'de-welfared', leaving millions of vulnerable people at risk. Are the societies fighting the right battle?

NOTES

1 The 'Gaitskell' Report was the Co-operative Independent Commission Report of the Commission established following the Edinburgh Congress of the Co-operation Union in 1955 to look at the state of the Movement, and published by the Union in 1958.
2 *Decanter Magazine*, May 1997.
3 Rochdale Pioneers Museum booklet, published and printed by the Co-operative Union Ltd.
4 Co-operative Independent Commission Report, published by the Co-operative Union in 1958.
5 Co-operative Union Ltd Information Services, May 1997.
6 *Corporate Governance & Corporate Control*, edited by Dr Saleem Sheikh & Pr William Rees.
7 Reference from *The Governance of Co-operative Societies*, Pr Brian Harvey.

8 None of the directors are part of the operational team. The report of the working group recommended that chief executives and financial controllers should be appointed to the board, as clearly a complete lack of direct executive knowledge and input on the board is undesirable.

Chapter 7

KEY PEOPLE

Introduction *101*
Chairman *102*
Executives *103*
Non-executive directors *106*
Conclusion *108*

'He had a clear and comprehensive view of weighty matters of business, a strong and unfettered will, a promptitude of decision, and a punctuality in execution unexampled, in their combination.'
From a tribute by the Circular to Bankers
on the death of Nathan Mayer Rothschild, 1836.[1]

Introduction

We consider in this chapter the key people in a company, and in the UK, these are, generally speaking, the members of the board and the chairman.

Firstly, a general comment: when looking at the composition of the board, it is imperative to bear in mind that members should be selected for the right reasons – to add value to the board. This most obvious of rules is by no means universally obeyed. In this context, two important points need to be remembered:

- *definition of roles* – all members of the board must be clear from the beginning as to their exact role in the company and what is expected of them, and to a certain extent vice versa; they should make clear what they expect from the company
- *management of relationships* – good relationships between members of the board, particularly between the chairman and the chief executive, and the chairman and the rest of the board, are vital to its effectiveness and success and therefore to the success of the whole company.

Furthermore, one of the most important elements in good boardroom practice is communication. It is important that board members should be able, and *feel* able, to speak out against other members if they feel something is against the interests of key stakeholders. An environment where everyone can feel comfortable with each other enough to have meaningful and constructive discussions is essential.

> **... their exact role *in the company*...**
>
> In this book we are talking not about putting a strait-jacket on the key members of the company, which is clearly obstructive, but about giving *constructive* help and guidelines. Here we are emphasising the importance of evaluation in the *individual* company, being as it is unique.

The chief executive–chairman question

Another important matter is the justification for combining the roles of chairman and chief executive. As discussed in Chapter 2, putting the same person in both positions can be seen in effect to put the individual in the impossible position of monitoring himself. The probability is growing that the supervisory structure will automatically separate the job of chairman from that of the chief executive in public companies. Until the law is changed, however, some companies may well continue to combine the two for perfectly valid reasons.² However, we would increasingly expect the two roles to be separated, and, what is most important of all, for the two roles to be clearly distinguished from each other regarding their supervisory and executive contents.

Chairman

The chairman is obviously a key person amongst key people. He or she provides the public face of the company and the leadership within the company. There is no template, as it were, for the ideal chairman for all circumstances. The focus of the job depends on the times and the company's state of development. One thing is certain, however: chairmen must have a clear view of where they want to go, both for the company and for the role of the board within it.

It is the chairman's job to ensure that there is the right balance between executive directors and those without an executive role, that the latter fit into the board and add value to it. The chairman should instigate a proper induction programme to ensure that the directors understand the company, its products, people and culture. Where the directors do not contribute, they should not be directors and ought not to be on the board. That evaluation is part of the chairman's job.

Sir Peter Walters views the chairman's primary responsibility as being to create a board which allows adequate discussion of major issues, bearing in mind the differences between executives and non-executives. He comments that because of the very different focus which each director brings, there exists a divide in the board. This is not, he says, for personal or self-centred reasons,

> but because of the knowledge, experience and focus which the executives will have regarding their own company and industry and the non-executives will have in much greater breadth from their wider experience and because they are less likely to be caught up in the personal challenges to meet targets that have become an integral part of international competitiveness.'[3]

Once again, the challenge is one of managing relationships.

The conduct of meetings is also a critical factor. A passive chairman is ineffective. Board meetings take up valuable time and need to be used properly in order to be meaningful. It is up to the chairman to ensure that there is a correct balance (for the company in question) between diplomacy, to smooth things over, and creative tension, to get the best out of people under some stress.

Being the company's main representative, the chairman needs to create and maintain a positive image of the organisation, both generally, in terms of the general public (more important to larger organisations), and specifically, in terms of the company's various stakeholders. He therefore has the responsibility of balancing the interests of these stakeholders. This is made easier, or at least safer, if the chairman is not an executive.

He has a key relationship with the chief executive and his executive colleagues, especially regarding the formulation of the strategic plan, and also regarding the political and social implications of major decisions, for example:

- major acquisitions/disposals, in terms of effects on community, public image, employees of all the companies in question, perhaps the environmental impact (eg retiring an oil rig)
- financial policies, in terms of changes in gearing, issue of equity, dividend policy.

In order to successfully carry out these duties, a chairman must possess a suitably strong character. Bain and Band prescribe that the chairman:

- be a strong leader
- have the intellectual capacity to deal with complexity and multidimensional issues
- be a capable communicator
- have both the energy and the time to get around the company and see the key executives in action on their own turf.[4]

The chairman's role is, therefore, one of leadership and vision: chairmen have to have a vision for the company and how it should be governed. That being so there is no room for a 'non-executive' chairman: it may be a part-time role, but the responsibility is full-time and cannot be abdicated. Chairmen are on call every day of the year, 24 hours a day.

Executives

The chief executive

While the chairman is a leadership figure, the chief executive provides the company with operational drive. He works closely with the chairman, as discussed above, to formulate strategy, and translates the vision of the company into profitable reality. He must also be a strong leader for management; the challenge here is clearly to balance the roles and the strong personalities of the chairman and chief executive and ensure a relationship which benefits the company. The chief executive should achieve the goals set out in the strategic plan:

> What we want is a CEO who is able, by virtue of ability, expertise, resourcism and authority, to keep the company not just ready for change but ready to benefit from changes, even to lead them. The CEO must be powerful enough to do the job, but accountable enough to make sure it is done correctly.[5]

Developing the strategic plan is the chief executive's most important responsibility. In doing so, he may well use the increasingly popular 10:3:1 model, which might be thought of in terms of Strategy:Goals:Tactics (ie long-term, medium-term and short-term). Strategy is usually thought of as the long-term policies of a company and the general direction, the methods and the ethics which the company is pursuing. In order to achieve the company's strategic objectives, the chief executive needs to set manageable, well-defined goals, the desired results of decisions which will affect the medium-term future of the company. To do this, the company requires tactics, short-term manoeuvres and targets which will, with each action taken, bring closer the desired result.[6] As the reader will notice, there are parallels with the art of war. The fact is that business, in this fiercely competitive free market system of ours, resembles the way in which war is planned and conducted. The ultimate objective of the chief executive, as of the general, is obviously to win the war and this requires shorter-term, more precise goals, such as the advancement of armies to a certain point by a certain time. Battles need to be fought along the way to fulfil these goals and objectives.

Indeed Kotler and others have expounded the idea of using the military analogy to explain the dynamics of achieving a tactical advantage over competition. John Saunders, discussing competitive strategy in *The Marketing Book*, spends quite some time on competitive strategy and war. The note[7] on page 109 gives a taste of the interesting insight he provides into the concept. He explains the sudden necessity in the 1980s to fight not just for market share, but for survival, as new and aggressive competition, especially from Japan, invaded western markets killing off whole industries – like the UK shipbuilding and motor industries and the US consumer electronics industry.

Apart from the strategic similarities between commerce and war, another exists in the necessity for good leadership, which is common to both environments.

The physical and mental demands of running a successful international business should not be underestimated. Command in any organisation, corporate, military or political, can be a lonely place, and an ambiguous one, where the wrong order can be carried out with as little questioning as the right one.[8]

The 10:3:1 model requires first of all a 10 year plan (often with the involvement of the chairman) which includes predicted effects of decisions on the community and other stakeholders (hence the chairman's involvement). This is followed by a three year plan which sets out the more specific goals of the company, such as target growth, market share, etc. Finally comes a detailed plan of what the chief executive believes the company can (or should) achieve this year and targets, such as sales and profit levels.

The chief executive is the operational driver of the company. He is concerned with making sure the company functions in the best possible way on both an overall level – (putting into practice all the elements of the strategic plan) and on a day-to-day level (introducing individual measures to ensure efficiency); in other words on both a macro and a micro scale. He has to select his executive team carefully and manage them effectively, so that their efficiency and effectiveness will filter down to the lowest levels of the company.

Executive directors

We can identify five important roles of the main board directors.

1. **Overseeing all subsidiary companies.**
2. **Corporate governance,** *re* **monitoring all stakeholders' interests.**
3. **Operational director of subsidiaries (elements of corporate governance in practice).**
4. **Functional management.**
5. **Regional management.**

What we are interested in here is the importance of governance in *all* these roles. It is named above as a separate role for emphasis and to point out that the directors have a responsibility to make sure that management is practising good corporate governance and that they in turn are doing the same for their divisions, and so on down the line. We cannot emphasise enough how good corporate governance should affect every part of a company's operations.

The directors have the knowledge of the company needed to develop strategy. For this reason it is vital that the chairman and chief executive consult properly with them during this process. The directors in turn need to consult heavily with their managers to ensure that regular, complete and accurate information reaches the board. They then have the responsibility to return from board meetings with the concerns and comments made on behalf of the various stakeholders, and to implement any changes agreed at the meeting. It is a two-way process, whereby they represent both the company on the board, and the various stakeholders (and the rest of the board) in their operational role within the company.

Non-executive directors

In recent years, much has been talked about the subject of non-executive, or independent directors. This section summarises what is generally agreed is or should be the chief roles of the non-executive director.

As discussed above, chairmen have to build a team and weld it together. To do that they can also benefit by the vision and independent perspective of directors who are not part of the operating management of the business. To us as authors, independence means independence of thought and attitude, rather than independence from the company of which they are directors.

Having outside directors can be very important as they may be best able to provide this independent perspective. They should also add lustre to the business, and it goes without saying, they need to be selected with care. In our experience, this is frequently abused, with appointments being made as favours to old friends or relatives. In certain areas, control is tighter; for instance, the regulatory authorities in the UK will vet the persons to be appointed to the boards of banks and building societies.

There are six main business (as opposed to regulatory) criteria usually found in the selection of independent outsiders to the board:[9]

1. To obtain specialist experience.
2. To give access to governments, authorities, opinion leaders, specialist sources of information, etc.
3. To provide an independent appraisal and check on management.
4. To strengthen the board in general business experience.
5. To give a new perspective on the company's direction.
6. To provide status.

Let us then consider the actual roles of non-executive directors. We can boil down their responsibilities into two broad types of role, the stakeholder representative role and the advisory role.

Stakeholder representative role

An independent director may represent particular key stakeholder groups, such as shareholders, employees or a major trading partner, or he or she may have a more general purpose, representing all interested parties. Clutterbuck and Waine[10] note that while in theory he is appointed to represent the interests of shareholders, in practice ' ... the effective independent director will balance the interests of all stakeholders'.

He or she is on the board to ensure that the company is acting in a responsible way, a way which favours the best, long-term interests of the stakeholders over shorter-term and sometimes personally profitable objectives of the executives. Clutterbuck and Waine define independence as 'not getting trapped into the attitudes, values and short-term objectives of the executive team'.

What is best for the company and what is best for each of the stakeholder groups (other, perhaps, than shareholders) is often not the same, an obvious example being restructuring which involves closing down large plants, causing major negative effects on the local community (see Chapter 3). The non-executive director needs to add balance to strategy so as to take into account both those directly involved with the company and those more distant who will be affected by its actions.

Adviser role

Non-executive directors may also be appointed in the guise of outside advisers to the company. They may be selected having had no previous relationship with the company (unless coincidentally they owned shares in it) but be brought in by the insiders because of the specific qualities or knowledge they can apply. It may, for example, be specialised technical knowledge, industry experience, market contacts or political influence.

With the globalisation of markets, the consequent disappearance of national borders and the formation of strategy units which cover groups of countries, companies are increasingly recruiting foreign non-executives, arguably an essential move anyway. This provides even more independence and knowledge of other systems of governance, as well as advice on particular national characteristics and possible business opportunities. This is just one example of the many positive uses of the tool of non-executive directorship, and of the benefits of advice which these directors can bring.

Conclusion

We have noted above that there is no template for being a chairman, a chief executive or a director, as every company has different needs and every individual has his or her own style. However, there are lessons to be learnt, not only from corporate failures, but also successes. As we look at what has been behind success or failure, it is possible to identify certain principles, requirements and procedures which therefore constitute good corporate governance. In Parts B and C we will go beyond academic (and often slightly unworldly) guidelines on the roles of key people, and translate the theory into what we hope will be a useful, practical guide on *how* key people can fulfil the roles discussed here.

Definition of roles, management of relationships and the importance of non-executives on the board are the most salient points made in this chapter. Let us end by emphasising that the outside, specialist knowledge of independent directors should be thought of as an opportunity, not a threat, as some senior executives and, ironically, even chairmen are still inclined to do. The fact is that it is very difficult to see potential problems when you are in the midst of them. And as Robert Burns wrote:

> O wad some power the giftie gie us
> to see oursels as ithers see us.

NOTES

[1] Taken from *The City of London*, Volume 1, by David Kynaston, Pimlico 1995.
[2] One argument is that leadership should be provided by someone who knows well how the company operates and cares for it; how can someone who only appears a few times a year do either? The benefits of separation, however, often outweigh the doubts, and these can be rectified to a certain extent if the supply of information is good and the individual possesses the necessary characteristics.
[3] *Corporate Governance & Corporate Control*, Saleem Sheikh and William Rees, Cavendish Publishing Limited 1995.
[4] *Winning Ways*, Neville Bain and David Band, MacMillan Business, 1996.

5 *Corporate Governance*, Monks and Minow, Blackwell Business, 1995.
6 All three stages must obviously coincide, which requires a lot of thought into aligning specific objectives and ensuring there is a common thread to the plan.
7 **The military analogy:** Kotler and others (1980, 1985) have explored how the ideas of the military strategists – such as Carl von Clausewitz, Sun Tzu and Liddell Hart – can guide competitive advantage. Taking military and commercial parallels is not a new idea. Clausewitz (1868) sees war as a social activity similar to others:

> War is a clash between major interests solved by bloodshed – that is the only way in which it differs from other conflicts. Rather than comparing it to an art we could more accurately compare it to commerce, which is also a conflict of human interests and activities ...

The military analogy shows four competitive positions: the defender trying to hold on to its existing markets, the challenger attempting to take market share, the follower and the nicher. Saunders goes on to describe the various defensive strategies, including 'position defence: the fortress', 'pre-emptive defence' and 'contraction defence: the hedgehog'; the confrontation strategies of the market challenger, including 'frontal attack', 'flanking attack' and 'encirclement' – while the flanking attack, for example, 'aims at a weak point in the competitor's defence, encirclement involves a multi-pronged onslaught that dilutes the defender's ability to retaliate in strength ... The aggressor can encircle competitors by producing an enormous variety of types, styles and sizes of products, including cheaper and more expensive models.' He quotes Honda as an example, who 'clearly encircled competitors in the motorcycle industry by model proliferation – launching a new model of motorcycle every two weeks!'. Followers, he says, 'succeed in industries where opportunities for product and large image differentiation are low, price sensitivity is high and where competitors are offering comparable services inadequately' (he quotes Compaq as a successful follower of IBM).

Finally, for the nicher, Saunders moves away from war to ecology to demonstrate that just as two similar species cannot exist in the same habitat and geographical area, so a company trying to model itself on the markets and organisations of another cannot survive if it is too similar to the leader – it will need to find a niche in which it is uniquely able to survive.
From *The Marketing Book*, edited by Michael J Baker, 3rd ed., Butterworth-Heinemann for the Charted Institute of Marketing, 1994.
8 Op. cit. 3, Sir Peter Walters.
9 There are, of course, many benefits and reasons for having independent directors; listed here are those most salient and relevant to boardroom effectiveness.
10 *The Independent Director*, David Clutterbuck and Peter Waine, McGraw Hill, 1994.

Chapter

8

FUTURE INFLUENCES

Introduction *113*

Parliament/DTI *113*

Stock Exchange *114*

Corporate sector pressure groups *116*

The Green movement *117*

Co-operatives and mutuals *119*

'In the financial year 1993–4 the [CalPERS] fund voted against 138 management proposals out of a total of 950 votes in 13 foreign countries'.

JOHN PLENDER
from *A Stake in the Future*[1]

Introduction

In the final chapter of this part of the book, we will take a quick look at the factors which may be likely to affect the state of corporate governance and make predictions about short- to medium-term developments.

Firstly, we can ask ourselves: who is currently watching the corporate governance debate; who are the interested parties? The answer would appear to include the following:

- Parliament/DTI
- the Stock Exchange
- corporate sector pressure groups
- the Green movement
- the co-operative movement and mutuals.

In the following sections we look at each of these and ask:

- how will they affect the state of corporate governance? and/or
- how will they *be* affected by developments in corporate governance?

considering for each:

- pressures from different sources, not least public opinion
- impact of corporate disasters
- possible developments in regulation
- political motives/pressures/opinions
- co-operatives and mutuals – could the sleeping giant be awakening?

Parliament/DTI

This is often the most public side of corporate governance issues. When a major scandal hits the headlines, the general public, with the assistance of the media watchdogs, takes its complaints and outrage to unsuspecting politicians and civil servants to find out how such a thing could have occurred and demands that they do something to stop it happening again. There has been a series of highly publicised corporate disasters in recent years – BCCI, Maxwell, Barlow Clowes, to quote but three – which have had a very damaging effect on public opinion of the corporate governance system. The truth is, of course, that there are probably no more incidents now than there have been in the past – who now remembers Emil Savundra and Fire Auto Marine Insurance in the 1970s, or John Bloom and Rolls Razor in the 1960s, for example? The fact is that there has been a lot more media attention recently, escalated by the case of Maxwell and his raid on the company pension funds, because of its impact on so many *ordinary* people.

Sometimes (though, as discussed in Chapter 2, fairly infrequently) governments are eventually spurred into taking 'decisive' action. However, the resulting measures often do not produce the desired effect and can smack of political 'bribery' towards special interest groups of supporters rather than a genuine desire to clean up the image of business. The Financial Services Act, a reaction to the pre-election financial 'scandals' of the 1980s, is a prime example: it was hugely expensive, caught many unintended targets, and failed to prevent the subsequent large-scale disasters of the 1990s – Maxwell, Barings, Lloyd's, etc.

This, and the effect on public opinion of recent 'fat cat' controversies in privatised UK utilities, has led to renewed calls for MPs to 'do something'. One response has been the steps to impose a windfall tax on utilities. There has also been a trend to more and more regulation. This is a cheap way for government to control industry. Setting up committees and commissioning reports and inquests – or better still, getting other people, like the Stock Exchange, to do it, can enable government to give the appearance of taking action without personally spending too much time and money. This may seem a little cynical, and we are against over-legislation, but we do feel a lot more could – and should – be done by those responsible for controlling industry for the sake of ordinary people.

Stock Exchange

The Stock Exchange is under increasing pressure regarding its role. It is still relying on history and tradition for its existence and has repeatedly failed, in recent years, to respond to the need to become a proper business concern rather than just a marketplace where one naturally goes to find and invest capital. The amalgamation of jobbers and brokers and the idea of advertising what you want to sell and linking up directly to interested buyers threatens a complete by-passing of the Stock Exchange. The demand for this direct trading – and the technology which makes it possible – coupled with competition from more liberalised foreign exchanges is decreasing market share, and the organisation seems incapable of reforming itself. John Plender in his important

FUTURE INFLUENCES

book on stakeholdership, explains the problems facing the London Stock Exchange, questioning, as we do, what continuing purpose it serves in this day and age:

> So disastrous was its [the London Stock Exchange] attempt to introduce a new system for settling transactions in the mid-1990s that the Bank of England felt obliged to take over the whole project. Internal quarrels, particularly over the reform of the Stock Exchange's dealing system, have contributed to the enforced departure of two chief executives in quick succession. And the exchange's system for dealing with international stocks and shares, known as Seaq International, has seen a serious loss of business to continental European exchanges.
>
> These tribulations owe much to the changing economics of running stock exchanges. In the days when the London Stock Exchange had a domestic monopoly, it was close to being a utility. It existed to enable mainly British investors to buy and sell securities and to permit companies to raise fresh capital. In today's deregulated global marketplace, stock exchanges are opening up in an attempt to win business from the established players. With technology taking securities activities away from dealing floors, it becomes harder to answer the question of what a stock exchange, traditionally the home of a physical marketplace, is really for.
>
> In such a world, the need for more sophisticated management becomes imperative. The London Stock Exchange has conspicuously failed to rise to the challenge. One reason is that it's a commercial business fighting for survival, even though it retains functions in which there is an important public interest. And *the balance between the various stakeholders – securities firms, investors and companies [seeking investment] – has been unevenly struck.*[2]

We highlight the last sentence as it exemplifies the thrust of this book – that stakeholders should form part of the strategy process. We will look at how this can be achieved, and how to work towards what we call *Goal Congruence* in the second part of this book.

Plender goes on to explain how this has not been considered in the Stock Exchange and what the effects are and will be:

> Because the big securities firms have invested heavily in the existing dealing system, they have been reluctant to move rapidly to a different system, even though many large investors, especially Americans who own not far short of 10 per cent of all the shares quoted on the stock market, would prefer this. And they know that most of the return on the exchange's investment in a new and expensive dealing system would accrue to institutional investors, not to the securities firms that put up the money. This means that any chief executive who wishes to sustain and enhance the exchange's competitive advantage is bound to quarrel with the owners of the business. The failure

115

fully to complete the transition from a club to a properly accountable commercial concern will lead to a progressive loss of market share. In its present form the London Stock Exchange is condemned to long-run genteel decline.

Corporate sector pressure groups

CalPERS

Corporate governance is such a major international issue now that the subject already has a substantial presence on the Internet (the World Wide Web). This summary of the California Public Employees' Retirement System is taken from an article written specifically for a corporate governance site produced by James McRitchie.

> CalPERS has $100 billion in assets, serves 1 million members and is administered by a 13 member board. Six are elected by various membership groups; the others are either appointed by elected officials or serve by virtue of their elected office. In contrast to the short time frame of most institutional investors CalPERS takes a long term perspective. Their average holding period ranges from 6 to 10 years.
>
> CalPERS equity strategy consists of making long term investments so it can be in a position to influence corporate governance. It targets poor corporate performers in its portfolio and pushes for reforms. These range from specific advice, such as arguing a few years ago that Sears and Westinghouse should divest poorly performing divisions and redefine their strategic core businesses, to more general advice. For example, CalPERS believes most need to expand employee training and shared managerial authority with lower level employees. Although CalPERS must often bear the full cost of monitoring, and other shareholders get a 'free ride,' the sheer size of its investments makes such monitoring worthwhile.

The authors wish to acknowledge their debt to this most useful of web sites.

PIRC

In the UK, PIRC (Pensions Investment Research Consultants) has, like CalPERS, put pressure on companies on corporate governance issues, but as a consultant for investors. Established in 1991, it provides shareholders with information on governance issues, including analysis of Annual General Meeting proposals and advice in proxy voting, through such media as company reports, including analysis of compliance with the Cadbury Code, a research service and a 'Corporate Governance Manual' of legal, regulatory and administrative issues. It also produces a regular 'briefing' called *PIRC Intelligence* for its clients which reports on ethical and other issues, shareholder campaigns and overseas trends.

While the organisation is supposedly the 'guardian of good corporate governance – and shareholder responsibility' (according to *Investor Relations Magazine*), it is perhaps too focused on the regulatory side of the issue, which we have questioned so often in this book. It is also quite negative in its approach to confronting perceived poor corporate governance. An example would be its conduct in the Shell episode (see Chapter 3), where it refused to back down in support of a shareholder resolution calling for improvements in its ethical practices, despite Shell's proposals to reform these, which addressed most of the issues in the resolution. As it happened, the Association of British Insurers decided to oppose the challenge, saying 'PIRC has never won a resolution or been successful in anything they've done.'[3]

The Green movement

In recent years there has been an abundance of environmental pressure groups, Greenpeace and Friends of the Earth being prominent, present at every ecological accident to highlight potential or actual dangers. These groups have often been criticised for being extremist, and anti-business, and so have tended to be viewed as obstructive rather than constructive. While there is clearly a need for tight environmental accountability, the attitude should plainly be one of working *with* businesses, not fighting against them, to clean up corporate practices. Conversely, companies should learn to do the same. In many ways they have been as guilty of extremism and obstinacy as the Green groups, only they are the ones who, guilty or not of charges brought against them, are the source of the controversy.

Companies seem, at last, to be taking this on board. Some, for example The Body Shop, have always made efforts not just to be 'green', but to make it part of their corporate philosophy. But the fact is that until fairly recently, projects which were attacked for being environmentally unfriendly went ahead anyway, unless the political battle was lost against the pressure groups and the projects were prohibited by governments or sheer force of public opinion. Now the Green movement has much more influence and is growing all the time, not because the pressure groups are more powerful, but because companies are realising that no matter how justified their decisions are, they have to react, and be seen to act, very quickly to public feelings. A good example referred to earlier was the Shell oil platform which was due to be dumped in the Atlantic to join many other wrecks, and ended up being towed into a Norwegian fjord. More importantly, Green or ethical issues are being absorbed into the corporate governance system, from the top down. As the workers at the bottom of the pile form part of this public feeling, hopefully they will meet in the middle!

The (forgotten?) consumer

Over the last 10 years environmental awareness and activism has increased exponentially, not within these pressure groups, but within the consumer market itself. And consumer activism is far more dangerous. Any company these days should, of course, realise that it ignores the consumer at its peril, but not all companies act decisively enough or in time to prevent consumer fears or suspicions from destroying them. Although consumer boycotts of 'unfriendly' products are on the wane, they are by no means history. The effect has been to make people more inquisitive about where the products they buy come from and how they were made. This means that while consumer opinion has 'matured', companies, having had a rude awakening to 'the Green phenomenon', have to tread very lightly and, once again, appear whiter than white.

Consequences

Corporate responsibility, as discussed in earlier chapters, is about *ethics*, and *morals*, not just about compliance with laws and regulation.[4] Companies need to be seen to incorporate these issues into their 'way of life'. Those that don't will get their fingers burnt – or worse. The same can happen by ignoring – or simply failing to realise that, despite their own research, public opinion does not approve of their actions, as Shell found out. Governments, too, are feeling this pressure, vis à vis issues such as the funding by the UK Government and the World Bank of the aid project to build a giant dam in Malaysia, widely seen as environmentally damaging, or actions supportive of unsuitable regimes, for example providing medical support to Saddam Hussein's regime in Iraq. These issues can not only damage governments, but whole countries, as in the action (or reaction) against French wines and other goods following nuclear testing in the Pacific.

The provision of information to shareholders is also an important factor here and the latter are under increasing pressure to use it at Annual General Meetings to vote against unethical or 'ungreen' decisions, or to sell their shares.

We have placed a lot of emphasis on the Green/ethical issue because we believe it will be one of the most significant influences on corporate governance in the years to come. As we have commented in previous chapters, the finger is no longer being pointed just at senior executives, but also at the shareholders, and as pressure to make the company more socially responsible increases, it will surely be in this direction.

Co-operatives and mutuals

We discussed the issues relating to the co-operative system in Chapter 6, and it seems that some of the aspects of their philosophy of mutuality and inclusiveness might be coming back into favour. Is the fact that some UK building societies have refused to follow the trend to convert to banks, for example, a sign of things to come? The huge success of co-operative movements around the world – a classic example being Mondragón in Spain – is proof that in certain environments they still work. After all, their style of corporate governance automatically ensures a certain amount of consideration to all interested parties, at least in principle.

But it is from the consumer perspective that we believe could emerge the most interesting developments. Consumer trends show a more demanding attitude towards producers. The paradox of simultaneous globalisation of tastes, and increasing individualism in demand, shows a need for ingenuity to satisfy the ultimate – though often forgotten – sovereign of the marketplace. Equipped with the necessary resources and qualities to catch a potential new tide of consumer desire for a softer, more caring approach to commercial relations, the sleeping giant, consumer co-operative movement, could well relaunch itself in the UK and lead the way in recapturing consumer confidence in business.

NOTES

[1] John Plender, *A Stake in the Future*, Nicholas Brealey Publishing, 1997.
[2] Ibid.
[3] Tony Baker, deputy director-general of the ABI, to the *Financial Times*, 29/4/97.
[4] As the CBI report of 1973 (see Chapter 2) said: 'The law sets minimum standards of conduct. But it does not, and cannot embody the whole duty of man; and mere compliance with the law does not necessarily make a good citizen or a good company.'

Part B

HOW TO PRACTISE GOOD CORPORATE GOVERNANCE

Implementing a practical operating system

Chapter 9

A NEW APPROACH TO CORPORATE GOVERNANCE

Introduction *125*

Corporate cultures and vision *125*

Principles of good corporate governance *127*

Five Golden Rules *128*

Good corporate governance is good management *129*

Corporate governance and the strategic management process *131*

The whole picture *132*

'When Bill Hewlett and I put together the initial plans for our business enterprise in 1937 ... (we decided) that we wanted to direct our efforts towards making important technical contributions to the advancement of science, industry and human welfare.'

DAVID PACKARD,
Chairman Emeritus, Hewlett-Packard Company[1]

THE FIVE GOLDEN RULES

Introduction

The public image of a corporation will quite accurately reflect the culture of that body. It follows, then, that good corporate governance has to be in the bones and bloodstream of the organisation since this in turn will be reflected in the culture. To carry the analogy further, in the same way that healthy blood and bones are reflected in the naturally healthy look of a person, so an organisation whose internal functions are healthy will naturally look so from an external perspective.

In this section of the book, therefore, we put forward what we believe are the key concepts in embracing good corporate governance. They represent the healthy look we have just described – embracing these principles will mean the company's culture and therefore public image will shine out as an example of an open, well and fairly run organisation.

We will also go further to propose a methodology to achieve this, one whose vehicle lies at the very heart of the business and is the driver of change – the strategy process. The methodology has as its base the standard elements of strategy formulation, but incorporates an analysis of all stakeholders, a procedure usually left out of the decision-making process, but crucial to the success of a strategy. The stakeholder analysis seeks answers to questions as simple as who are our stakeholders (which is often a fuzzy issue in itself) and ranging to what do they personally want or expect from the company.

Finally, but most significantly, in that we are not aware that it has ever been done before, we present a model (fully extrapolated in Appendix A) whereby results of the stakeholder analysis can be mapped, producing a visual measurement of performance against stakeholder expectations.

Corporate cultures and vision

The quotation at the beginning of this chapter expresses the early aspirations of two entrepreneurs when they started their business. Nearly a lifetime later, the principles these two men espoused at the beginning have become part of the ethos of the business they founded.

Similarly, Ernest Butten shortly after he founded the management consultancy Personnel Administration in 1943, issued a document which he called the PA Charter. The clear vision behind this document shines through, and was to drive the business forward through his sale of the business into trust for its staff and well through his retirement 25 years later. 'EB's' presence permeated the company and guided its behaviour for a generation. His belief in the importance of communication, persuasion and salesmanship became an enduring part of the PA culture and is illustrated by his letter to one of the authors as a young man.[2]

Fig 9.1 Culture and vision – the PA Charter

THE PA CHARTER

Our objective, stated in 1944 and repeated in 1953, is:

To build PA into the leading organisation of its kind in the world, consisting of men who are acknowledged authorities on the various branches of Management, to create new and improved procedures which can be taught readily to Industrial and Commercial Staffs and thus raise the standard of Management in the interests of the community as a whole.

The first step is to build up a Management Consulting Organisation to render beneficial service to individual firms in return for substantial fees. In this way, a growing source of revenue should be forthcoming. During the course of this consulting work, experience will be gained, the field for our work will be widened and improvements in our methods will, to a certain extent, automatically result.

With the assurance of an expanding source of revenue, the next step is to build up a Management Research Organisation, devoted to the development of New and Improved Techniques and to distribute the knowledge so gained for the benefit of all.

There will thus be two main sides to our work – Operating and Research. There must, however, always be the closest co-operation and liaison between these two sides and the work of each will frequently overlap.

When the Research side has established a reputation for rendering worthwhile benefits to Industry and Commerce, there is no reason why it should not be approached by individual firms, groups of firms, whole industries and even Government to assist in solving specific problems. Fees for this work would augment the revenue derived from our Consulting Services to finance further the expanding Management Research and Development, Educational and Training Centres, Administrative Staff Colleges, etc.

Ernest Butten
Chairman

Butten went on to create the elements described in the Charter: he acquired a Nash mansion at Sundridge Park near Bromley in Kent in 1955 and established his management centre in which he set up the management research operation he had foreseen. His management consultancy went on to become one of the world's leading businesses in this field.

This intention and ability to create a vision and turn it into a way of life for the company may be regarded as nothing unusual until one compares a supposed entrepreneur and builder of multinational corporations, Robert Maxwell, whose empire collapsed after he died, with another entrepreneur and business builder, Thomas J Watson, whose creation, International Business Machines, is still a global force to be reckoned with over 80 years after he founded it.

Principles of good corporate governance

From the above examples, we can draw some conclusions and formulate a short set of rules regarding the practice of good corporate governance. All the 'goodies', to a great degree, abided by these rules. All the 'baddies' to a large extent ignored them. The principles underlying these rules are:

- ethical approach – culture, society; organisational paradigm
- balanced objectives – congruence of goals of all interested parties
- each party plays his part – roles of key players: owners/directors/staff
- a decision-making process in place based on a model reflecting the above giving *due* weight to all stakeholders
- stakeholders treated with equal concern – albeit some have greater weight than others
- accountability and transparency: to all stakeholders.

Hence, with due respect to Milton Friedman who is quoted as believing that *the social responsibility of business begins and ends with increasing profit* we contend that running the business successfully is not *simply* about market domination or shareholder value.

And good corporate governance is not *simply* about a battle between distant, disloyal institutional shareholders and greedy directors, but about the ethos of the organisation and fulfilling its clearly agreed goals.

These goals may be set by the entrepreneur who starts the business, but they are accepted by all parties as being high-minded and in everyone's interests. This is notwithstanding the fact that some parties have bigger stakes and some benefit more than others. And, of course, different parties want different things from the company. There has to be, therefore, a process of identifying the different needs and, as much as possible, harmonising them. This is the starting point for the smooth running of the business. Once dissonance in the common goal creeps in, the danger of the standard of corporate governance deteriorating rises steadily.

Clearly external regulation can only play a limited part in ensuring that such a deep-seated and beneficial culture as that described above exists. Equally clearly, however, the task of ensuring this desirable state belongs to the various stakeholders, who can and should, through their proper participation, bring this about.

Five Golden Rules

As we have iterated, this section of the book lays out and explains the holistic approach by which we believe an organisation can ensure that a state of good corporate governance exists, or is brought into being if its existence is uncertain. It takes the view that there is an over-riding moral dimension to running a business[3] and that the standard of governance will depend on the moral complexion of the operation. Hence the approach developed is based on the belief that:

- the business morality or ethic must permeate the entire operation from top to bottom and embrace all stakeholders
- good corporate governance is an integral part of good management practice also permeating the entire operation, and not an esoteric specialism addressed by lawyers, auditors and sociologists.

The principles of this approach are framed in relation to the conventional way of looking at how a business should be properly run.

FIVE GOLDEN RULES

1. **Ethics:** a clearly ethical basis to the business.
2. **Congruence of goals:** appropriate goals, arrived at through the creation of a suitable stakeholder decision-making model.
3. **Strategic management:** an effective strategy process which incorporates stakeholder value.
4. **Organisation:** an organisation suitably structured to effect good corporate governance.
5. **Reporting:** reporting systems structured to provide transparency and accountability.

This approach recognises that the interests of different stakeholders carry different weight, but it does not, by any means, suggest that those with a major interest matter and the rest don't. On the contrary, all stakeholders should be treated with equal concern and respect, and though, for obvious reasons, the methodology we will propose involves taking major stakeholders into greater account when formulating strategy, it is designed to generate all round support because of the fact that every stakeholder, no matter how small, is given the opportunity to express a view. It is key to the approach that organisations truly respect the minority interests. Like the spirit of the US constitution,[4] the approach can be said to embrace liberty, equality and community, but like the US economy, it aspires to produce the most powerful and effective result in the world.

Good corporate governance is good management

The regulatory approach to the subject would regard governance as something on its own, to do with ensuring a balance between the various interested parties in a company's affairs, or more particularly a way of making sure that the chairman or chief executive is under control, producing transparency in reporting or curbing over-generous remuneration packages. This indeed is what the Cadbury recommendations and the Greenbury Report are all about. However, the reader will be aware from Part A that we regard this as much too limited a view of governance.

The essence of success in business is:

- having a clear and achievable goal
- having a feasible strategy to achieve it
- creating an organisation appropriate to deliver
- having in place a reporting system to guide progress.

Very many books have been written to advise on how to do this, and of course, this is what is described as good management.

Good governance is about achieving the stakeholders' goal, and delivering success in an ethical way. Hence it follows that it must entail an holistic application of good management, and that is the theme of the remainder of this part of the book.

To demonstrate the totality and the need for an holistic approach, Figure 9.2 (a modified illustration from an earlier book[5] by one of the authors), shows the pressures on a large organisation.

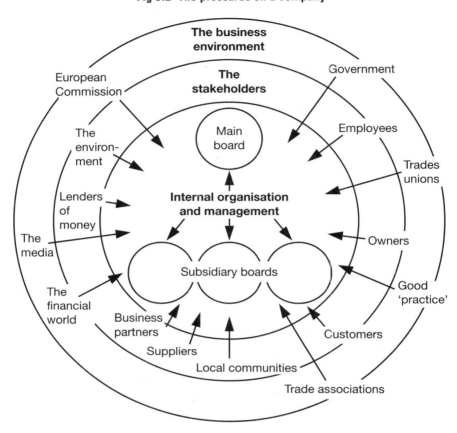

Fig 9.2 The pressures on a company

It is important that a wide perspective is taken when considering corporate governance because we cannot emphasise too strongly our belief that good management practices will deliver good corporate governance. Compliance with checklists of regulations and codes, in the setting of bad management or a lack of commitment to good management, will *NOT* deliver good corporate governance. The longer-term consequences of this externally-applied regulatory approach will mean more and more rules, held in less and less regard, producing less and less effect.

This may spawn a small industry of specialist advisers in corporate governance and lobby groups (which has already started to happen), but the result will benefit neither business nor its customers.

Corporate governance and the strategic management process

George Bain, Principal of London Business School, pointed out to us that the big advantage of the shareholder model over the stakeholder model in management terms is the simple goal it presents: maximise shareholder value. No such simple target attaches to the stakeholder approach, and yet without a clear goal, management faces an impossible task in trying to do its job properly – what exactly is its job?

In our 30 years of working with and observing management in all kinds of situations, a general rule stands out: the governance, the goals and the strategy of a business must be compatible, and there must be congruence between the expectations of the various interested parties. Clearly, this means that:

- there is a common view as to the ethic by which the business is conducted
- the views of all interested parties are taken into account when deciding the goal
- an appropriate weighting is given to those views to arrive at a conclusion as to how to achieve the greatest good
- a strategy is formulated to attain the chosen goal which takes account of the likely behaviour of the various interest groups
- an implementation programme is drawn up which makes the necessary organisational arrangements to fulfil the strategy and to protect the interests of the various stakeholders
- the implementation programme includes reporting systems which ensure transparency and regular feedback on matters which affect them to the various stakeholders.

This and the next five chapters of this book are devoted to the process whereby a board, and the main stakeholders, can ensure that the company complies with the Five Golden Rules of good corporate governance. Since we believe that good governance is all about good management, we make no apology for presenting the totality of a strategic management model so that the elements which are more specific to this subject are placed in context. The reader can adapt the model to his or her preferred taste, but the approach we have chosen draws on Michael Porter, whose ideas are now widely accepted and adopted. The overall process is summarised in Figure 9.3.

Fig 9.3 Corporate governance and the strategic management process

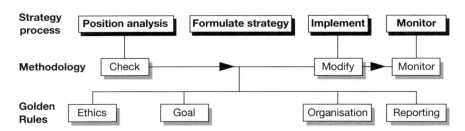

The whole picture

The key to our approach and the methodology developed to achieve good corporate governance lies, as we said at the beginning, in building the concepts we put forward into every part of the business. Figures 9.4a and 9.4b put this into context – they show that everything starts and finishes with the strategy process. It is the vehicle for starting the whole process and the destination for all the results obtained from the analyses, and the vehicle for corresponding changes in policy and organisation. In Chapter 12 we will look in detail at how the strategy process (as summarised in Figure 9.3) should be carried out to incorporate stakeholder involvement,[6] but from an overall perspective, here, we can see how the Golden Rules approach relates to the whole business.

A NEW APPROACH TO CORPORATE GOVERNANCE

Fig 9.4a The stakeholder approach and the strategy process

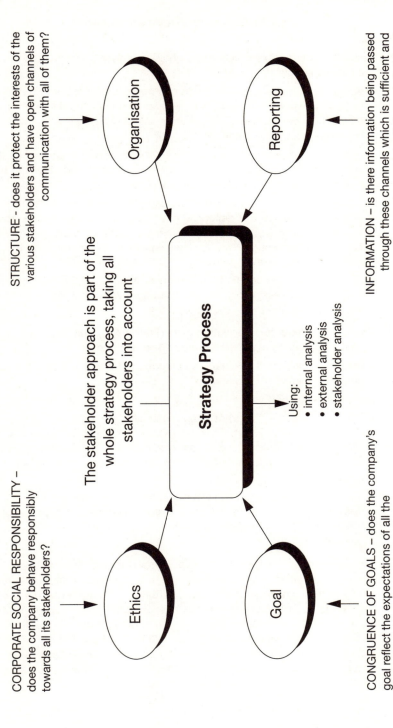

Fig 9.4b A summary of the methodology

1. Using the internal, external and stakeholder analyses, we can find out a balanced view of:

   - *ethics:* what the board thinks of the company's ethical behaviour may not be the same as what other stakeholders think – the differences may simply be due to lack of communication (which will show up later) but need to be reconciled

   - *goal:* the crucial part of the process – if the company's 'agreed' goal is found to be significantly different from what stakeholders want, the goal will have to be adapted or changed completely

   - *organisation:* we talked earlier of ensuring the company has an organisation capable of delivering good corporate governance – from the stakeholders' point of view, then, this means ensuring accountability through direct contact with all stakeholders, which may be unclear or even unknown

   - *reporting:* here we can find out how much the stakeholders know about the business, which can be compared with what they should know, or what the board *think* they know.

2. We can then feed the information gathered *back into* the strategy model and use it to make any changes necessary to:

   - the ethical stance or the resources made available to improve the company's image, for example

   - the goal – the general direction in which the company is moving

   - the organisation – this process automatically opens up communication channels if they were lacking before, but these will need to be rationalised; it will also have opened our eyes to any structural or operational inefficiencies, etc which are affecting our stakeholders

   - reporting systems – having opened up these channels, it is then possible to monitor progress and ensure stakeholders are getting all the information they need and this function, too, will have to be rationalised.

3. When a strategy has been selected and implemented, the steps taken above will mean we can evaluate progress of the strategy and the effect it is having on stakeholder attitudes to the concepts addressed by the Golden Rules – particularly usefully, ethics and the goal. This will be aided further by the stakeholder model referred to in the Introduction. As Figure 9.3 shows we will need to monitor all four elements – including the organisation and the reporting systems themselves – to ensure continuing high standards and that we are receiving accurate, timely information to feed back into the model.

The next five chapters deal with the particular issues within each Golden Rule. What is important to remember is that the procedures explained in them are all part of the methodology we have just described. That is, the main *focus* of each concept will be at different stages of the strategy process, but they will have relevance throughout, since the methodology demands that we take all the Rules into account at each stage. So rather than think of these as separate actions, they should be thought of in the context of an overall process of applying this holistic approach to corporate governance.

Further, as explained in the introduction to this chapter, there are basically two levels to our approach to implementing good corporate governance: one is the principle of good governance, represented by the Golden Rules as set out above, the other is the methodology, where we are checking, modifying and monitoring the company to comply with these rules. This means that on one level we are saying how important it is to be accountable – through transparent reporting, and on the other level we are saying that in the second stage of the methodology above we are making changes to the organisation to make this possible. It is for this reason that the fourth and fifth Golden Rules (Chapters 13 and 14) are both connected to organisation – in the modification stage of the methodology (corresponding to the implementation stage in the strategy process). However, we have deliberately made reporting a distinct rule not only because of its distinct importance, but also because, as the third stage of the methodology dictates, we need to use the reporting systems we have set up to monitor compliance with all the Golden Rules and progress of the strategy. This is represented in Figure 9.3 and the full version in Figure 12.1.

Finally, the main advantage of adopting this approach is that, as the reader will have noted, there are no complicated, isolated processes that need implementing – the methodology uses the strategy model already in existence (rationalising where necessary to tighten procedures) as the vehicle for change, which is simply a matter of incorporating new or improved systems.

PART B · HOW TO PRACTISE GOOD CORPORATE GOVERNANCE

NOTES

[1] *The HP Way*, Harper Business Books, 1995.
[2] A letter from the founder of PA showing his strong commitment to a sales-oriented culture.

2, ALBERT GATE,
KNIGHTSBRIDGE,
LONDON, S.W. 1.
01-235 6060.

21st August 1968

Dear Nigel,

<u>re Salesmanship</u>

Under separate cover I am sending you the following books:

OPEN THE MIND AND CLOSE THE SALE - Wilson
THE PSYCHOLOGY OF SELLING - Cash & Crissy:
   Vol. 1 - A Point of View for Salesmen
   Vol. 2 - The Use of Appeals in Selling
   Vol. 3 - Motivation in Selling
   Vol. 4 - Personality and Sales Strategy
   Vol. 5 - Tactics for Conducting the Sales Call
   Vol. 6 - The Salesman as a Self-Manager
*SALESMANSHIP - Alfred Gross
SELL YOUR WAY TO SUCCESS - Tack

which may help you to master the important art of "putting across ideas," whether you are selling a product or dealing with a Client, or consulting with fellow Directors in a Board Room.

                With all good wishes
                Yours sincerely,

                Ernest E. Butten

* to follow

EEB/AM/2AG - Enc.

---

[3] See Chapter 2, where we discuss the concept of the corporation as a 'moral person'.
[4] *Freedom's Law*, Ronald Dworkin, Oxford University Press, 1996.
[5] *Corporate Governance*, Sheridan and Kendall, Pitman Publishing, 1992.
[6] The authors would like to acknowledge their debt to Johnson and Scholes, whose full and clear expression of how the strategic management process works must by now have passed into the manual of good practice in most well run companies. The authors are particularly indebted to them for their thoughts on a stakeholder audit which they have used as the basis for that most difficult of tasks: how to judge the weight to be given to the interests of the various stakeholders.
ref.: *Exploring Corporate Strategy, Text and Cases*, Gerry Johnson and Kevan Scholes, Prentice Hall, 1993.

Chapter 10

A QUESTION OF ETHICS

'The bigger issue in [consumers'] minds was one of corporate ethics and responsibility. They were making strong ethical judgements about business practice and corporate brands.'

From an investigation by Ogilvy & Mather entitled 'Ethical Marketing: Is it Worth it?'

RULE 1: THE ETHICAL APPROACH

The first Golden Rule is that the business morality or ethic must permeate an organisation from top to bottom and embrace all stakeholders.

As part of the overall investigation, therefore, it is essential to start with a diagnostic of the ethical approach underlying the business. Just as widespread bribery and corruption in society are recognised as being inimical to the development of a healthy economy, similarly the lack of a high standard of ethical behaviour in a company is inimical to trust and loyalty, which in turn has a detrimental effect on the health of the company over the longer term.

It may be argued that an owner can run a business in whichever way he or she wishes, and at first glance there would appear to be a case for this so long as no other shareholders are involved, and only his or her money is at risk, and of course with the acquiescence of the employees and trading partners. However, in many years of observing different standards of behaviour in different business circumstances, one recognises the relationship between the perception of ethics which permeates an organisation and the degree of trust and loyalty present among employees and between staff and management. The conclusion one reaches is that loyalty and trust have a significant value in terms of the efficiency and effectiveness with which a business can be run, and the concomitant cost of control systems needed.

In other words, a highly ethical operation is likely to spend much less on protecting itself against fraud and will probably have to spend much less on industrial relations to maintain morale and common purpose.

An experienced eye and ear will recognise the ethical stance of a business within a fairly short while from talking to directors and senior management, and this will be rounded out by discussions with a representative sample of staff, particularly those concerned with customers and personnel management. It will almost certainly be confirmed by a conversation with the finance director and an appreciation of how the money matters are dealt with.

Clearly it is necessary to deploy rather more than gut feeling in examining a business's position in regard to business ethics. Below we pick up the methodology taken from Figures 9.4a and 9.4b.

CORPORATE SOCIAL RESPONSIBILITY – does the company behave responsibly towards all its stakeholders?.

Ethics

1. Using the internal, external and stakeholder analyses, we can find out a balanced view of:
   - *ethics:* what the board thinks of the company's ethical behaviour may not be the same as what other stakeholders think.

Here we are first checking how the company measures up on ethical issues. It is unwise to trust the feelings of the board, as has been proven on many occasions (for simplicity we quote Shell again). No matter how ethical a company thinks it is, it needs to make sure – from an external viewpoint – that it is beyond reproach. So the board will need to listen especially carefully to its stakeholders; the investigation by Ogilvy and Mather quoted above involved extensive research into consumer attitudes towards corporate brands and concluded that a strong ethical stance is and will be increasingly vital to successful consumer marketing.

JOHNSON AND SCHOLES ON BUSINESS ETHICS[1]

Ethical issues concerning businesses and public sector organisations exist at three levels:

- at the *macro* level there are issues about the role of business in the national and international organisation of society. These are largely concerned with assessing the relative virtues of different political/social systems, such as free enterprise, centrally planned economies, etc. There are also important issues of international relationships and the role of business on an international scale
- at the *corporate* level the issue is often referred to as corporate social responsibility and is focused on the ethical issues facing individual corporate entities (private and public sector) when formulating and implementing strategies
- at the *individual* level the issue concerns the behaviour and actions of individuals within organisations. This is clearly an important matter for the management of organisations, but it is discussed here only in so far as it affects strategy, and in particular the role of managers in the strategic management process.

A report produced in 1981[2] found 10 stereotypes or roles of organisations in

Ethics, to quote Lord Moulton, can be defined as 'obedience to the unenforceable'. In our view the successful companies in the next century will heed this maxim. It's not simply about doing good; in any case, few companies could support so extreme a philosophical positioning. Economic pragmatism will always hold sway. What it is about is really understanding and nurturing all the relationships that a company has with its publics from staff to supplier to consumers and ensuring that the corporate philosophy puts their needs and values at the centre of its vision.

The concept of ethics is clearly an ambiguous, intangible one, as the word 'unenforceable' reflects. Being 'ethical' means different things to different people. This means that the importance each respondent places on ethics will reflect different issues. In other words, this is about stakeholder *perception*. If stakeholders feel the company is not being ethical, it makes no difference whether they are thinking about damage to the environment or price differentiation (between customers or groups). If the board's perception of ethics is the former, it may justifiably feel that it is an ethical business, but this is irrelevant if the stakeholder is concerned with price differentiation and believes that the company is guilty of gross price differences which they find unacceptable.

---

business ethics. Quoting these, Johnson and Scholes identify four broad groupings, which are summarised below.

1. Those organisations believing, after Milton Friedman, that the only social responsibility of business is to increase its profit, and that it is government's responsibility to provide through legislation a suitable framework of duties and responsibilities under which business will operate for the greater good.
2. Those believing in the above, but who recognise that well-managed relationships with external stakeholders are beneficial, and give rise to the need to monitor behaviour to catch and stop short-term practices of doubtful ethical provenance for the sake of the long-term business benefit.
3. Those believing that stakeholder interests need more explicit incorporation in the objectives of the business, and that performance means more than just the bottom line, for instance retaining uneconomic jobs in deprived areas, or not trading in products perceived as harmful, though a balance clearly needs to be maintained to preserve the long-term health of the business.
4. Those founded in response to a community need, where financial considerations are secondary to society needs, and the balance is usually so weighted that finance becomes simply a constraint on providing primarily for the interests of the beneficiary as the most important stakeholder

Through the stakeholder analysis, and to a certain extent through the internal and external analyses (in that the processes employed by the company can be seen at a glance and so judged), a lot of information can be gathered about the ethics of the company and the perceptions held by interested parties. A major part of the research programme needed for the stakeholder analysis will involve respondents giving values[3] to the main issues associated with ethics, including how they feel the company delivers on these issues. They will include:

1. General views on ethics – what and how important the issues are, such as:
   - consideration and protection of the environment
   - fair trading, especially with poor countries
   - defending human rights, for example non-exploitation of workers in poor countries
   - not investing in countries with unacceptable regimes
   - supporting local communities
   - fair treatment of staff.

2. Particular stakeholder views/angles, such as:
   - customers' beliefs when *purchasing* – how much do ethical issues actually affect their buying behaviour?
   - employees' moral values – how important is it for them to work in an ethically sound company?
   - shareholders' feeling of responsibility – to what extent do they feel obliged to enforce ethical behaviour?
   - local community's interest – how much are they interested in the company's *active* involvement in the community?

We pointed out in the last chapter that many concepts in this process will be unfamiliar to many stakeholders. Here, the problem lies in not knowing company policy and so being unable to judge the company. In quantitative research, therefore, it is necessary to give them something more tangible and real to base judgement on – anyway, qualitative research should be carried out which will allow more extensive probing. In this case, the sort of ideas that can be used as proxies are:

- encouraging people to recycle
- involvement with local charities and community groups
- allowing/encouraging fundraising for charity
- staff who are happy in their work.

The fact that these do not cover issues such as fair trading is irrelevant. Respondents can only judge what they see. Further, if they do want to know more about company policy but do not have the means, they will have the opportunity later to make this known, too, with questions on organisation (see Chapter 13) – as represented by the proxy of communication. What is relevant, as the second point covers, above, is how *important* the question of ethics is to them as a stakeholder (which overlaps, not surprisingly, with the next rule, the goal).

NOTES

[1] Extracts from: *Exploring Corporate Strategy, Text and Cases*, Gerry Johnson and Kevan Scholes, Prentice Hall, 1993.
[2] *Facing Realities: The European Societal Strategy Project*, summary report produced by the European Foundation for Management Development and the European Institute for Advanced Studies in Management, 1981.
[3] The mention of 'values' refers to the construction of the model described in Chapter 9. It is a way of simply quantifying stakeholder perceptions of the company, thus enabling better monitoring and prediction of future changes when formulating strategy. Fuller explanation of and reference to the model is deliberately avoided in the main body of the book – the reader may wish to read Appendix A before reading further, to understand better where these chapters are leading.

Chapter 11

TOWARDS A COMMON GOAL

The right goals *147*
Checking the goal *149*

'Clouds of smoke, even laughter, engulfed the room as the figures revealed an achievement it had taken nearly a decade to create: Pepsi had surpassed Coke in sales as the leading soft drink sold in the nation's supermarkets. "This is what I've longed for during my entire career," Kendall exulted, "to beat Coke fair and square."

JOHN SCULLEY
From *Odyssey Pepsi to Apple*[1]

RULE 2: CONGRUENCE OF GOALS

The right goals

The second Golden Rule is that the business should be targeting an appropriate goal which properly reflects the expectations of the stakeholders. 'Properly' in this context means that it has been arrived at after due consideration of all the interests concerned, and an appropriate weighting which recognises that the various stakeholders have different claims on the organisation. A misjudgement of the weighting may do serious damage to the totality of the business, and a lack of understanding of the need for congruence between the aims of the different stakeholders may make the business impossible to run at all.

We give below a case study to illustrate these problems. It is based on real events and though the details have been changed to preserve anonymity, the principles are reflected in the modified story.

Case study: Losing sight of the need for a common goal

An industry sector group operated as a trade association within the engineering industry, with members drawn from all the leading UK engineering firms. After one particularly reflective general meeting, it was decided that the industry would benefit if a new organisation was set up to introduce self-regulation into that sector, to eliminate the cowboy operators.

An organisation, which we shall call Directorate for Optimum Operating Methods and Enhanced Designs, or DOOMED for short, was established for this purpose with a brief to introduce new standards and encourage sector companies to join the organisation and become accredited to the new standards. The organisation was set up as a company limited by guarantee with the shares held by the industry sector trade asssociation, and the guarantee being underwritten effectively by the leading engineering companies.

One of the conditions of gaining approval for such an operation was that a board of directors should be set up to govern the DOOMED organisation, whose members were selected to be representative of all the parties likely to be involved. This was a standard condition for the organisation to be accredited by its own regulatory body and required the appointment of directors drawn from the ranks of suppliers, customers and the trade association, with a couple of academics thrown in for good measure. Interestingly, this did not include representatives of the general public as final consumers of the products being certificated, and neither was the chief executive made a director, so all the board members were non-executive.

Over the next few years, nearly 50 per cent of the firms in this sector were prevailed upon to join the organisation and become accredited, and the first objective seemed to have been achieved. Then the problems began to emerge, which highlighted the lack of goal congruence which had been built in from the start. The problems were triggered by the very success of gathering members since this alerted potential competitors to the possibilities in this new market which had been created. First one, and then another certification body started approaching members with a 'cut-price' offer, using the same standards which had been developed by DOOMED – a practice they were perfectly entitled to adopt – and cutting back on the number and extent of monitoring visits.

The conflicts of interest now became apparent when management drew the board's attention to the rapidly deteriorating trading position and asked for guidance in determining a strategy to remedy the situation. The reactions were varied:

- the directors representing larger suppliers insisted on there being no dilution of standards, pointing out that this process would eliminate the smaller competitors who would go for the cheaper certification, thereby damaging their reputation in relation to the market leaders and hence losing market share; in fact the certification process should probably be made more demanding and more expensive to hasten the departure of the smaller firms
- the directors representing smaller suppliers felt that the proper solution was to reduce the demands of the monitoring process and cut the prices to compete with the new entrants; in any case, they had been saying for some time that they themselves could not afford the current fees and had been warning of the likelihood of cut-price competitors entering the market
- the directors representing customers were in favour of a reduction in fees, since this was clearly what the market was indicating, but they also believed that standards ought not to be reduced with the implications for an inferior product; DOOMED was the first in the field and still the market leader and the experience curve surely indicated that their operating costs must therefore be lower than the new competitors. DOOMED must cut its costs to reduce its prices while maintaining standards.
- the academics agreed with all the arguments above and felt that it was too early to be able to predict how the market might develop; in any case, the organisation was committed by its constitution to continue imposing high standards on its members – any change would surely require a constitutional conference. So, since the bank balance was still healthy with undistributed reserves from the earlier successful years, DOOMED ought to leave any radical decision for another 12 months while it watched developments and use its reserves to fund any shortfall in trading cash flow

- the chairman in this situation felt unable to give any clear direction to management, and the matter was deferred to the next quarterly board meeting.

The chief executive, charged with running a successful organisation, and denied guidance from the board, of which he was not a member, faced a rapidly deteriorating trading situation which required a fresh assessment of the market, and a new strategy. Clearly the board was riven by conflicts of interest, so he decided to go direct to the shareholders.

At this point, he realised that the trade association was the shareholder, but that it held the shares effectively as a trustee for the big engineering firms, and they appeared to have only a marginal interest in an organisation which was peripheral to most of their businesses. They provided directors to sit on the governing council of the trade association, but most of these were very senior directors in multinational corporations who had little knowledge of DOOMED and even less interest in being sucked into discussions about its trading problems. If pressed to express a view, it would be: 'close it down if it has become a problem'. In reality *no one* could speak for the shareholders of DOOMED.

The chief executive's frustration with the market pressures and the growing need to agree a strategy to address them was then coupled with despair at realising that there was *no* goal that could possibly be elicited from shareholders or board. In effect his job was not do-able.

His despair turned to clinical depression and resulted in a nervous breakdown. He never worked again.

DOOMED appointed a replacement chief executive, but failed to address the contradictions inherent in its constitution. Its trading position deteriorated and soon it was subsumed into a rival regulatory body, and in due course it disappeared.

The lesson is very clear. DOOMED was set up with no attempt to ensure that there was a commonly accepted goal amongst the various interested parties. This made it impossible to provide the chief executive with a proper brief beyond simply recruiting members and writing standards. When market pressures required a market strategy, none was, or could be, forthcoming. The organisation had no long-term future, and the chief executive had an impossible job.

Checking the goal

As we discussed in Chapter 9, corporate governance issues are relevant throughout the strategy process, but the *focus* of each issue occurs at a different stage. In view of the need for congruence in stakeholder expectations, it is clear that checking the goal – and the ethics, as we stressed in the previous chapter – is of fundamental importance. In other words, the major efforts, here, will come in the position analysis, so that from the beginning we know what our stakeholders want. This knowledge is the foundation of the strategy process, on which the building blocks of strategy can be confidently placed. Knowing we will have support for the strategy – or at least that we can easily check this[2] – turns the process away from a purely business exercise to one which is based on the realities of our operating environment.

With this in mind, we remind the reader that the procedures described in these chapters are by no means separate exercises but part of the whole process of applying the holistic approach we advocate. Below, therefore, is the most relevant part of the methodology, taken from Figures 9.4a and 9.4b.

CONGRUENCE OF GOALS – does the company's goal reflect the expectations of all the stakeholders?

1. Using the internal, external and stakeholder analyses, we can find out a balanced view of:

   - *goal:* the crucial part of the process – if the company's 'agreed' goal is found to be significantly different from what stakeholders want, the goal will have to be adapted or changed completely

Since stakeholder expectations will usually be different, to a greater or lesser extent, from the perceptions of the company, the goal will therefore need to bring these into line – in the process moving to achieve congruence of goals. This process is displayed in Figure 11.1. As part of the strategic (position) analysis described below, we detail a model through which the stakeholder expectations can be determined and weighted for input to the corporate goal and strategy. At this stage we shall limit ourselves to describing a goal discussion meeting at which management can explore the extent to which the organisation's current goal appears to be both clear and appropriately representative of the aspirations of the stakeholders.

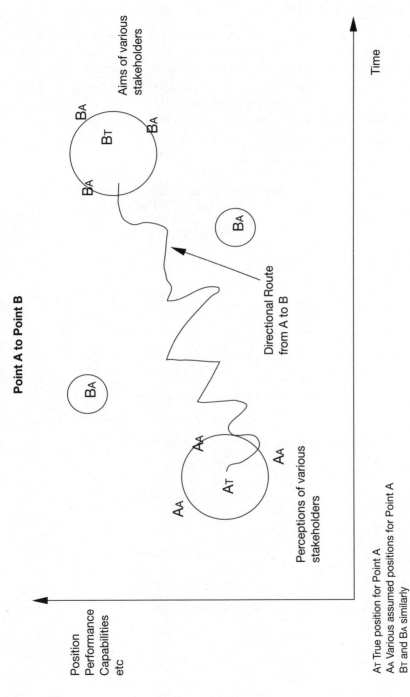

Fig 11.1 The goal – aligning perceptions and expectations

Goal discussion meeting

We give here as an illustration of a goal meeting the agenda for a discussion meeting held by a client of one of the authors prior to the commencement of a project to determine a new strategy.

The purpose was to review the board's understanding of the goal of the corporation so as to give added focus to the strategy study. Additionally, the aim was to understand how closely this provisional goal reflected the expectations of the various stakeholders.

LARGE CONSUMER SERVICES LTD (LCS)
GOAL MEETING OF GROUP BOARD, JANUARY 1997

AGENDA

Time

13.00 Introduction
- setting the scene
  - background
  - agenda

13.05 Review of background briefing paper
- covers: current vision, recent technical development, the competition, industry trends, demographic trends, company history
- questions arising – insofar as not covered by subsequent discussion

13.10 Discussion of what constitutes a suitable goal

13.10
- statement of key issues to be faced
  - current mission statement
  - industry characteristics and consumer trends
  - likely industry response

13.15
- statement of key features of goal
  - continuous improvement in present business
  - entry into new related business to dominate
  - compatibility with history and core beliefs

13.20
- contribution from each participant in turn
  - executive directors
  - non-executive directors

14.20
- summing up
  - views expressed

14.30	**Break**
14.50	**A new concept**
14.50	• bones of an idea
15.00	• how it could be piloted in LCS
15.10	• brainstorm ideas – reactions – open discussion
15.40	• summing up – collective view (key concept, modified as necessary?)
15.50	**On-going strategy project programme** • overview of total programme • requirements from Board members
16.00	**Close**

The above meeting proved very effective in getting the board to consider:

- how to focus on an appropriate and feasible goal
- how to approach such a goal taking into account the interests of the various stakeholders and giving proper weight to the culture and core beliefs of the business.

NOTES

[1] Donald M Kendall, powerful chairman of Pepsi Co, had just learned from Nielsons' market research figures that he had achieved his career ambition, which had thus become the goal of Pepsi Co management. John Sculley's book, *Odyssey Pepsi to Apple*, was published by Collins in 1987.

[2] This, of course, will depend on the successful modification of the organisation where necessary, in the fourth stage in the strategy process. Having opened up the channels of communication, though, the process of rationalisation, as explained in Figure 9.4a, will make these concrete, and the implementation of a continuous monitoring process will enable us to obtain quickly and easily the information we need.

Chapter 12

THE WHOLE PICTURE

Internal analysis *159*
External analysis *171*
Stakeholder analysis *180*
Confirm or change goal *191*
Formulating strategy *195*
Implementation *202*

'The job of management is to maintain an equitable and working balance among the claims of the various directly interested groups – stockholders, employees, customers and the public at large.'

FRANK ABRAMS,
chairman of Standard Oil Company of New Jersey in an address in 1951[1]

RULE 3: CORPORATE GOVERNANCE AS AN INTEGRAL PART OF THE STRATEGY PROCESS

The third Golden Rule is that good corporate governance requires an effective strategic management process to be in place.

By this we mean that the company is organised and run according to rules which:

- set a goal matching the duly considered expectations of the stakeholders
- work out a feasible strategy to achieve that goal
- put in place an organisation which can carry out the strategy and attain the goal
- establish a control and reporting function to permit management to drive the organisation effectively and make necessary adjustments to the strategy or even the goal.

Anything less rigorous will only achieve success by accident and will be vulnerable to all kinds of unexpected events.

This chapter brings together everything in this section of the book – as we explained in Chapter 9, the strategy process is the beginning, the middle and the end of translating the concepts of our holistic approach into a practical system of good corporate governance. The methodology in Figures 9.4a and 9.4b showed it is the starting point – through the position analysis, the vehicle for driving the company in the direction the stakeholders wish – through the strategy formulation stage, and the means to change and monitor the organisation to reflect stakeholder expectations through the final, but ongoing stages of the strategy process. This is represented in Figure 12.1, which shows how a standard strategy model can be adapted.

Following this model and to demonstrate the process we will assume the role of analyst at Good Corporate Governance Limited (GCG). We will go through the points to be covered and the procedures needed to arrive at a strategy for the company, as summarised by the steps below (see Figure 12.1). The process is set out in such a way that when doing it for real,[2] the structure can be used to produce the final reports.

PART B · HOW TO PRACTISE GOOD CORPORATE GOVERNANCE

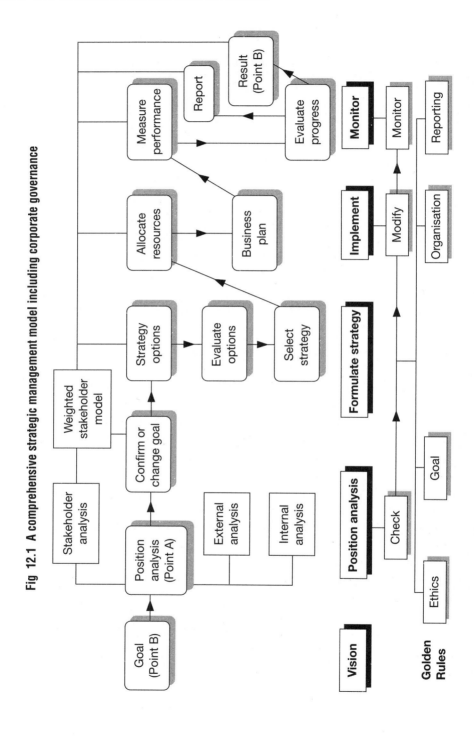

Fig 12.1 A comprehensive strategic management model including corporate governance

Covered in this chapter are:

a. Position analysis, addressing where the company is now, which comprises:
- internal analysis – an assessment of the organisation's internal position
- external analysis – an assessment of the external business environment within which the organisation is operating
- stakeholder analysis – an assessment of the company's stakeholders, their perceptions and their expectations.

b. Formulation of strategy, which comprises:
- generating strategic options
- evaluating and assessing the suitability of each, taking proper account of the various stakeholders' expectations
- making a choice.

The final two stages of strategic management are mainly dealt with in the next two chapters, namely:

c. Implementing the strategy.
d. Monitoring progress.

Particular reference is made to the way in which these affect the interests of the various stakeholder groups.

Internal analysis

In carrying out an internal analysis, we aim to:

- understand existing and potential resources available to GCG
- evaluate the business's strategic capability
- assess its potential strengths and weaknesses
- identify opportunities for short-term performance improvement within the existing strategy.

We will therefore need to:

- review all our internal resources
- review available external resources
- highlight key resources
- assess and analyse the company's value chain
- compare our present position with past performance and with best industry practice, as a benchmark
- find out how existing GCG resources are being allocated to enable us to correct any imbalances

- summarise the key issues and highlight deficiencies that have come to light as a result of the whole analysis.

Hence, this internal analysis will show the areas in which the company can improve and what it is capable of potentially. By analysing our resources, both internal and external, and identifying the strengths and weaknesses of the value chain, we highlight GCG's current competitive position, enabling us to realistically assess the company's development potential. Figure 12.2 shows how this stage of the position analysis is used to assess strategic capability.

Review internal resources

We will need to document all resources under GCG's direct control. We can divide this as follows:

a. **Tangible resources** including:
- buildings: distribution, age, etc
- property portfolio and investment
- other fixed assets (eg plant and equipment)
- product range (goods and services).

b. **Financial overview** including:
- balance sheet strength and financial soundness
- trading margins achieved
- shareholder returns
- ratio analysis.

c. **The workforce** including:
- distribution by age, grade, length of service, division, part/full time
- skills and training: quality and quantity
- earnings compared with industry averages
- labour turnover.

d. **Intangibles** including:
- company history and heritage
- brand value or goodwill
- loyalty
- links with local communities, interest groups, etc.

THE WHOLE PICTURE

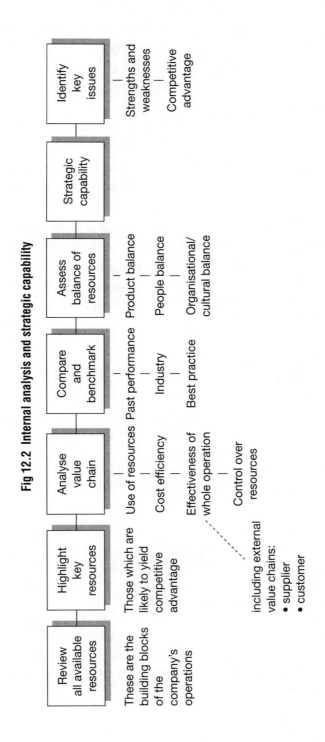

Fig 12.2 Internal analysis and strategic capability

> **THE STRATEGY PROCESS**
> INTERNAL ANALYSIS
> - Review internal resources
>   - a. Tangible resources
>   - b. Financial overview
>   - c. The workforce
>   - d. Intangibles
> - Review available external resources
>   - a. Trading contacts
>   - b. Customers
>   - c. Shareholders
> - Highlight
> - Analyse value chain
> - Compare and benchmark
> - Assess balance of resources
> - Identify key issues
>
> EXTERNAL ANALYSIS
> STAKEHOLDER ANALYSIS
> CONFIRM OR CHANGE GOAL
> FORMULATING STRATEGY
> IMPLEMENTATION

Review available external resources

This analysis aims to produce a statement of *all* the resources available to GCG. So here we will document resources not directly owned or under our control. These will cover:

a. **Trading contacts** including:
  - customer and supplier partnerships and geographical alliances.

b. **Customers** including:
  - length of relationships, loyalty.

c. **Shareholders** including:
  - closeness of relationship, loyalty and support.

Highlight

The analysis will start to highlight those resources which are likely to confer a distinctive competitive advantage in the marketplace, as opposed to simply enabling the business to exist.

It will also be instructive at this stage, having assessed the business's financial resources, to consider these at a strategic level from the point of view of the expectations of our major stakeholders. For instance these might be:

- **shareholders:** growth in shareholders' funds via excellent profits plus the availability of cash to pay a consistent dividend
- **bankers:** financial soundness and interest cover
- **employees:** financial soundness but not excessive profits at the expense of wages
- **suppliers:** financial soundness and liquidity to pay on time
- **customers:** ability to survive as a supplier and to supply consistent quality without making excessive profits at their expense
- **local community:** strength to maintain existing level of employment or even to expand it.

Analyse value chain

Michael Porter said that a business can be seen as a value chain. Goods and services accumulate value at each stage of production, whether it be the assemblage of different parts to build a car or the development and construction of an accounting model. All organisations in an industry have a similar value chain, and will be profitable so long as revenues exceed costs. Management should understand both their own value chain and those of their competitors.

The documentation and highlighting of resources undertaken so far is just that. It will not in itself help us understand how well these resources are being employed, which is key to the success of a strategy. We will therefore use value chain analysis to evaluate GCG's operational performance in terms of efficiency and effectiveness, and undertake a comparative analysis with our competitors as a benchmark. Knowing our own strengths is important, but it is irrelevant if we do not know those of our competitors. As Sun Tzu, a Chinese general of the fourth century BC, said:

> If you know your enemy and know yourself, you need not fear the result of a hundred battles. If you know yourself but not the enemy, for every victory gained you will also suffer a defeat. If you know neither the enemy nor yourself, you will succumb in every battle[3]

The purpose of this stage of the strategic analysis is to understand how the various activities in the company's value chain underpin its competitive advantage in the marketplace. Using this approach, we will categorise GCG's activities into two broad types:

- *primary* activities, basically concerned with the processes by which raw materials are turned into finished products or services and delivered to the final consumer by a series of enhancements or adding of value
- *support* activities, basically the functional activities which the organisation sets up to optimise performance of the value adding processes.

In following this approach, we will therefore:

- identify our primary and support activities
- identify sources of competitive advantage
- assess cost efficiency, and
- analyse the effectiveness of the whole operation.

Fig 12.3 The Value Chain

Support Activities					
Organisation/ Management					
Human Resources					
Technology					
	Supply Chain Mgmt	Operations	Distribution	Marketing and Sales	Customer Service
	Primary activities				Margin

a. Identify primary activities

We will group these into five main areas, as in Figure 12.3:

- **Supply chain management:** how we obtain our raw materials – who are our suppliers, how efficient are these suppliers,[4] etc?
- **Operations:** how we turn these raw materials into finished goods or services
- **Distribution:** how we physically get these products to our customers – if not end users themselves, are these maximising value on the way to the end user?
- **Marketing and sales:** how we inform our customers (actual or potential) of our product offerings
- **Customer services:** how we support customers after purchase – including installation, repair, training, spares, etc.

Having established this grouping, we will then need to gather details for each area on:

- processes involved
- facts and figures:
  - resources used
  - efficiency
  - effectiveness
- value added

writing up a summary of findings and conclusions.

b. Identify support activities

Here, there are three main areas to assess (though these can be divided up or more added):

- **Organisation/management:** the management style and culture, eg command and control vs autonomy – is the current structure aiding maximum value?
- **Human resources:** including skills/training
- **Technology:** investment in/use of new technology to enhance value through efficiency improvements, for example

Again, having established this grouping, we will need to gather details for each area on:

- purpose
- process
- facts and figures:
  - resources
  - effectiveness
  - efficiency

writing up a summary of findings and conclusions.

c. Identify 'cost or value drivers'

These are factors which seem likely to sustain competitive advantage. To do this we need to:

- look for key linkages, especially in the internal value chain – eg low cost supply linked to geographical position
- look for links between primary activities – how they influence value creation, eg high stock levels help high service levels
- watch for lack of harmony between primary activities
- look for links between primary and support activities – to support competitive advantage, eg unique procurement system linked to local distribution points
- assess linkages between support activities – eg linking HR and technology
- assess sub-optimisation – eg excess stocks lead to higher mark-ups to cover carrying costs, hence lower competitiveness
- assess potential for collaborative arrangements between different organisations in the value chain to:
  - reduce costs
  - increase competitive edge.

d. Assess cost efficiency

These 'cost or value drivers' should then be checked for efficiency, using the standard tools of:

- economies of scale
- supply costs
- product process design
  - capacity fill
  - labour productivity
  - material yield
  - working capital utilisation
- the experience curve/relative market share – this should be applied to all parts of the value chain, and related to activities not goods or services.

e. Analyse effectiveness of the whole operation

Having identified and detailed the processes used to make and distribute our products to customers, assessed how our resources are being used and the cost efficiency of production processes, we are now in a position to analyse how well the whole business uses (*all* available) resources to most effectively meet the needs of our customers in the most efficient way possible. In this examination, because it is important to ensure effectiveness *throughout* the value chain of a product – including processes over which we have no direct control – we need to take into account external supplier chains which provide GCG with goods and services, and also customer value chains which lead to the final consumption of the product. Since the final consumer will benefit, it is logically also beneficial to all contributors to the value chain to ensure maximum effectiveness. Therefore, while the questions below are geared towards GCG itself, they need to be asked, at least to some extent, of our suppliers and (if not end users) our customers.

Since customer satisfaction is of primary importance, we will first ask some basic questions to ascertain whether we are achieving this, paying special attention to cost and value drivers in the analysis:

- How well do our goods and services match the needs of our customers?
- Is the cost of unique features recovered in higher prices?
- Are supporting services up to customers' expectations?
- Are communications systems to customers adding value before, during and after the sale?

- Are we customer-orientated when measuring performance? Are targets based on accounting/budgeting rather than value?

Now we will ask more general questions:

- Is GCG creating value *throughout* the system?
- Do we have our priorities clear? What are our 4–5 key value-enhancing measures?
- Do we have complete control over our resources? Is information timely, enough to influence decisions?
- To what extent can we evaluate and influence the creation of value? For instance in regard to:
  - buildings: security, maintenance
  - products: stock control, quality control, losses
  - human resources: control of key personnel, leadership
- What use can be made of:
  - vertical integration
  - central specialisation
  - Total Quality Management.

In the analysis of GCG's value chain, the interests of our various stakeholders will become apparent, and using the information gained here, we can develop ways in which their particular expectations can be better addressed.

To take two examples, this might, for instance, result in:

- improved working conditions for employees as part of a re-engineering of the production process, paid for by efficiency improvements
- improved services for customers, coupled with delivering efficiency improvements, leading to improved profits for shareholders.

THE STRATEGY PROCESS
INTERNAL ANALYSIS
• Review internal resources
• Review available external resources
• Highlight
• Analyse value chain
a. Identify primary activities
b. Identify support activities
c. Identify 'cost or value drivers'
d. Assess cost efficiency
e. Analyse effectiveness of the whole operation
• Compare and benchmark
a. Past performance
b. Industry
c. Best practice
• Assess balance of resources
• Identify key issues
EXTERNAL ANALYSIS
STAKEHOLDER ANALYSIS
CONFIRM OR CHANGE GOAL
FORMULATING STRATEGY
IMPLEMENTATION

Compare and benchmark

We have used the value chain approach to understand and assess how well the company is managing its activities and resources to enhance value, and the linkages between these activities to sustain its competitive advantage. We will now look at comparisons and trends over a period of time to see how the organisation has chosen or been forced to change its behaviour and performance over the preceding years. This will give an insight into how the relationships with the various groups of stakeholders has evolved, which can be illuminating. The emergence of incompatible expectations can often be traced in these comparisons, together with the growing inevitability of the resulting problems.

We will make three broad comparisons:

a. Past performance

An historical comparison of internal resource movements and trading performance can be instructive. If we consider the deployment of resources in relation to the company's value chain and make comparisons over a number of years, we are likely to uncover significant changes. We will use financial ratios from a Dupont type analysis like:

- turnover/capital employed
- sales/employee.

We may also usefully compare non-financial measures like:

- quality and service levels
- geographical distribution and customer profiles
- employee age and skill levels.

This exercise can often highlight developments which were not previously readily apparent, and uncover concealed changes which will progressively have a major impact on the business.

b. Industry

Knowledge of the industry within which we are operating is essential, so we must compare our past performance with that of our major competitors and the industry as a whole, using the same or similar measurements and over a similar period of time.

A caveat in relation to benchmarking performance is that the domestic industry may be underperforming in relation to overseas competitors or the industry as a whole may be under pressure from alternative products or services. We will consequently need to watch for whole industry trends to identify larger scale over or under-performance.

The key is the *relative* peformance of the business.

c. Best practice

To supplement industry norms, it is prudent to look for 'best practice' and establish 'benchmarks' of performance. So, for example, we can use:

- competitor profiles
- benchmarking for key activities.

Assess balance of resources

We have considered the resources available to the business and the way they are deployed in producing and selling the company's products and services through its value chain, and have compared the trends over a number of years, both internally and in relation to its competitors. It is now appropriate to look at whether the company's resources are suitably balanced, or whether the business is suffering or likely to suffer from an inappropriate bias. The three aspects to this examination are:

- *Product balance* – using product portfolio analysis, we can see the extent to which the various activities and resources in GCG complement each other or are unrelated. It will also show up any over-reliance on a particular product.
- *People balance* – the degree of balance of people within the organisation, taking particular account of the skills and personalities of our key people.
- *Organisational/cultural balance* – the degree of flexibility within the organisation to meet known uncertainties. Does excessive rigidity, possibly through a command culture, create a vulnerability?

We should consider here the expectations of the various stakeholder groups and assess whether the balance reflects the intended weighting of their various interests. This is dealt with later in this chapter, but examples here might include excessive investment in a particular business division due to the powerful personality of an ambitious divisional head, or the continuing group level support of a loss-making subsidiary due to the influence of a powerful shareholder with a specific interest in it.

Identify key issues

The last part of the internal analysis is to pull out the key issues from all the detailed analysis and express them in two summary analyses:

a. Strengths and weaknesses

It is at this stage that we can make an assessment of the organisation's major strengths and weaknesses. These can be summarised from all the detailed work carried out in the various pieces of analysis comprising the internal analysis. We can then map them against the assessment we will make, following the external analysis, of opportunities and threats, to determine the strategic implications. This is the point at which all the detailed findings of this resource-based analysis come into play when they are used as a basis for deciding future action.

b. Competitive advantage

We will now compare our strengths and weaknesses with those of our competitors. We will ask especially:

- how closely owned are they, and how easily might they be taken by a rival?
- how long will they last before they become obsolete or superseded?
- how easy would it be for a rival to acquire the same skills or to develop similar ones?

This exercise will indicate how robust and hence how valuable are the various key strengths. Further, as Michael Porter has recently said,[5] competitive advantage is not about the individual strengths themselves – skills, resources or activities, for example, unique to GCG – which provide its competitive edge, but the unique way in which they fit together. The sum is far more difficult to emulate than the parts.

External analysis

The second part of the position (or strategic) analysis process is the external analysis. Here we aim to:

- understand our business environment:
  - current industry structure
  - the nature of the competitive forces
- evaluate GCG within its industry structure:
  - the business relative to competitors
  - the 'drivers of change'
- summarise the key issues arising from the whole analysis, which will enable us to assess our competitive position:
  - opportunities and threats
  - potential sources of competitive advantage
  - short-term improvement potential within the existing strategy.

Understanding the business environment and the positions and perspectives of the various stakeholding groups is a key element in ensuring continuing congruence of goals. As the business climate changes, the positions of the different groups will change, and what once seemed harmonious and co-ordinated may become progressively fragmented and unharmonious.

The external analysis is summarised in Figure 12.4

Assess the nature of the marketplace

We will first of all look at how stable and predictable is the martketplace in which we are competing. Understanding our environment will enable us to better judge the type of strategy to pursue and react to changing conditions. We will use two measures:

- **static v changing:** a marketplace is rarely completely static or its players would go stale. But its variability is relative, depending on such factors as the economic cycle and the product life cycle – mature markets are generally more stable than those in which a new product is being sold, with new entrants appearing all the time. If conditions are dynamic, we need to pay more attention, and look at the future state of the environment, not just the past. No assumptions may be made, especially when considering the relationships with the various parties who have a stake in the future of the business

PART B · HOW TO PRACTISE GOOD CORPORATE GOVERNANCE

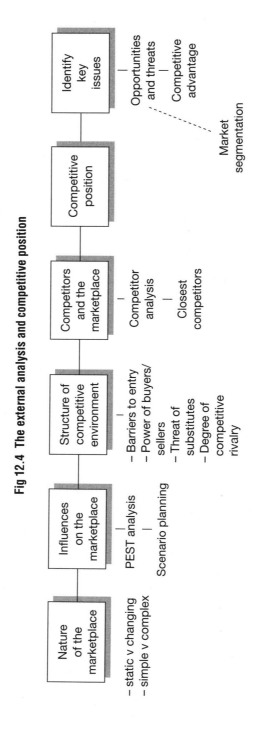

Fig 12.4 The external analysis and competitive position

- **simple v complex:** here we need to look at the number and variety of influences on our operating environment. We then need to find and have at our fingertips the necessary information to be able to handle these influences. Complex shareholder groupings need special attention, for instance, as do production sites in areas of great unemployment.

Examine influences on the marketplace

Now that we know what the main characteristics of the marketplace are, we need to examine what most influences this state – that is, the drivers of change – an example of which is changing demography, which may progressively eliminate our customer base, or at least change customers' requirements.

We will use two analytical techniques, PEST analysis, and scenario planning.

PEST analysis

PEST stands for Political, Economic, Socio-cultural and Technological, and entails an examination of the macro environment under these four broad headings. We will use this checklist to cover the major issues or influences.

Political/legal	Economic
monopolies legislation environmental protection laws taxation policy foreign trade regulations employment law government stability	business cycles GNP trends interest rates money supply inflation unemployment disposable incomes energy availability and cost
Socio-cultural	Technological
population demographics income distribution social mobility lifestyle changes attitudes to work and leisure consumerism levels of education	government spending on research government and industry focus of technological effort new discoveries/development technological transfer speed rates of obsolescence

Plainly, the position of the various stakeholder groups is highlighted by considering them under each of the above headings. The result may confirm existing perceptions or it may cause their attitudes and expectations to be seen in a new light.

Scenario planning

We can also use scenario planning to illustrate the longer-term effect of major trends. It entails:

- applying a small number of key assumptions to the industry
- showing the impact on the overall market and the main competitors.

As a guide to the robustness of a proposed strategy over the longer term we can usefully construct one or two outline scenarios against which the strategy can be tested. At the extreme, does the goal of the company still make sense, taking into account the likely evolution of the aims of its various stakeholders?

To look elsewhere to demonstrate, how does the development of the global insurance market sit with the hopes and expectations of the Names at Lloyd's, particularly when the management has to consider the future of the business as a whole? Will the stake of the Names be given an appropriate hearing against that of the new corporate stakeholders, and where do the employees fit into the equation? Ultimately, it will be determined by what the customers, ie the insured, want, and this stakeholding group will have the major influence in determining the actions which ensure the survival of Lloyd's as a business.

Analyse the structure of the competitive environment

We will now move from the broad view to the focused, and address the immediate competitive environment. In doing so, we will make use of Michael Porter's well-known five forces analysis. This is a structured way of looking at the competitive environment surrounding a business so as to understand the competitive forces at work. The process is illustrated by Figure 12.5.

We consider below the five forces which Porter described as the key influences on the business competitive environment. This is helpful in looking at the stakeholder groups represented by the company's trading partners, and putting in perspective the expectations of the other two major stakeholder groups, the owners and the employees.

> **THE STRATEGY PROCESS**
> INTERNAL ANALYSIS
> EXTERNAL ANALYSIS
> - Assess the nature of the marketplace
> - Examine influences on the marketplace
> - Analyse the structure of the competitive environment
>   a. Threat of entry
>   b. Power of buyers/sellers
>   c. Threat of substitutes
>   d. Competitive rivalry
>   e. Key questions arising
> - Know our competitors
>   a. Competitor analysis
>   b. Strategic group analysis
> - Identify key issues
> STAKEHOLDER ANALYSIS
> CONFIRM OR CHANGE GOAL
> FORMULATING STRATEGY

a. Threat of entry

The threat of entry by newcomers is governed by the barriers to entry. We can group these barriers into:

- economies of scale
- capital requirements of entry
- access to distribution channels
- cost advantages independent of size, eg experience curve
- expected retaliation
- legislation or government action: protecting established operators
- differentiation and the ability of a newcomer to achieve this.

b. Power of buyers/sellers

The suppliers and customers can be considered together since all organisations are both buyers and sellers, and both groups have similar effects in exercising constraints on strategic freedom and margins. It is important to be aware of their power when considering them as stakeholders, and what expectations they may have.

Fig 12.5 Michael Porter's five forces analysis

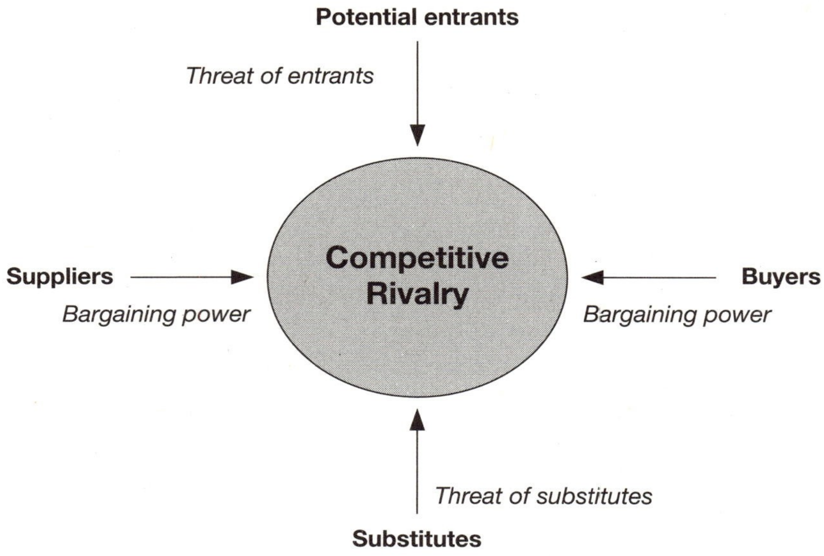

```
                    Potential entrants
                           │
                    Threat of entrants
                           ▼
                    ┌─────────────┐
   Suppliers ─────▶ │ Competitive │ ◀───── Buyers
  Bargaining power │   Rivalry   │      Bargaining power
                    └─────────────┘
                           ▲
                    Threat of substitutes
                           │
                      Substitutes
```

Supplier power is indicated by the following:

- there is a concentration of suppliers
- there are high switching costs from one to another
- there is a powerful supplier brand
- the supplier can integrate forward to threaten the customer
- the customer is of little importance to the supplier.

Buyer power is indicated by the following:

- there is a concentration of buyers, and especially if the buyer volumes are high
- alternative sources of supply exist
- material cost is a high percentage of total product cost, driving the buyer to shop around to find the best price
- the buyer can threaten backward integration.

c. Threat of substitutes

We will now look at how likely and possible it would be for competitors to replace our products in the marketplace. The key questions we need to ask are:

- does substitution pose a real threat of obsolescence to the company's products?
- how easily and cheaply can buyers switch from the existing products to the new ones?
- how can switching costs be increased to deter substitution?

d. Competitive rivalry

The degree of rivalry and intensity of competition in the marketplace has a major influence on the trading performance of the players in that market. To find out how sharp the competition is, we can consider:

- the extent to which competitors are in balance; equally matched firms will compete more fiercely
- how slowly the market is growing; a fast growing market will provide pickings for all, whereas a maturing market will put pressure on all
- high fixed costs which may lead to price wars as firms are driven to seek volume to recoup these high fixed costs
- the possibility of introduction of much increased capacity which will clearly put pressure on all existing players, potentially ruining the margins presently earned
- lack of differentiation between competitors, producing the same effect as a market full of evenly balanced players
- the acquisition of weaker players by stronger ones, raising the average effectiveness of the competition
- high exit barriers leading players to remain in the industry when normal economics would incline them to abandon their business.

e. Key questions arising

Following an examination of the business environment and the market forces at work within it, we need to highlight those factors which most affect GCG's operational freedom. The most important questions we need to ask are:

- what are the key forces at work?
- are there any underlying forces driving change?
- what are the likely changes?
- how do these affect particular competitors and the competitive position

Know our competitors

Having considered the competitive environment at an industry level, we now need to understand the company's position relative to competitors, and the implications for its strategy. We will therefore:

- perform a detailed analysis of our main competitors
- attempt to group the competitors and identify to which group GCG appears closest and where that group is in the marketplace.

a. Competitor analysis

This entails assessing our main competitors in the same way as we have GCG, that is producing a detailed study for each showing the impact of environmental influences and the competitive forces at work in the marketplace. Thus for each competitor we must try to determine and document:

- the objectives of that organisation
- its resource strengths
- its performance record
- its current strategy
- its presumed underlying core beliefs or guiding principles.

The more that is known about the main competitors, the easier it is to predict their future actions, and to get a proper perspective on the company's own views of the market.

b. Strategic group analysis

The next step is to find out which are our closest competitors – and hence our greatest threat – by forming finely defined groupings, and placing ourselves in one of these. Each group will represent organisations with similar strategic characteristics, following similar strategies or competing on similar bases. We will therefore:

- select two to three sets of characteristics, drawn from
    - extent of product diversity
    - extent of geographic coverage
    - number of market segments served
    - distribution channels used
    - extent of branding
    - marketing effort
    - service quality
    - technological leadership
    - cost position
    - pricing policy
    - level of gearing
    - ownership structure
    - size

- assess the ease of mobility between one group and another
- assess likely market changes or strategic opportunities.

When we compare these with our own situation we can place GCG into one of the groups we have formed. The purpose of this is to ensure that the company is competing against its true rivals and not missing the real enemy, and to learn from the behaviour of its real competitors.

Identify key issues

In order to understand fully our external operating environment, we need to bring out the most strategically important messages that we have received from carrying out the external analysis. We can then, as we discussed earlier, put GCG's strategic capability (concluded in a similar way from the internal analysis) in the context of the marketplace. This is covered in the next section when we summarise everything as a basis for strategy formulation. Here, then, we will identify the opportunities and threats that exist in the marketplace, and the consequent competitive advantage we may have.

a. Opportunities and threats

We are looking here at the general attractiveness of the market in which we are operating, in terms of the major political, economic, social and technological influences analysed earlier. There may also be opportunities to exploit weakness in the competition, for example, an ailing competitor in our strategic group. We will also look at market segmentation and whether there are new ways to segment the market to our advantage, as this is a key to *making* new opportunities.

Market segmentation
Market segmentation is key to market dominance. It is relative market share that counts, and if the company is a relatively weak performer in relation to several much stronger rivals, we may have to find new ways of looking at the market to create a strong, defensible and profitable position. To do this we will:

- define the market in terms of appropriate factors such as:
  - characteristics of people
  - purchase/use situation
  - user needs and preferences for product characteristics
- assess the attractiveness of different market segments

- assess the existing and potential relative market share in each segment
- assess the benefits of focusing in one or more segments.

The more deeply we understand the market, the better we can create and sustain a dominant position, and the less we are likely to develop weakness. The key here is knowing our customers, and if anything gets to the heart of what the business is for, and what the goal is all about, this is it.

b. Competitive advantage

We will now compare our position in the marketplace with that of the competition – here we are looking purely from outside the company; we will carry out a complete analysis after we have looked at and understood our stakeholders. So here we are attempting to get an independent view of our competitive position. To determine this, the sorts of question we will need to ask are:

- how well does our current direction match the trends and consumer behaviour in the market …
- … and that of our main competitors?
- are there any areas where we dominate or have a major impact, say, in an important geographical area?
- how level is the playing field? Is the competition stiff with no clear leader?

This relates back to the first stage of this analysis when we examined the nature of the marketplace, but is more focused on the individual players; it basically summarises our position relative to our competitors, with the objective of identifying weaknesses and sources of competitive advantage.

Stakeholder analysis

We discussed earlier the need for congruence of goals of the various stakeholder groups. The practical way to do this is through a stakeholder analysis. This is how we ensure that the strategy we choose will be supported by those whom we expect to carry it out and others affected by it. Or rather, it ought to be approached the other way round: that is, we listen to our stakeholders *before* deciding on where to go from here. Our objectives here are to:

- find out stakeholder perceptions; how does GCG perform/deliver on:
  – ethics
  – organisation
  – reporting
- understand the goals of the stakeholders
- map these findings for reference in the strategy selection process.

As outlined in Chapter 9, these findings will have to be duly weighted to reflect the different levels of interest and power of the various stakeholders, while maintaining an appropriate balance to ensure that power is not too concentrated in one individual or group.

The stakeholder analysis process is summarised in Figure 12.6.

Fig 12.6 The stakeholder analysis

NB – *The reader will note that we have approached the next section slightly differently from the sections on internal and external analysis, since the research involves much more field work than the mainly desk-based research of the other two analyses. Thus we set out the methodology in some detail and give a layout for the final report at the end. It must be said, however, that this report should really be a summary of the key points to gain maximum effect, and that the rest of the data should be fed into the model explained in Appendix A. For obvious reasons, reference to the model is made frequently during the methodology; so although we provide explanations of how the various parts fit into the model, we recommend that the reader reads Appendix A before – or while – this section is read.*

Stakeholder survey

The survey will combine quantitative and qualitative research to obtain from the five main stakeholder groups (customers, shareholders, employees, suppliers and the community) both depth and breadth of knowledge. It should, therefore, include larger scale questionnaire-based research and discussion-based interviews and focus groups on how stakeholders feel the company is delivering on the four elements (representing the other Golden Rules) – ethics, goal, organisation and reporting.

a. Ethics

Corporate social responsibility – does the company behave responsibly towards all its stakeholders? Particularly:

- environmental/human rights issues
- support for local community/society in general
- honesty/transparency
- fair treatment of staff
- responsibility regarding pensions/consideration of pensioners.

b. Goal

Congruence of goals – does the company's goal reflect the expectations of all the stakeholders? Particularly:

- what do stakeholders want from GCG?
- what would they expect from a leading player in GCG's industry sector?
- what will be needed for the future?

c. Organisation

Structure – does it protect the interests of its various stakeholders and have open channels of communication with them? Particularly:

- management style and culture (dealt with internally in Chapter 13)
- operational effectiveness and efficiency
- accountability

d. Reporting

Information – is there information being passed through these channels which is sufficient and accurate enough to satisfy all the stakeholders? Particularly:

- transparency
- do they want to know more about the company's activities?
  - trading results
  - community projects/activities
  - donations (political/charitable)
  - future plans.

When conducting the stakeholder analysis, there will be difficulties in transposing these four elements (representing four of the Golden Rules) into concepts understandable by the stakeholders, especially those with a lower level of interest or involvement in the running of the business, so proxies will need to be assumed to obtain the information required using more familiar content and language. These will need to be based on physical evidence: *ethics*, for example, could be represented by the placement of recycling points on company premises to encourage recycling, staff who are friendly and responsive (giving an impression that the company looks after its staff), and support for charities, say, by encouraging fund raising schemes. For *organisation*, we can find out stakeholders' perceptions of operational efficiency and effectiveness, such as prompt delivery of goods or good working conditions. We can also probe for opinions on communication, since this is fundamental to corporate governance, for example:

- how frequent, and one or *two way* communication
- availability of ways of expressing views as stakeholders, for instance:
  - customer service
  - staff consultation meetings
- how *important* are these to stakeholders?

The questionnaire

Having looked at the issues that need to be covered in the analysis, let us briefly look at the sort of measurement we will need to use to get stakeholder responses.

a. ethics

How does GCG rate on:

- environmental/human rights issues?
- support for local community/society in general?
- honesty/transparency?

- fair treatment of staff?
- responsibility regarding pensions/consideration of pensioners?

This is not a detailed sociological survey, but a means of obtaining an overall view of the way the company's general behaviour is perceived, though the use of focus groups can prove interesting in finding out the participants' opinions on what ethics are and how they perceive us.

b. Goal

This will clearly vary from group to group, and the purpose of gathering this information is to ensure that all parties' interests are understood, and taken into account to the appropriate degree. Comparing this with our own business goals will show us the extent to which we are fulfilling their expectations and data from all the groups will tell us how much congruence there is between these different interests. We may ask:

- what are the stakeholders' expectations?
- are they aware of GCG's 'agreed' goals?
- do they approve of them?
- how close are they to their own goals?

c. Organisation

Here we aim to pick up both outside perceptions amongst owners and in the marketplace, and well-informed inside experience. On the structural side, we can ask:

- what are the stakeholders' views on the effectiveness of the organisation in achieving a proper balance of the interests of all the stakeholders?

On the communications side we can ask:

- what channels do stakeholders know about to communicate with GCG?
- do they use these channels?
- how easy/convenient/user-friendly are they?

d. Reporting

To check the effectiveness of the accountability of the management and the transparency of its reporting, we will ask:

THE WHOLE PICTURE

- how much do stakeholders know about GCG?
- is it enough, or would they like to know more?
- can/do they get information *when* they want it?

The stakeholder model which we have been referring to will need some explanation here. As indicated in the introduction to Chapter 9, this model allows the mapping of the company's performance against stakeholder expectations for these four elements. The way this is done is to use these questions to form carefully worded statements, which are scored out of 10 – for perceptions (ethics, organisation, reporting) the score represents agreement (or not) with the statement, and for expectations it rates how important the particular issue is to the respondent. This is fully explained in Appendix A.

Frequencies

Once the survey has been completed, all the scores will need to be collated. Figures must be kept for the model within the grouping used in the research, ie geographical/demographical, division, and so on. So at this stage all we have is truly *raw* data, which we can use for diagnostic purposes (see Appendix A). Before averaging *between* groups is done, to arrive at overall, and more meaningful (and digestible) figures, these groups will have to go through the weighting process, with the help of information from the internal and external analyses, such as sales per area, division, account, etc.

> **THE STRATEGY PROCESS**
> INTERNAL ANALYSIS
> EXTERNAL ANALYSIS
> STAKEHOLDER ANALYSIS
> - Stakeholder survey
>   a. Ethics
>   b. Goal
>   c. Organisation
>   d. Reporting
> - *The questionnaire*
>   a. Ethics
>   b. Goal
>   c. Organisation
>   d. Reporting
> - Frequencies
> - Weighting
>   a. Background
>   b. The power/interest matrix
> - Mapping
> - Implications/applications for the strategy process
> CONFIRM OR CHANGE GOAL
> FORMULATING STRATEGY
> IMPLEMENTATION

Weighting

Background

The weighting process is based on the premise that individuals will exercise influence through belonging to one or more groups which share their expectations. Through these groups they will attempt to influence the organisation's strategy. External stakeholders may seek to influence strat-

185

egy through links with internal stakeholders. Understanding stakeholders and how they are likely to influence the company is a key part of the assessment of strategic options. It is also at the heart of good corporate governance.

The first thing we need to bear in mind is that there will always be conflicts of expectations between the various interested parties. Indeed, it is normal for conflicts to exist regarding the importance and/or the desirability of many aspects of the company's strategy. These differences of opinion can arise in relation to the introduction of measures to improve trading performance. For instance:

- cost efficiency measures introduced through capital investment can cost jobs
- in order to grow, short-term profitability and cash flow may have to be sacrificed.

> The key to the whole stakeholder approach is that we keep in mind at all times
> - a good balance of power
> - the overall survival of the company, and
> - the common goal.

Compromises have to be made, and it is important to understand the expectations of different stakeholder groups and to weigh these in terms of the power they exercise. Mapping out the various expectations helps us understand the core beliefs, and this, together with an understanding of the power structure, is necessary to assess future strategies in relation to their cultural fit and how easy or difficult change will be.

The power/influence matrix

At this point we need to identify all our stakeholders, whether by individual, with the more influential ones, or by grouping, with the lower levels. We can then place each of these individuals or groups into categories, depending on their willingness to get involved in decision-making and their ability to influence this process, thus indicating the type of relationship we need to nurture with each group. To do this, we will need to make judgements on:

- how likely each group is to press its views
- whether they have the capacity to do so
- the likely impact of their expectations on future strategy.

A table can be used to group stakeholders in this way, and this is shown in Figure 12.7 (we will still keep the five main groups separate). It is based on:

- **Propensity to act**
  - will act
  - may act
  - unlikely to act

- **Ability to influence**
  - have significant power
  - do not currently have significant power, but could get it
  - do not currently have significant power, and unlikely ever to be able to get much.

Fig 12.7 The power/influence matrix

Stakeholder group:..

		Hi	Propensity to act	Lo
		will act	may act	unlikely to act
Hi	has power	A1	A2	A3
Ability to influence	could get power	B1	B2	B3
Lo	can't get power	C1	C2	C3

This is clearly judgemental, but represents an informed approach to deciding how much weight to attach to the wishes of each group. If the stakeholder group was customers, for instance, propensity to act could equate to loyalty and ability to influence could equate to buying power.

The next stage is to decide on the degrees of weighting, ie the amount of weight or value given to each group. Suggested values and consequent calculations are demonstrated in Appendix A, but here we will set out some principles, based on some useful ideas by Johnson and Scholes,[6] with which we can start to assess the power structure of our stakeholders:

> **Within** an organisation, the following are the usual **sources** of power:
>
> - seniority within an hierarchy
> - personal influence
> - personal freedom of decision-making
> - control over key resources within the business
> - key specialist knowledge or skills
> - significant influence over the business environment.
>
> Useful **indicators** of power for internal stakeholders are:
>
> - status of the individual or group
> - size of their budget
> - representation in powerful positions on boards or committees
> - symbols of power, such as type of company car, size of office.
>
> Regarding **external stakeholders** the usual **sources** of power include:
>
> - shareholding
> - buyer or seller control over key resources or products
> - involvement through holding a key place in the value chain, like control over distribution
> - key knowledge and skills in relation to the value chain
> - influence through powerful links with key managers.
>
> Useful **indicators** of power for external stakeholders are:
>
> - large shareholding
> - how their status is perceived by the company's own staff, and how they behave towards them
> - how difficult it is to switch suppliers or replace a lost customer
> - how much at arm's length the other party is treated in any negotiating arrangements.

Overall, the exercise to weight stakeholder expectations serves as a useful way of assessing where the political efforts should be channelled during the development of new strategies.

Returning to Figure 12.7, here are some examples of the different stakeholder groups:

A1 These are clearly the key stakeholders, with power and a willingness to act, so their expectations are paramount. They are likely to include key directors and major institutional shareholders, but also key customer groups.

A2 This category might include significant shareholders who have thus far shown little interest in the company's actions, but might be moved to call an EGM, and migrate to A1 if the company's behaviour was seen to damage their interests.

B1 This category could include trade unions in a sensitive area of employment which have committed themselves to resist job-destroying reorganisations, and whose involvement on behalf of their members in strategic discussions regarding such action is clearly advisable.

B2 This category could include the management and key staff of a subsidiary company which, in certain circumstances, could be motivated to propose a buy-out of the business with support from a trade buyer.

C1 This category could include environmental groups which, generally speaking, have little real power, but live by the publicity arising from their willingness to act. The key danger here is that if their cause gains big public support in the face of unwise behaviour by the company, they may, against the odds, acquire real power.

C3 This category could include company pensioners, traditionally quiescent (though this may be changing) and with very limited power. There is a clear moral case for treating this group properly, though they are likely to have little impact on the company's plans.

Hence, this stakeholder weighting can show:

- to what extent the ethics, goals and strategy match the wishes of the most important stakeholder groups
- who are the groups most likely to give trouble or derail the strategy, and who the supporters are likely to be
- how much work is likely to be needed to stop stakeholders from becoming an active hindrance to implementing the strategy
- to what extent action is likely to be required to protect the interests of the weaker stakeholders.

Mapping

With all the scores weighted and in place in the model structure we are effectively constructing, we can now plot this data in charts which clearly show how well or poorly GCG is performing on a number of different issues. These charts can be compared with each other, across the various stakeholder groups, and used for a variety of purposes, including benchmarking delivery against expectations, a particularly useful measurement which shows up very clearly on such a chart (see Appendix A). On the highest level, we can plot weighted average scores for all five main stakeholder groups on all four elements of the research, to see if there is one particular group which had radically different opinions from the rest. This, and similar exercises on lower levels, can be used to adjust weighting and later on, strategic choice, to reflect the three fundamental principles to this approach: balance, survival and the common goal. This is also discussed briefly in Appendix A.

Implications/applications for the strategy process

In terms of the input which the stakeholder analysis makes to the goals and strategy, traditionally, the business culture has a major influence on the expectations of stakeholders. This in turn influences the goals and strategies of the organisation. So the goals and strategies tend to be formulated by the dominant stakeholder – usually management! In the best governed situations a proper balance must exist, and the stakeholder analysis represents a methodology to ensure that this is appropriately built into the strategic management process and its implementation. Hence:

- at the highest level, the corporate goal and any related mission statement must express the key values of the business and the expectations of the various stakeholder groups
- at the level of corporate targets there is a need for statements of objectives to be met on behalf of a variety of stakeholders, including customers, suppliers, employees and local communities affected by the company's operations.

As we have said, when we carry out this analysis we are working towards setting up a model. Therefore once the initial work has been done, it will simply be a matter of adjusting and adding to the model. This is why the process laid out in Figure 12.6 is shown as a circle, representing the function of continuous monitoring. However, for the purposes of a report conveying, as we discussed earlier, the salient points (rather than *all* the data), we will therefore need to, as it were, 'break off' from the circle to channel these findings back into the continuing strategy process. In the process, we can bring in some background information which will serve as reference to where we want to go from here. By this we are referring to what we shall call *heritage*, that is, the historical and cultural background against which the current operational environment is set. This need not be an overly detailed part of the report, particularly since the senior members of the company responsible for formulating strategy, should already be aware of their own heritage. That said, it should also serve to force the whole board – indeed the whole company – to re-assess the relevance and benefits (or the opposite) of the existing or traditional paradigm.

Confirm or change goal

The last three stages have comprised the position analysis which has enabled us to understand where we are now, 'Point A'. Here we can look again at the broad goal decided on in the goal discussion meeting (see Chapter 11) to see if:

- we have the necessary strategic capability to achieve it
- it is feasible given the nature of the marketplace
- it reflects congruence of the expectations of all our stakeholders.

While this will already be apparent to a certain extent through doing the analyses above, it is helpful to summarise the key influences before making a decision to proceed with the goal or not. The first step is therefore the SWOT analysis.

At this point, the findings from the internal and external analyses can be brought together, as indicated earlier, putting GCG's strengths and weaknesses against the opportunities and threats that exist in the marketplace. By breaking each action up into smaller sections, it becomes clearer what needs to be done and how to do it. So first we can simply measure GCG against certain indicators without distinguishing between the positive and the negative.

Market attractiveness and business strength

To come to any kind of conclusion about the various aspects of the market, we must first consider the different market segments by reference both to their intrinsic attractiveness and to GCG's strengths in relation to those markets. Thus, using a strengths/attractiveness matrix, or a directional policy matrix, as it is sometimes called, indicators can be based on:

Business strength	Market attractiveness
market share	market size
sales force	market growth rate
marketing	cyclicality
customer service	competitive structure
R & D	barriers to entry
manufacturing	industry profitability
distribution	technology
financial resources	inflation
image	regulation
breadth of product line	workforce availability
quality/reliability	social issues
managerial competence	environmental issues
political issues	
legal issues	

We can then assess the position of GCG in relation to our competitors in the various segments by drawing on this directional policy matrix.

SWOT and stakeholder views

In carrying out the analysis above, we will see which factors are positive and which are negative and place them accordingly into the SWOT matrix; at this stage we can add any other information, such as specific product strengths or gaps in the market. We then turn to the stakeholder analysis to display (via a summary of the findings) how their expectations will affect the selection of a strategy, for example, whether approval will be forthcoming in exploiting certain opportunities, say, in foreign investment.

An example of this – let us assume for GCG – is shown in Figure 12.8.

THE WHOLE PICTURE

Fig 12.8 SWOT and stakeholder views

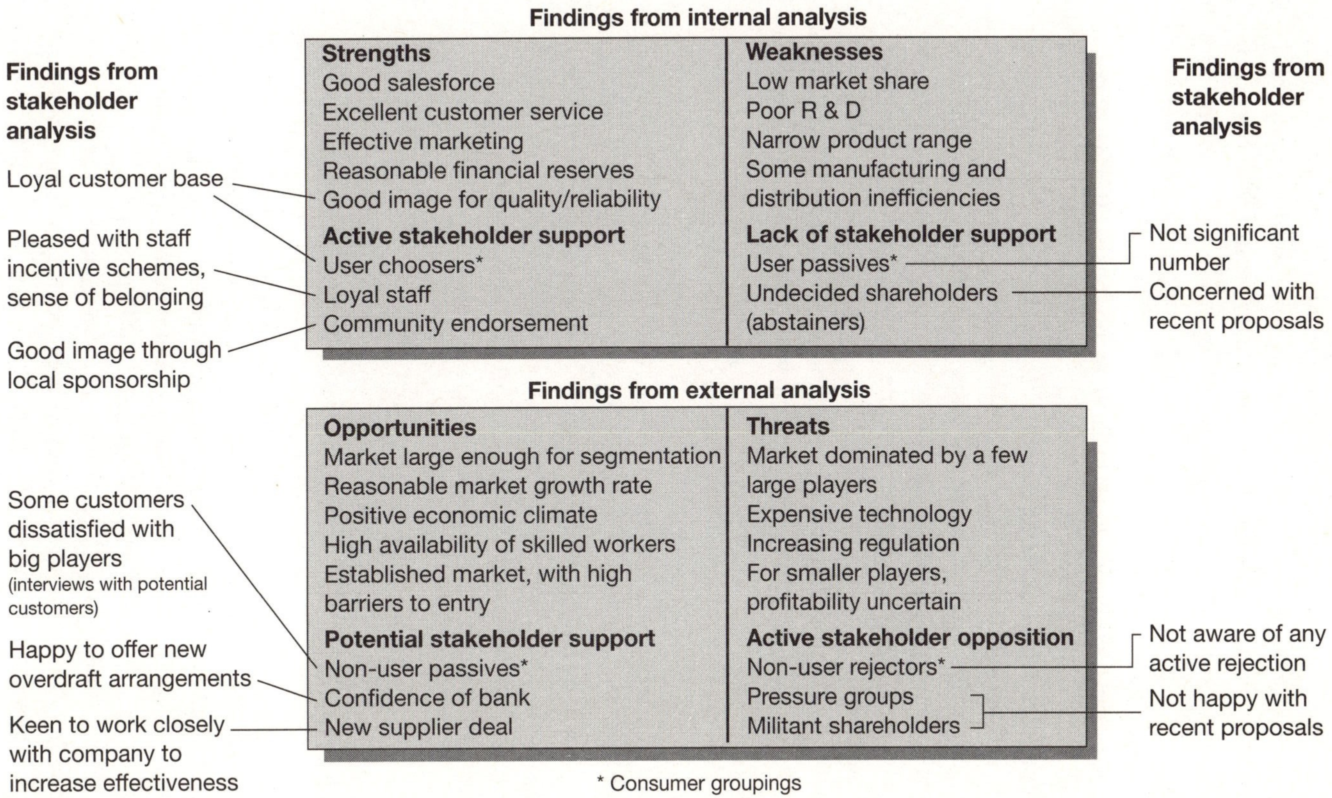

Findings from internal analysis

Strengths
- Good salesforce
- Excellent customer service
- Effective marketing
- Reasonable financial reserves
- Good image for quality/reliability

Active stakeholder support
- User choosers*
- Loyal staff
- Community endorsement

Weaknesses
- Low market share
- Poor R & D
- Narrow product range
- Some manufacturing and distribution inefficiencies

Lack of stakeholder support
- User passives*
- Undecided shareholders (abstainers)

Findings from external analysis

Opportunities
- Market large enough for segmentation
- Reasonable market growth rate
- Positive economic climate
- High availability of skilled workers
- Established market, with high barriers to entry

Potential stakeholder support
- Non-user passives*
- Confidence of bank
- New supplier deal

Threats
- Market dominated by a few large players
- Expensive technology
- Increasing regulation
- For smaller players, profitability uncertain

Active stakeholder opposition
- Non-user rejectors*
- Pressure groups
- Militant shareholders

Findings from stakeholder analysis (left)

- Loyal customer base
- Pleased with staff incentive schemes, sense of belonging
- Good image through local sponsorship
- Some customers dissatisfied with big players (interviews with potential customers)
- Happy to offer new overdraft arrangements
- Keen to work closely with company to increase effectiveness

Findings from stakeholder analysis (right)

- Not significant number
- Concerned with recent proposals
- Not aware of any active rejection
- Not happy with recent proposals

* Consumer groupings

In studying the information in the summary, our choice of the type of goal and strategy is clear. It shows a company with a small, but loyal customer base, clearly loyal because of a reputation for quality and reliability, and excellent customer service. This is within the context of a large, growing market dominated by a few big companies, putting pressure on smaller companies through effective cost leadership obtained using expensive technologies.

GCG evidently needs to look at niche marketing. By defining better our core skills, or products, and the particular type of customer we can best match these skills to, we can effectively dominate this segment. Further, the signs are that we can attract customers from our competitors by offering this distinct, more personal service which the big players lack. Our position is further strengthened by a sound balance sheet, backed by confident bankers; co-operative new supply arrangements which will help our drive to improve the whole of the value chain; local sponsorship paying off by adding to our good image; but most importantly, strategically speaking, we have a workforce which believes in us, and this will be key, in terms of motivation, in planning a new initiative.

All these factors are clearly positive, but only in the context of a new approach to the business. We will need to tread very carefully, particularly with the potential threat of shareholder action hanging over us, but without the courage to change the way we work and break with tradition, somewhat, we will be forced out of the market completely by our powerful rivals. The overall survival of the company is at stake here, and we need to make all parties – particularly our shareholders – see that. We are then ensuring the balance of all the stakeholder interests.

Conclusions

We now have at our fingertips all the information necessary to decide whether the desirable overall goal is, in principle, both suitable and feasible. Since the development of a detailed strategic plan is a significant piece of work, there is little point in embarking on this if there is uncertainty as to whether the overall goal is still appropriate.

For instance, from the stakeholder analysis, it may have become apparent that the main shareholders have become unhappy with the company's overall direction. This might arise from a range of possible issues such as:

- an ethical matter, like being in the armaments business or tobacco, or trading in countries with unacceptable regimes
- a security of capital matter, such as having a significant exposure to a country with an unacceptable level of risk of structural instability.

In these circumstances it would be wrong to devise a strategy for maximising the market share and profitability in these fields, however commercially attractive this might otherwise appear.

A second reason for reconsideration would be if the perception of Point A – where the company is now – was so widely adrift of the reality disclosed by the three reports produced in the position analysis that there was clearly no realistic possibility of achieving the desired goal. This might seem far-fetched, but it is not nearly as unlikely as might be thought. The ability of management and owners to deceive themselves about the state of the market in which they are operating and their own capabilities and reputation continue to surprise.

We will assume that the broad goal is appropriate, so the next step is to examine a range of plans to achieve this goal.

Formulating strategy

This has three steps (see Figure 12.1) namely:

- generate several optional strategies to achieve the goal
- evaluate and assess the suitability of the various options
- choose the most appropriate strategy.

Generating strategic options

We will generate more than one option so that the route we prefer is tested as thoroughly as possible by comparison with other possibilities. There are three parts to the process of developing strategic options:

- the basis of the strategy, and here we consider generic strategies
- the direction by which the generic strategy can be pursued
- the alternative methods by which the strategy might be accomplished.

> **THE STRATEGY PROCESS**
> INTERNAL ANALYSIS
> EXTERNAL ANALYSIS
> STAKEHOLDER ANALYSIS
> CONFIRM OR CHANGE GOAL
> - Market attractiveness and business strength
> - SWOT and stakeholder views
> - Conclusions
>
> FORMULATING STRATEGY
> - Generating strategic options
>   a. Generic strategies
>   b. Directions for strategy and methods for development
> - Evaluating strategic options and selecting strategy
>
> IMPLEMENTATION

a. Generic strategies

Michael Porter in his book, *Competitive Strategy*, argued that there are only three basic strategies by which a business can achieve sustainable competitive advantage (see Figure 12.9).

Fig 12.9 Porter's generic strategies

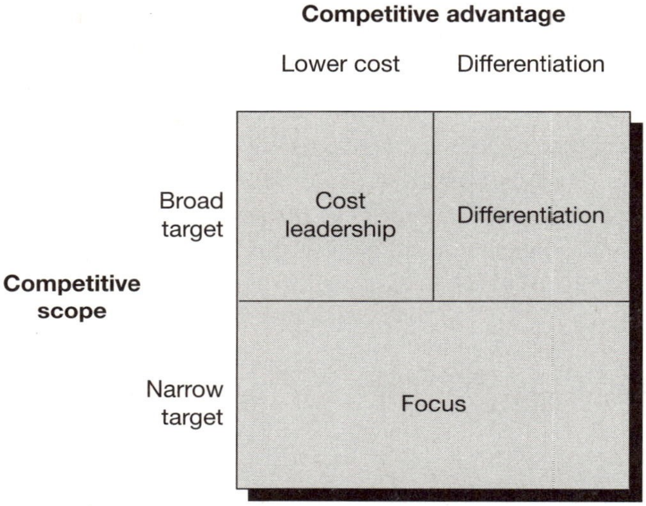

	Competitive advantage	
	Lower cost	Differentiation
Broad target	Cost leadership	Differentiation
Narrow target	Focus	Focus

(Competitive scope on vertical axis)

These three strategies, as put forward by Porter, are:

- **Cost leadership** – where a business aims to be the lowest cost producer in its industry. To achieve this, it must beat all its competitors in finding and making use of all possible means of minimising costs to achieve a competitive advantage, and if it can succeed in this, and maintain this success over an extended period, while maintaining selling prices at or near the industry average, it will achieve an above average performance. Generally speaking, this strategy is taken to be that of the market leader, and it is expected that the company with the highest relative market share will earn the best profits. It was interesting to observe that quite shortly after Tesco's market share finally surpassed that of its old rival Sainsbury after a nearly 20 year chase under the leadership of Lord MacLaurin, its profitability also overtook Sainsbury's for the first time, and has remained higher.

- **Differentiation** – where a business aims to differentiate itself from the competition by emphasising some aspect that is particularly desired by the customers, in such a way as to establish itself as uniquely well qualified in the customers' minds to supply that product or service. If it can maintain that differentiation, it should be able to charge a higher price, and as long as the extra margin on price exceeds its extra marketing costs in establishing its uniqueness, it will outperform the average. It is generally understood that a business which cannot achieve market leadership has to spend substantially on marketing to achieve differentiation to sustain its position. Avis, for many years, sustained its number two position to Hertz in car rentals by advertising that 'we try harder'.
- **Focus** – or niche strategy, where a business targets a particular market segment or segments and focuses on these to the exclusion of all others, thereby becoming the premier supplier within these niches, and hence able to charge a premium price and achieve above average returns. The difficulty with niches is that they may close suddenly and unexpectedly and turn into graves. An exploiter of niches must be prepared to be quick on his feet.

b. Directions for strategy and methods of development

Having made a choice of generic strategy (or confirmed which one we are currently following), we will now look at the different directions in which we can develop our strategy. This is summed up by Figure 12.10, based on the Ansoff matrix.

This book is not primarily about strategy but is concerned that an effective strategic management process is in place to ensure a good system of corporate governance, so we shall not go into detail here on the elements in Figure 12.10, which are a familiar part of management books.

Similarly, we shall limit ourselves to pointing out that for each different direction in which a strategy may be developed there are three options for that development:

- in-house development, which may offer greater development of expertise and control, but which may prove more expensive
- acquisition of the desired business or products, which may be cheaper in the short term but may hold more risk
- joint ventures or alliances, which have become more popular in recent years, particularly in relation to cross border link-ups. The track record of these has, however, been patchy.

Fig 12.10 The direction matrix

	Domestic market	Non-domestic market
Non-core business expansion	**DIVERSIFICATION** eg Sainsbury DIY Homebase	
Format extension in core business	**PRODUCT DEVELOPMENT** eg TESCO Metro	**MARKET DEVELOPMENT** eg TESCO acquisition of Catteau in France
Current product offer	**PENETRATION** eg TESCO acquisition of William Low	

Level of risk: Low → High (horizontal)
Level of risk: Low → High (vertical)

In each of these three areas, the views of the stakeholders are very important, and our choice must always reflect the best interests of all concerned.

Evaluating strategic options and selecting strategy

The process of evaluating and selecting the strategy is all about determining which plan is most likely to get GCG from Point A (where we are now) to Point B (where we want to be). Figure 12.11 summarises this process.

In evaluating and selecting a strategy we must:

- decide the suitability of the various available strategic options, by asking questions such as:
  - how robust are they when considered against the strategic view of the marketplace derived from the external analysis?
  - how feasible are they when considered against the picture of the company and its capability shown by the internal analysis?
  - how well do they match the expectations of the various interested parties displayed by the stakeholder analysis?

This will be made easier by the exercise described earlier of gathering and summarising key information, which can be kept readily available for quick and easy consultation

Fig 12.11 Strategy evaluation and selection

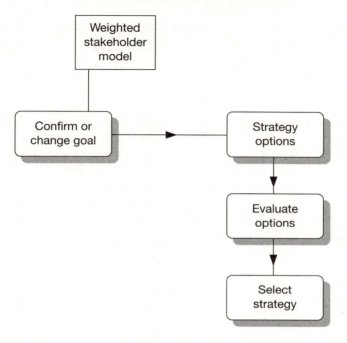

- determine the appropriate detailed criteria by which to assess and rank these options, and apply them. Hence against each of the above, key measures will be selected, both financial, such as:
  - market share
  - return on sales
  - growth in shareholders' funds

  and non-financial, such as:
  - customer satisfaction
  - employee development
  - industry reputation.

This process is designed to ensure that the evaluation and selection process builds in the stakeholder values and expectations described above, so that the implemented strategy protects their interests. A balance needs to be struck between backing a hunch and 'paralysis by analysis'.

Finally, it should be noted that, while the actual strategy selected will be the one which best fits the criteria, in the course of implementation the original objectives may be modified to some extent. This is a not-infrequent development – what Henry Mintzberg describes as 'emergent strategy'- and often the way in which theory is turned into practice.

The following case study seems to encapsulate a number of important lessons in strategy and stakeholder participation. Clearly the more confidential aspects cannot be given, but the broad picture tells its own story.

Case study

DEARDEN FARROW

In the late 1980s, one of the authors was asked by Ray Whittaker, the senior partner of Dearden Farrow, a leading firm of UK Chartered Accountants, to conduct a strategy study for them. He was about to retire and was concerned to leave the firm set on the right road.

The firm's expressed goal was to be an international full service practice in direct competition with what in those days were the Big Eight. Dearden Farrow ranked well up in the second tier at number fourteen, or thereabouts. This meant providing the full range of services, which at that time consisted of:

- auditing
- taxation advice
- financial and accountancy services and business advice
- company secretarial

There was growing concern about the pressure on profits, and the low average remuneration per partner, which was a fraction of that of the Big Eight. It was felt, particularly by some of the more able and ambitious younger partners, that some of the older partners were not pulling their weight and the fees earned per partner reflected this.

The firm's view of the market was that, as a second tier firm, they could look naturally to second tier companies, who would be comfortable with them, and would be happy with the rather lower fees Dearden Farrow charged them. They had a network of UK offices, and internationally, they looked to relationships with similar firms in other parts of the world to provide an international capability to those of their clients who needed it.

There were no special, world quality services offered, but partners relied on their personal relationships with clients which they felt provided a better service than could be offered by the partners of the Big Eight.

Similarly, they looked to recruit articled clerks whom the Big Eight had considered but had turned down. They were thus able to pay them a little less.

The strategic analysis showed that:

- internally, the efficiency of the firm was indeed significantly inferior to that of the larger competitors, and they were always going to struggle against the ability of the larger firms to invest in the best people and to develop new products and services to keep up with the times. The efficiency problem was addressed

by tightening the internal client accounting systems and retiring several partners and the profitability rose to more acceptable levels. Sadly, the overworked managing partner took this as a direct reflection on his own performance and resigned from this role
- the external analysis, however, indicated a severe problem. Application of the Porter-type analysis showed clearly that the firm had no realistic prospect of achieving its goal. There was no clear market leader, but the top four firms had nearly five times the UK revenue of Dearden Farrow, and internationally were over 40 times larger, and were integrated partnerships in a way that Dearden Farrow was not. Their market strength and cash flow power were overwhelming in relation to the small competitors. Clearly, the only realistic independent strategy was to become a niche player in some area of specialism and close the UK branch network, focusing all resources on a limited range of services
- the key stakeholders were customers, partners and staff. The customers showed their longer-term expectations by voting with their feet, and there was a slow but deadly draining away of the larger, quoted clients to the Big Eight. The partners were unwilling to see this long-established and respected firm reduced to a couple of offices in London and wanted to maintain a national business, and clearly there would have been substantial job losses for the staff in a major contraction
- the only feasible strategy in these circumstances, and therefore proposed by the author, was that Dearden Farrow would have to set up a three- to four-way merger with other firms from its peer group to create a business of a similar size to the leading firms, Peats (as it was then), Cooper Brothers, Price Waterhouse and Deloittes (as it still was). It would have to headhunt a charismatic chief executive to lead the process since (in the author's view) none of the partners, able accountants though they were, possessed the necessary qualities of vision, leadership, experience and ruthlessness to come out on top at the end of such an exercise
- the reactions of the key stakeholders were salutary:
  – the younger partners accepted this strategy as securing their future in a larger business
  – the senior partner in waiting, understandably, was never persuaded that he could not fulfil the role, though sadly the point was proved when he suffered a heart attack a few months later and had to convalesce for a number of months. His view though prevailed and no headhunter was approached.
  – the partnership as a whole could not bring themselves to take such a big step as a four-way merger and took rapid steps to approach just one of their peer group, with whom they had closer relations than the others. They then tied the knot with Binder Hamlyn, and the name Dearden Farrow was lost for ever
- the result, of course, was that two medium-sized firms then became one larger, but still medium-sized firm, and Binders still faced the same problems as before.

Only a few years later Binders, suffering the same problems that had faced Dearden Farrow, decided to approach one of the current giants, Arthur Andersen. The difference this time was that this was not a merger of equals but a take-over of the smaller firm's UK-quoted client base, and the stresses broke up the Binder partnership in the process.

The lessons from this case study are that the wishes of the larger and most financially important members of that all-important stakeholder group, the customers, were for their supplier to provide them with the services of a top firm, and they associated this with the size of the very biggest firms. The other stakeholder group, the younger partners, would probably have gone for the four-way merger, and with a new and experienced leader, the firm would have survived. Taking insufficient account of these key stakeholder groups' wishes and expectations produced an unrealistic goal and a catastrophic strategy.

Implementation

When assessing the feasibility, and therefore acceptability of the strategy for GCG, we need to consider how it can be implemented. At this point, it is worth reminding ourselves that three things have to be in place before implementation can be commenced:

- agreement on the present position – Point A
- agreement on the desired future position – Point B
- agreement on the strategy to get from A to B.

Point B has not truly been defined until a practical implementation plan has been drawn up, since the whole exercise is clearly pointless unless the selected strategy can be implemented. As a further check on the robustness and clarity of thinking about Point B, we should ask ourselves the following questions about our current position:

- have we got clear objectives: business, financial and stakeholder?
- have we defined the business: markets being served, needs being supplied, and means of supplying those needs, products, channels of distribution, etc?
- are we clear on the basis of competition: key elements of GCG's competitive advantage and critical skills to beat the competition?

- have we acquired and allocated the necessary resources?
- do we have a clear idea about an implementation route?

Strategy implementation is often called the *action* stage of strategic management. It is considered by many with experience to be the most difficult element, and the one most likely to derail the whole process.

The main activities we need to perform are to:

- plan and allocate the necessary resources
- plan any necessary organisational changes
- write the business plan with detailed financial forecasts and budgets
- build in a system to monitor progress and feed back information to management to enable the strategy to be kept on course or appropriately modified
- project-manage the whole process
- set up a long-term strategy evaluation process to monitor the effectiveness of the strategy.

By now, we will have incorporated the stakeholder model into monitoring systems so that throughout the implementation process we can keep a check on how stakeholders are reacting to the strategy. This will go a long way towards ensuring the agreed strategy will *not* derail at the hands of dissenting parties. Indeed, the strategy should be designed to bring together the goals of all the stakeholders to achieve a common direction and philosophy, and we can use the model to measure progress towards this.

Planning and allocating resources

A strategy will fail if the resources vital to its success are not made available. This means that:

- at the corporate level we are mainly concerned with the allocation of resources between different parts of the organisation, be they business functions, operating divisions or geographical areas. But if there is a requirement for an overall increase in resources, this must be properly planned for
- at the business unit level we have to consider the value chain and address resource requirements through the whole chain, recognising which activities are of greatest importance to successful implementation of the strategy and ensuring that these are planned with particular care. In this process it is critical that we understand how the detailed resource plans at operational level underpin the overall strategies of the business units

- at the stakeholder level, we need to think about how we balance resource allocation to achieve maximum overall satisfaction. This goes back to the weighting process, of course, and will depend on how demanding particular stakeholders are for resources for their interest in the company, taking into account its competitive importance. If we ensure all stakeholders are informed of the strategy and of the efforts to incorporate their expectations, this should not prove overly difficult.

Planning organisational change

The people in an organisation are the means by which a strategy is implemented, so the way in which they are organised is of key importance. The position analysis carried out will give clear insights into pros and cons of the present way of organising the business, and the strategic plan will indicate desirable modifications.

Guiding the decisions about organisational change will be:

- clear-headed logic about the natural way to organise in the most effective way, disregarding the baggage of current practices
- paying due regard to the experience of the past in assessing what appears to work well and what appears to give problems
- putting in place the mechanism to deliver the agreed strategy, with whatever modifications and additions are needed.

Into this process must be built the means of providing appropriately for the needs of all the various stakeholders to ensure that their interests are properly taken care of.

This is addressed more fully in the next chapter.

THE STRATEGY PROCESS
INTERNAL ANALYSIS
EXTERNAL ANALYSIS
STAKEHOLDER ANALYSIS
CONFIRM OR CHANGE GOAL
FORMULATING STRATEGY
IMPLEMENTATION
- Planning and allocating resources
- Planning organisational change
- Writing the business plan
- Setting up a monitoring and reporting system
- Project management
  a. deliverables
  b. benefits
  c. controls
  d. review
- Long-term strategy evaluation

Writing the business plan

The strategy is implemented through a series of business plans for each of the business units usually covering the next three to five years. A typical framework for such a business plan will consist of:

1. Mission statement
2. Goals
3. Role in the group
4. Overall strategy statement
5. Products and services
6. Marketing
7. Production
8. Procurement
9. Information systems
10. Organisation
11. Finance
12. Assessment of risks
13. Implementation plan

Each section will have several sub-sets.

Setting up a monitoring and reporting system

The requirements of a monitoring and reporting system and the resources required to put such a system in place will be part of the business plan. A good system provides the instruments whereby management and all the other stakeholders can be made aware of progress in implementing the agreed strategy. Without first-class systems there can be a dangerous lack of necessary information, or worse, wrong information. All too often, monitoring and reporting systems are designed without adequate regard for the big picture, and with an almost total focus on financial aspects. The stakeholder model has already been constructed following the analysis, so this, as we have said, will form part of the system of transparency and accountability.

This is dealt with more fully in Chapter 14.

Project management

Finally, the strategic plan and related business plans will only be successfully implemented through good project management and a good implementation programme. This is not the place to go into the intricacies of project planning, and we will simply draw attention here to the need to include in the programme certain important modules.

a. Deliverables

- establish the deliverables throughout the project and the actions necessary to deliver them. These embrace the planned objectives in regard to each category of stakeholder
- agree a basis for measuring the deliverables
- define a delivery model for each category of deliverable, and use the

model to produce a time schedule for each deliverable, which will then become part of the project control system
- assemble the elements into a project plan embracing the whole implementation programme, and allocate responsibilities for managing and executing each part of the programme
- set up a mechanism to measure progress on a regular basis against the delivery model to assist project control.

See Figure 12.12.

Fig 12.12 Example of deliverables model

Stakeholder group: Customers								
	Year 1				**Year 2**			
Deliverable	Q1	Q2	Q3	Q4	Q1	Q2	Q3	Q4
Point of sale in number of stores	20	50	100	100	100	100	100	100
Staff training in number of stores	5	30	60	100	100	100	100	100
Attitude reorientation in number of stores		20	40	60	80	100	100	100
Product range extension	1,000	1,200	1,400	1,500	1,500	1,500	1,500	1,500
Sales per sq. ft. £	10	11	12	13	14	15	16	16

b. Benefits

- establish a benefits model to allow the success of the strategy to be measured, and related back to delivery
- use this model to assess the value of any suggested changes or enhancements to the plan
- make sure that all the stakeholders receive their appropriate benefits.

See Figure 12.13.

Fig 12.13 Example of benefits model

Stakeholder group: Customers								
	Year 1				Year 2			
Customer satisfaction	*Q1*	*Q2*	*Q3*	*Q4*	*Q1*	*Q2*	*Q3*	*Q4*
Ethical perception	6.0	6.2	6.4	6.6	7.0	7.5	7.5	7.5
Convenience	6.4	6.4	6.4	7.2	7.4	8.2	8.2	8.2
Value	7.1	7.2	7.3	7.4	7.5	7.6	7.7	7.8
Complaints level	6.8	6.9	7.0	7.2	7.5	7.8	8.0	8.0
Complaints handling	7.2	7.8	8.2	8.2	8.2	8.2	8.2	8.2

Figures represent scores out of 10

c. Controls

- plan a comprehensive set of control mechanisms, including:
  - management responsibility and authority structures
  - implementation teams
  - asset and other resource controls
  - software control tools
  - financial controls
  - cost management mechanisms
  - work plans and schedules
  - detailed action responsibilities
  - appropriate reporting systems.

d. Review

- ensure that a review mechanism is in place:
  - identify milestones or checkpoints
  - check deliverables at these points and modify the future programme as necessary
  - check benefits are being achieved by all stakeholders.

Long-term strategy evaluation

Strategy evaluation is the final stage in the strategic management process, and represents the need of GCG's management to know how well our strategies are working. We will therefore need to:

- review the external and internal factors which have been the bases for the current strategies
- review the stakeholder weighting model to ascertain if there are any significant changes in the views of the different groups
- measure performance
- take corrective action.

We must periodically evaluate the strategy being implemented, since:

- achieving success today does not guarantee that success will be achieved tomorrow in a potentially changing business environment
- the very achievement of success by its nature changes the circumstances and is likely to create new and different problems, which will need prompt action.

To evaluate the ongoing success of the chosen strategies, we may review:

- whether there are inconsistencies between different constituent parts of the plan, which tend to show up in continuing management infighting
- whether the strategy has taken into account all the relevant factors or whether there are omissions, which give rise to incompatible objectives
- the ongoing practicability of the strategy in terms of the adequacy of the resources needed to achieve successful implementation
- how successful it has been in creating significant competitive advantage in the marketplace.

In practice, since external factors will certainly have changed since the creation of the strategy, and there will similarly have been changes in the internal circumstances of the business, this periodic evaluation will usually point up the need for at least some changes. The corollary is that if we do not contemplate any changes because there is no re-evaluation of the strategy, it will probably not be delivering the desired results, and we will be putting the interests of at least some of our stakeholders at risk.

NOTES

[1] Quoted from an article by Robert Reich in the *New York Times*, 5 January 1996, reproduced in *Prospect* (and quoted by John Plender in *A Stake in the Future*).
[2] As stated previously, we have had the advantage of going through the whole process for real (hence the title of the book, Real World Corporate Governance!) when writing this, and we have proved that a lot of the theory – including our original ideas – is impractical. In this Part B, therefore, we have made adjustments to reflect a practical, rather than theoretical approach, and we have removed most of the jargon of strategy, choosing instead to empathise with the short-of-time analyst to produce an easy to read, plain English account of what needs to be done.
[3] Quoted in *The Marketing Book*, 3rd ed., Edited by Michael J Baker, Butterworth-Heinemann for the Chartered Institute of Marketing, 1994.
[4] Clearly just as important as our own efficiency is that of our suppliers and customers to maximise value for the end user. As the process involves knowing our suppliers and customers better, this will make closer the relationships, providing opportunities for further value enhancement.
[5] From an interview in the *Financial Times*, 19 June 1997.
[6] *Exploring Corporate Strategy – Text and Cases*, 3rd ed., Gerry Johnson and Kevan Scholes, Prentice Hall, 1993.

Chapter 13

SHAPING UP

Principles of organisation *214*

The board and corporate governance *215*

Brief for the board *215*

Board structure *217*

Appointment and removal of directors *221*

Induction and training *223*

Board effectiveness *224*

Accountability *224*

'We trained hard – but every time we were beginning to form up into teams, we would be reorganised. I was to learn later in life that we tend to meet any new situation by reorganising, and a wonderful method it can be for creating the illusion of progress while producing confusion, inefficiency and demoralisation.'

The famous words of Roman General Caius Petronius: Petronii Arbitri Satyricon, AD 66

RULE 4: ORGANISING TO DELIVER GOOD CORPORATE GOVERNANCE

The first three rules of good corporate governance are about an ethical approach to business, a clear and sensible goal which represents an appropriate balance of the collective wishes of all the stakeholders, and a strategy process which reflects the stakeholder approach to business. In order to implement the strategic plan which has been developed to achieve the agreed goal, the organisation[1] must reflect these three rules. With an inappropriate organisation in place, the goal will not be achieved, and the approach to business will be vulnerable to a falling short in ethical behaviour. Furthermore, any relationship between the way the business is being run and the expectations of the various non-managerial stakeholders will be purely coincidental.

Let us first, then, look at the methodology outlined in Chapter 9. During the last three chapters, we have looked at checking, by means of a position analysis, ethics, the goal, organisation and reporting systems. As we pointed out, the analyses carried out will highlight any areas which need changing, particularly concerning our stakeholders. At the end of the last chapter we briefly examined how a strategy should be implemented, including the sorts of organisational changes needed to get from Point A (where we are now) to Point B (the goal). This reflects Point 2 of the methodology, set out below, taken from Figures 9.4a and 9.4b.

STRUCTURE - does it protect the interests of the various stakeholders and have open channels of communication with all of them?

2. We can then feed the information gathered *back into* the strategy model and use it to make any changes necessary to:

- **the organisation** – this process automatically opens up communication channels if they were lacking before, but these will need to be rationalised; it will also have opened our eyes to any structural or operational inefficiencies, etc, which are affecting our stakeholders

We will not go into the detailed operational side of the organisation here, since working out appropriate improvements and planning changes is a matter for individual companies to determine. However, we do emphasise the need to open new channels of communication and rationalise existing ones; clearly this also is the basis of the fifth Golden Rule and in the next chapter we will discuss the *uses* – and benefits – of good reporting systems.

Principles of organisation

There are two key elements to be considered when designing the appropriate organisation.

Shape

There are five basic types of organisation structure:

- *simple* – an organisation run by an individual, with little formal structure, unworkable beyond a certain size
- *functional* – an organisation based on the functional elements, sales and marketing, production, finance, and found in smaller, more focused businesses, and the divisions of larger ones, since the structure gives rise to a big co-ordination requirement as businesses grow
- *multi-divisional* – an organisation combining functional business units with central support services, and requiring more sophisticated management techniques, but useful to serve the development of product/market businesses in a larger company
- *holding company* – suitable for the larger organisation in which the centre exercises little day-to-day operational control but behaves more like an investment company
- *matrix* – representing a significantly more complex way to organise, with business, functional and geographical dimensions sharing responsibilities, and leading in different circumstances; a structure praised for focusing skills and experience but criticised for confusing ultimate responsibilities.

Style

There are three basic styles of management:
- *strategic planning* – with the centre operating as an overall planner, developing a detailed central plan and laying out roles for the divisions

- *financial control* – where the centre sees itself as a shareholder or banker for the divisions with little desire to get involved in defining their individual product/market strategies
- *strategic control* – where the centre allows the divisions to develop their own plans and approves them against an objective to implement an overall strategy and achieve a balance between the divisions.

The implementation of the strategic plan must ensure that the organisation is framed to embody the most appropriate shape and style of management to achieve success, and that it is constructed to serve the needs of all the key stakeholding groups.

As Bob Garratt points out in the title of his recent book: *The fish rots from the head* (HarperCollins Business). We therefore direct this chapter at the top of the company, the board. The lead comes from the board, and success or failure generally begins here.

The board and corporate governance

We have stressed our conviction that:

- good corporate governance is an integral part of good management
- good corporate governance can be assured by following the Five Golden Rules.

As far as the board is concerned, therefore, our approach is to look at normal good practice and ask to what extent current procedures need to be augmented to comply with our five Rules.

We shall examine this under the following headings:
- brief for the board
- structure of the board and sub-committees
- appointment and removal of directors
- induction and training
- effectiveness monitoring
- accountability.

Brief for the board

The generally accepted role or brief of a board of directors is to:

- approve the corporate goals, and the strategies formulated by management to achieve these goals

- appoint the managers who will run the business to carry out the strategies
- monitor progress, benchmarking against the industry norms, and take any necessary corrective action to keep the organisation on track
- report back to the owners on their stewardship
- operate effectively as a board, monitoring the board's own conduct for efficiency, effectiveness and good practice.

The brief for the board should *not* include second guessing management or trying to do their job. To the extent that the members of the board are also executive managers, they may report to the board in those capacities but must listen to others reporting, and must make board decisions in the very different capacity of that of a board director.

In the light of the Five Golden Rules, we need to amplify the board's brief in the following ways:

- the **corporate goals** which the board has to approve must be arrived at in the manner we described in Chapter 11, reflecting the expectations of all the stakeholder groups in an appropriate way, particularly the three key groups: customers, staff and owners. It should go without question that every member of the board, including the chairman, should understand the reasons for selecting the particular goals, but in our experience this is one of the first checks required, and a strategic management process is the best way to assure this
- the **strategies** prepared by management to achieve these goals must therefore be formulated in accordance with good strategic management practice, and again taking into account the interests of the various stakeholding groups. It is surprising how many organisations are budget-driven and only look at the bigger picture when it is forced upon them by a trading crisis
- **appointment of managers** to carry out the strategies must take into account the overall requirements, not simply those required to deliver to one or other stakeholder group. Hence favouring owners by appointing a person with a reputation as a ruthless cost-cutter to carry through a programme to produce a major uplift in profit and cash for dividends for owners would not be good practice if it was at the expense of the long-term relationship with customers, or at the expense of necessary investment in infrastructure or staff. This may seem simply common sense stated in these bald terms, but it is surprisingly easy for this bias to happen
- **monitoring progress** means monitoring against the expectations of all

the stakeholder groups, not simply focusing on trading performance and the building of short-term value for shareholders. Similarly, benchmarking performance means comparison on a range of measures, a number of which are non-financial. Likewise, corrective action means, for instance, that the board itself ought to be addressing the issue of an under-performing chief executive, not simply relying on absentee shareholders to exercise force majeure through their voting rights at an Extraordinary General Meeting

- **accounting** for their stewardship is extended to being accountable to all the key stakeholder groups for the progress towards achieving the various objectives which the strategic plan has determined in regard to each particular stakeholder group, not simply addressing the shareholders through interim and annual reports
- **effective operation** by which the board conducts itself in an effective way. Addressing this formally is a relatively new concept for most boards. We would extend this in the context of good corporate governance to include a regular check on the company's ethical stance and behaviour. As we described in Chapter 10, this is not about espousing the latest politically correct fads, but goes to the heart of the way business is conducted and the way the directors and employees of the company behave.

Collectively, these are the elements which make up the brief for the board of directors of the company. It will be clear to the reader that this brief is applicable to all companies, from the smallest to the largest. It requires the company to have an agreed goal and a practical plan to achieve the goal, and for the board to be held responsible for its achievement. The survival and commercial success of the company are likely to be at the heart of the agreed goal, but if the stakeholders were to wish otherwise, for instance through a financial package which was acceptable to each of the various groups, and which would terminate the business as an independent entity, then that would be the goal to follow, notwithstanding the personal ambitions of key directors.

Board structure

In small businesses the board structure will be simple, consisting of the chairman and chief executive, who may be the same person, and the most senior and trusted managers, who will often be the heads of the key functions: sales, production and finance. In larger, more complex organisations there will be a main or group board and subsidiary companies with their own boards, and the chairmen of the main subsidiary companies will usually sit on the main board. Many books have been written on how these should be structured, and what role the chairman should play.

The Cadbury Committee laid down guidelines for the structure of a board of directors which included separating the roles of chairman and chief executive, and ensuring a minimum of three independent directors. The committee's brief was much narrower than that which we have set ourselves, and we would therefore expect that adherence to our Five Golden Rules would cover everything that Sir Adrian's committee set out to achieve. In this section, therefore, we will concern ourselves with the way in which management can properly comply with the Rules. The board should be structured to fulfil the brief described above and logically, the directors should be in a position to:

- keep a watching eye over the ethics pertaining in the company, starting at the top, and percolating through the whole organisation; this might once have been taken for granted – or again it might not – but these days it merits addressing formally
- understand, discuss and take decisions on the multi-faceted goals; this may appear obvious, but it requires experience and possibly training too, and these can by no means be taken for granted
- ensure that the company is run under a strategic management regime which will assure that the appropriate efforts are made to achieve the agreed goals, and that the directors will be competent to understand the monitoring reports which indicate progress towards these goals
- ensure that the organisation is structured in such a way that, from board level to the smallest local branch, the agreed goals are not prejudiced by a bias towards one or other stakeholding group
- take so seriously their accountability to all the stakeholders that they ensure regular reporting and transparency of progress; we cannot emphasise too strongly that the well understood value of transparency in any free society as a bulwark against tyranny applies equally to the board of a company in regard to its accountability to its stakeholders.

How should the board be organised with these requirements in mind? We can address separately:

- the qualifications required of the people to be considered as possible directors

- the way the board may be organised, with sub-committees and administrative support.

The first point to make is that there is no distinction in English law between one type of director and another, and the concept of 'non-executive' or even 'independent' has no significance. Once a person is appointed as a director he or she must fulfil a useful role as a director, and the attempt to categorise directors into different groups is both misleading in law and unhelpful and divisive in management terms. In our view, there are simply directors.

The second point to make is that each director must fulfil a specific role with a clear brief. To this end, each director ought to be appropriately qualified for the role into which he or she is cast. This may seem obvious, but anyone with experience of the way in which boards are staffed will know that practice varies enormously.

Example

On joining the board of one of the major multinational oil companies a recent non-executive appointee explained his brief and induction training to us as follows: 'They said to me "Don't worry about that, we regard you as highly experienced, so we haven't planned any training for you, and in regard to your brief, you'll soon work out for yourself how you can be most useful"'.

There are three ways in which people may be qualified to become directors of a company, and to perform the roles described above:

- proven ability in running a significant part of the existing business
- knowledge, experience and contacts in an area of business, geographical or market, that is part of the company's chosen goals, and in which it is currently relatively weak
- knowledge and experience in a skill area highly relevant to the company's business and in which it is currently relatively weak, and in which it has not yet employed the necessary staff to fill the gap.

In terms of how the board is organised, it is always useful to have standing sub-committees to perform regular tasks and thereby to make the board's meetings more effective. While we disdain the situation in which more time is spent in meetings than in real action, we believe that the vital task of ensuring that the Five Golden Rules are properly abided by should be put in the hands of a *corporate governance sub-committee*.

This committee will have as its brief the task of ensuring that:

- the ethical behaviour of the company is above reproach
- the corporate goals represent the balanced interests of all stakeholders
- there is a proper system of strategic management in place
- the organisation is appropriately balanced to protect the interests of all stakeholders
- the accountability is comprehensive and transparency is the rule.

It will be responsible specifically for looking after the interests of the various key stakeholder groups:

- customers
- owners
- employees
- suppliers
- other trading partners
- local communities in which the company is a significant employer.

The corporate governance sub-committee should be served by a support function, which may be as little as an administrative assistant, or may be a small office, and it should link into the main functions of the organisation. For instance:

- marketing for customer relations
- company secretary for owner relations
- personnel for employee relations
- purchasing for supplier relations
- public relations for local community relations.

It will maintain a link with each stakeholder group and publish regular reports in enough detail to ensure transparency.

The distinction between this committee and the audit committee will be clear to everyone who recognises the distinction we have drawn between corporate governance as the way of conducting business, and corporate governance as a balance between institutional owners and boards of directors. The audit committee will still have its place as a means of ensuring that the internal audit function is doing its job – and paying for itself by keeping the audit fee lower than it might otherwise have been! The external auditors will review the work of the corporate governance committee as part of the audit, and study its minutes, to determine whether it has been properly fulfilling its brief. They will thereby check on behalf of all stakeholders whether their interests are being properly looked after, and though this will not be a statutory requirement, they will include a comment on this in their report to members. The absence of such a report will give its own clear message to the world.

The remuneration committee is probably the most effective technical way to deal with the remuneration of board members, but the public perception is that these committees are self-serving in that too many of the same group of non-executive directors sit on each others' committees and are disinclined to be as hard on each other as they perhaps should be. Consequently there is little restraining influence on levels of pay, and indeed the system tends to drive pay higher than it would otherwise go. There is a clear role for the corporate governance committee, as part of its concern with ethics and fulfilling the expectations of all stakeholder groups, to cast a critical eye over the results of the remuneration committee's work.

Appointment and removal of directors

The appointment of directors, and their removal, should be handled like the appointment and removal of employees generally, from top management to the least skilled and lowest paid:

- the organisational requirement is identified
- the job is specified to carry out that requirement
- a person specification is drawn up of what is needed in the way of qualifications, experience and personal attributes from candidates
- a short list of candidates is identified, and an appointment made from this list.

Similarly, removal results from a persistent failure to perform, which has been identified from regular performance appraisals, and following which no adequate improvement has resulted.

Like many other principles in this book, this may appear to be so obvious that it does not need stating. However, anyone with experience knows that appointment to the board in many companies can often be looked on as something very different. It may be, for instance:

- a reward for long and loyal service
- a mark of seniority to buy an employee's continued loyalty
- a step to ensure a balance of support for the chairman.

In our view, the brief for the board creates the job specification and the related person specification follows. Hence the specifications for the different directors' jobs should reflect the needs described earlier, and should be set out clearly in job descriptions, just as is required and expected for management generally. In our view, they should all represent positive parts of the brief, each contributing to the attainment of the agreed goals. There should be no element of confrontation for its own sake in the way the tasks are drawn up. The checks and balances introduced should be seen as a positive contribution to keeping the business moving in the right direction. With these criteria in mind, there will be no place for a job focused purely on the negative role of keeping an eye on the chief executive. Nor will there be a role for acolytes of the chairman, placed on the board to provide reliable support for him. In broad terms, in a unitary board, the directors' roles are likely to be grouped into:

- directors representing operating units of the business, and in the full-time employment of the company
- directors representing key stakeholders, for instance owners or partners in joint ventures or strategic alliances, who will only spend a part of their time on the company's payroll
- directors who bring important connections or skills associated with new markets, and whose experience and wisdom can be helpful in establishing the business in those markets, but who will only spend a part of their time working with the company.

As we discussed earlier, we have avoided the term 'non-executive director', as we believe it is misleading and divisive. In a similar way, the more fashionable term 'independent director' can be challenged on the grounds that no director can be truly independent, as each represents one interest or another, and all have a common interest in the continued health of the business. Furthermore, they all draw directors' fees! The auditors are expected to provide true independence. This inability of any director to be truly independent of all vested interests highlights the importance of the elements of ethics and congruence of goals embodied in our Five Rules of corporate governance.

The person specifications will then be drawn up to match the specific job specifications, and full thought given to the qualifications, experience and personal attributes referred to earlier. If headhunters are used, they are likely to go through this process rigorously, but they will be dependent on the client spelling out its view of the requirements of the job. If outside recruitment consultants are not used, and, of course, outside help is unlikely to be enlisted for internal appointments to the board, it is nevertheless equally important that the same degree of care is taken.

Much has been written on the appointment of non-executive directors – though very little on their removal – and even more on the personnel management processes involved in internal promotions, and we do not propose to go into more detail here.

Our message can be summed up as:

- all directors share an equal responsibility for the positive achievement of the company's goals, and for the company's compliance with the Five Golden Rules of good corporate governance
- directors should be appointed who are appropriately qualified to fulfil the board's brief
- directors' performance should be monitored and underperforming individuals should be replaced.

Induction and training

The incoming non-executive director of the multinational oil company to whom we referred earlier was a retired very senior civil servant, and had been used to a structured environment. He was surprised, to say the least, at the casual way in which his new job had begun. In fact, none of the more junior employees would have been treated that way, and nor should he have been.

There should be a properly thought through induction programme, possibly with a programme of visits to head office and key sites. The chairman should introduce new directors to the existing members of the board if this has not already happened during the appointment process, and should give them the opportunity for private meetings away from himself. This will give them the chance to gain a deeper insight into both the company and the chairman himself.

The appointment process should start with a job specification and conclude with a letter of appointment which spells out the content of the job specification, just as for an employee. Subsequently, just as with someone like a trainee manager, a training process should be applied which:

- ensures that all directors have attained the same minimum level of competence that the responsibilities demand. Two very different skills in this category might be:
  - training in strategic thinking

– training in board room procedures and effective meetings
- provides additional training for those directors whose special duties require this. Examples here might include:
– language and culture training for a director with the responsibility for a part of the business in a part of the world unfamiliar to him or her
– training in chairmanship for a prospective new chairman.

Board effectiveness

The board of directors is no different from any other management function in the company in that it must operate as effectively as possible. The rest of the company is under regular scrutiny from its superiors, but *quis custodiet custodes*?

There have been many books written about the effective conduct of board meetings and the most effective way to chair these, and we will do no more than refer to these here.[2] However, the point we would make is that there should be a mechanism in place to monitor the board's effectiveness, and the results of this monitoring should be fed back into the process so that a high standard of effectiveness is maintained, and everyone knows how to contribute to this. Hence there will be protocols by which the board's business is conducted, covering:

- the role of the chairman
- procedures and practice in the course of meetings
- circulation of materials sufficiently in advance of meetings to be useful
- the use of meetings to take decisions as opposed to meetings to air issues.

Ultimately it is the chairman's responsibility to ensure proper conduct of meetings, and effectiveness monitoring should be both directed to serve him, and transparent so that he is obliged to act on the messages it sends.

Accountability

Finally, the board of directors is responsible to the stakeholders for achieving the agreed goals. It exercises this responsibility by its actions, and the stakeholders are made aware of its progress by the communications it receives from them. This is the final operation that closes the loop, and without which no one has a proper idea what kind of a job the board is doing. That is why we describe it as the fifth Golden Rule of corporate governance. Transparency is the watchword here and is dealt with in the next chapter.

NOTES

[1] By 'organisation', we are, of course, using the term not to mean 'company' but the way in which the company is organised, ie, its structure, as Figure 9.4 explained.
[2] For example, *The Company Chairman*, by Sir Adrian Cadbury, Director Books, Simon & Schuster International Group, 1990.

Chapter 14

'IT'S GOOD TO TALK'

Customers *232*
Owners *235*
Employees *238*
Suppliers and trading partners *240*
Community *242*

*'Never play by the rules. Never pay in cash.
And never tell the truth.'*
The Three Rules of Wall Street, according to F. Ross Johnson,
president and chief executive officer, R J R Nabisco[1]

RULE 5: ACCOUNTABILITY AND REPORTING TO DELIVER GOOD CORPORATE GOVERNANCE

We closed the last chapter with the remark that without an effective process of reporting back to the stakeholders, no one can have a very good idea as to how well the board is doing its job. This is the reason that we have elevated the reporting function to the status of a Golden Rule. A good reporting system is the key to accountability, and transparency is the key to a good reporting system. For this reason:

- The Cadbury Committee made specific recommendations that 'the report and accounts should contain a coherent narrative, supported by the figures, of the company's performance and prospects'. Section 4 of the code, dealing with reporting and controls, stated that it was 'the board's duty to present a balanced and understandable assessment of the company's position'. It recommended that 'the directors should explain their responsibility for preparing the accounts next to a statement by the auditors about their reporting responsibilities'. It also caused consternation by recommending that 'the directors should report on the effectiveness of the company's system of internal control' and '… that the business is a going concern, with supporting assumptions or qualifications as necessary'. These disclosures are in effect exclusively related to the relationship between the City and the boards, and take little account of the interests of the other stakeholder groups. This is not a criticism of the committee, which was following its brief, but a reflection on the interests and concerns of those who set the brief.
- The Greenbury Committee spelled out 12 disclosure provisions in regard to directors' pay, and recommended that the chairman of the remuneration committee should attend the AGM of the company and be prepared to answer shareholders' questions. The provisions regarding disclosure of the pension side of top people's pay represented a very real blow for transparency and accountability. The problem was that the subject became so complex, with actuaries trying to square the very different views of pension funds and industrialists over what the value of these payment really was, that transparency went out of the window, and headline journalism became the messenger and the message. Furthermore, the committee inadvertently stumbled into a tax minefield

over its call for a change in the nature of the tax liability related to these payments. It wanted the sale of option shares to be subject to income tax, instead of capital gains tax, when the option was exercised. This meant that all the smaller shareholders would be brought into the tax bracket and illustrated the committee's apparent complete disregard for any shareholder groups other than the board and senior management.

In practice, the reader will recognise that something much more comprehensive is required to ensure accountability and transparency. Just as we have taken a broad view of corporate governance, compared with the narrow view generally taken by the City institutions and its followers, so we take a broad, holistic view of accountability and the reporting process.

In this chapter we are looking at setting up channels of communication, but the *message* here is how these channels and the reporting system as a whole should be used to:

- ensure all stakeholders are happy with the proposed strategy
- monitor progress from Point A to Point B in the strategy
- ensure, as the sections below dictate, that stakeholders are receiving all the information they require

INFORMATION – is there information being passed through these channels which is sufficient and accurate enough to satisfy all the stakeholders?

2. We can then feed the information gathered *back into* the strategy model and use it to make any changes necessary to:

- **reporting systems** – having opened up these channels, it is then possible to monitor progress and ensure stakeholders are getting all the information they need and this function, too, will have to be rationalised.

Logically, therefore, we need systems which have the following characteristics:

- they serve all the significant stakeholder groups:
  - customers
  - owners
  - employees
  - suppliers and other trading partners
  - local communities
- in total they communicate the intention to run the company under systems of good corporate governance, and in particular they have very specific objectives in relation to each target group. Following the methodology, they will include the four elements of:
  - *ethics:* projecting the ethos which permeates the company, and thus communicating to all stakeholders an image of the ethical company which the board is striving to create and operate
  - *goal:* reporting on the progress made by the company towards the agreed corporate goals, and in particular fulfilling the specific interests of the particular stakeholders addressed in the communications received by them
  - *organisation:* showing that the company is organised effectively to achieve the goals that have been communicated to all the stakeholders, and to look after their individual interests
  - *reporting:* demonstrating through the high quality of the communications that the accountability and transparency rule of good corporate governance is both understood and being adhered to
- in their execution, high standards are in place to ensure that the communications are easy to understand and provide the information required by the recipients, in line with their expectations referred to above
- the systems provide regular communications to all stakeholder groups, and whilst there is an appropriate weighting between the needs of the various groups, no group is neglected, for instance through allowing address lists to become out of date.

The process of setting up these systems is summarised in Figure 14.1.

Let us now consider what this means for each of the stakeholder groups in turn, and what ought to be the parameters for each reporting system.

Fig 14.1 A model for reporting systems

Customers

Purpose

In determining the company's trading goals, and preparing the strategic plan, the board will have approved certain objectives in relation to its customers. The marketing department will have made its own detailed plans, as part of the subsequent business plan, to develop relations with the whole customer base, and there will be specific plans for key accounts. Including the need for regular communications with customers in a book on corporate governance may seem odd, but the reasons are straightforward:

- there can never be too much attention paid to good relations with this key stakeholder group, and in the experience of the authors, excellence in this area can certainly not be taken for granted, even in the largest and best run of companies
- communications with customers tends not to be regular, but intermittent, driven by marketing plans which require new brochures and catalogues, updated price lists, special promotions and the like
- the existing communications may not adequately reflect the long-

standing interests of the customers, but rather will tend to concentrate on arousing (and supplying) new needs. Communications in the context of good governance need to pay particular attention to reflecting the company's focus on looking after the customer's current and anticipated interests and concerns
- the communications with customers need to take into account the communications with the other stakeholder groups and project the same good corporate governance message in a co-ordinated way, designed to reinforce it.

The overall purpose therefore has to be to develop customer loyalty and the belief that the company is the kind of supplier with whom the customer wants to maintain a long-term relationship

Content

The specific content will be determined in detail by the marketing department as part of its short and longer term plans, but following the four elements of the methodology, it will include:

- *ethics:* a regular message about the company's ethical position, illustrating this through some recent example of good corporate behaviour
- *goal:* a reminder of how the company understands the interests of its customers and is constantly working to improve the products and services it supplies, in anticipation of its clients' future needs, illustrated perhaps by a recent example of a customer problem solved by the company's insightful and innovative approach
- *organisation:* a reminder that the company has organised itself sensibly in a way that takes into consideration the interests of the customers as a key stakeholder group, for instance by describing the work of a customer-facing department which has been set up to improve the handling of customer queries or complaints
- *reporting:* a description of the content, and possibly an outline of the whole communications strategy, to show how this has been designed to further the aims of good corporate governance through accountability to each stakeholder group, and openness and honesty in the communications process. This could be illustrated by showing how some part of the content demonstrates this approach, for instance by dealing frankly and openly with an instance of product failure, and showing how the company went that extra mile to compensate the customers for any losses incurred.

Distribution

The channels for delivering communications to customers should be well-established by any self-respecting marketing and sales function. Lack of use of certain channels, such as not taking the opportunity of introducing an ethical element into packaging, or lack of control, such as using offensive debt collection letters, can both convey the wrong messages to customers. Regular channels of communication include:

- promotion and advertising, both through physical media such as brochures and posters, and through electronic media like television and Internet web sites
- the bidding and ordering process, including responses to requests for proposals and submission of tenders, through direct mail and mail order catalogues, to the receipt and acknowledgement of customers' orders
- the display, packaging and labelling of products and services
- the regular communication in the course of ongoing business, which includes letters, reports, invoices and the debt collection process
- social communication, including such matters as invitations to social events.

It should also be remembered that there may be a customer beyond the immediate one, for instance where a company is supplying partly assembled products. The interests of the customers further down the chain should be recognised as being of significant importance to those higher up the supply chain and taken into account in the target marketing. This goes back to the value chain approach in which efficiency and effectiveness should abound *throughout* the chain so the end user benefits – since this of course will in turn go back to benefiting everyone in the chain.

Frequency

The principle underlying the communication with customers, as with all the other stakeholders, is that there should be regular contact. Clearly, with customers there will be intermittent contact as business is conducted, and the existence of this must be taken into account when a plan is devised to ensure regular contact. Hence, contact will arise from such regular transactions as:

- bids and orders
- invoicing and debt collection
- complaints and claims adjustments.

Additionally, there will be periodic marketing campaigns with customer mailings. However, we list below some further examples of occasions when a company may take the opportunity to make contact with its customers in such a way that its ethical approach to business – as well as its ability to be 'on the ball' is demonstrated:

- helping customers in trouble, for instance where a client may have suffered a fire with resulting stock losses, and could be helped by urgent deliveries or an extension of credit
- letters of condolences to valued customers who have suffered personal bereavement or other loss
- similarly, letters of congratulation to clients who have achieved success or benefited by some good fortune
- letters acknowledging good customers by thanking them for their business, their regular prompt settlement of invoices or other helpful behaviour.

Owners

Purpose

The efforts of Cadbury and Greenbury, particularly, as well as PIRC and others, have been directed towards the relationship between the board and the owners, and their key recommendations regarding reporting are referred to at the beginning of this chapter. This may appear to be well-trodden territory. However, in approaching this with our broader perspective on corporate governance, we would say that the purpose of communicating with the owners needs to be re-examined. It should reflect more than just glossy statements of performance and compliance and really show them how their money is being used, as well as informing them of any problems along with the measures being instigated to solve these problems. Again, transparency is the key word and therefore, perhaps simplicity.

Content

The document required by the Companies Act and the Stock Exchange is, of course, the report and accounts, though as we will discuss below, this is not the only means of communicating with shareholders. Whichever forms we use, the content should include:

- *ethics:* conveying to shareholders, and in may ways equally importantly

to other long-term financial stakeholders such as debenture holders, bank and other lenders, the company's concern with ethical behaviour
- *goal:* reminding the owners of the company's goals for them as a stakeholder group and to demonstrate the progress made towards achieving them, covering such targets as market value of the shares, earnings per share, dividend growth, interest cover, repayment of borrowings
- *organisation:* showing that the company has made appropriate organisational arrangements to look after the owners' interests, and this ought to apply to the interests of small shareholders, who often feel themselves virtually disenfranchised, as well as those of institutions
- *reporting:* displaying through the quality of the communications that the company takes this aspect of its duties very seriously – with complete and accurate information.

We would add to this by giving our views on the formal document, the annual report, in the context of our holistic approach to corporate governance:

- the regulatory requirements have to be complied with, and all auditors are expected to be totally familiar with these – this clearly must be treated properly – and sincerely – in the report
- in many cases, in order to include the information summarised above, it may well be necessary to restructure the report to highlight, or make specific reference to the four elements outlined above; since this stakeholder group – particularly the larger shareholders – will probably have more of an interest than others in the management of the company from an accountability point of view, we add this to the four. Thus:
  – a section on ethics will be a new feature for many companies
  – methodically, comprehensively and consistently, from one year to the next, reporting against the various shareholder goals may represent an unfamiliar level of discipline and rigour for some companies
  – incorporating in the report evidence that there is a system of strategic management in operation will almost certainly involve a new approach to the document, and the traditional finance director and company secretary will not be the most obvious of people to conceptualise this. In an earlier book, *Finanzmeister*,[2] one of the authors described the finance director of the future pan-European business, who is multi-lingual and multi-cultural, and has a strategic approach to business which positions him or her to succeed the chief executive. This person may be relied upon to understand the content of this report to shareholders.

- communicating to shareholders the aspects of the organisation which have been specially set up to look after their interests, and describing what needs they serve and how they can be used, is likely to represent for many companies a degree of thoughtfulness and consideration for owners well beyond the present listing of the address of the various offices and branches, and the names of the principal officers.
- specifically commenting on the communications and their purpose, and inviting responses as to their effectiveness are part and parcel of fulfilling the objective of transparency and full accountability through excellence in communication.

Distribution

The normal distribution channels to owners are:

- the share register – the most common, and well-trodden, route
- general meetings of members – for most companies addressing physically only a very small number of members, though representing personally and by proxy probably nearly the whole membership.

Other channels, which ought not to be neglected, include:

- the sales and marketing process: only a minority of companies treat their shareholders as possible customers, and the idea of using them for such purposes as concept testing, or piloting new campaigns might be an unexpectedly successful way for some companies to improve the understanding between owners and management of the business their company is involved in, and to promote a feeling of involvement
- local and national advertising, usually only used when the board wishes to raise money or fend off a possible takeover, but available 365 days a year to further good communications with shareholders and encourage involvement and a sense of responsibility.

Frequency

With shareholders, the annual accounting routine gives rise to an annual mailing of a full report, and with larger companies there will usually be an interim report of some description as well. However, the frequency of communication with owners ought not to be driven by the statutory requirements coupled with the financial accounting timetable. In practice, there ought to be a combination of:

- regular reporting: covering all the standard items
- occasional reporting: addressing items of significant interest to owners.

Employees

Purpose

The employees of a company are the third key stakeholder group, and the goals of a well-run company in regard to their interests could include the following:

- raise their remuneration into the top quartile for all levels of staff
- improve the pension scheme and related benefits
- introduce health and safety improvements to working conditions
- undertake staff development programmes to raise educational standards, retrain staff in new skills, and improve the worth of all staff
- undertake a programme to improve management practice and procedures, for instance by introducing an Investors in People programme or getting accredited to the ISO 9000 standard
- create social and welfare schemes to provide valued facilities for staff, and promote the sense of corporate loyalty
- ensure full employee awareness of the company's overall strategic goals, and the part to be played by the various groups of staff in different divisions and regions, so that they may perform their jobs as effectively as possible.

Communications with employees should have the clear objective of reminding staff of these mutually agreed and desired goals, and demonstrating progress towards achieving them. They should not simply represent a vague notion of keeping the employees aware of the names of the management and communicating an emasculated version of the corporate strategy. There have been a number of cases which demonstrate the quintessential value of and the direct benefits from investing in people. The John Lewis Partnership, with its mutual philosophy, is a fine example of this, and so is Unipart – we will look at these companies in a little more detail at the end of the next chapter.

Content

The contents of communications to employees clearly must be governed by the specific goals referred to above. Hence an overall programme is needed to ensure that all the elements which have been promised to staff are actually dealt with in the various communications during the course of the year. Just as the board of directors has a monthly agenda for its meetings in which all regular items are addressed, similarly, the communications with staff must appear regularly, and comprehensively address all the items of regular interest.

At a minimum, the content should include:

- *ethics:* reminding the workforce of the company-wide commitment to ethical behaviour and encouraging initiatives to further the ethical image
- *goal:* progress towards the openly stated goals regarding furtherance of employee interests
- *organisation:* encouraging ideas for improvements and informing them of opportunities to discuss their views – thus showing them that they *are* valued, not just as workers but as people, with the potential to improve the well-being of the whole business. Both companies quoted above have proved that this alone can bring about increased efficiency and effectiveness
- *reporting:* information regarding the company's trading performance, including details of recent big orders, comparative operating costs in relation to competitors, sales prospects, and threats and opportunities in the marketplace, as well as any other information regarding the company which the staff are likely to be concerned about, like significant stakebuilding in the shares by investors.

Distribution

Typical devices for internal communication are:

- bulletin boards
- employee handbooks
- house magazines
- suggestion systems
- presentations
- payslip inserts
- public address systems
- employee meetings
- telephone
- fax
- e-mail/intranets (which can cover most of the other means listed here)
- Internet and Web sites
- letters and memos.

All these and other methods are means of two-way communication with employees, and have their place.

Frequency

The general rule is that communication should be regular and manageable. Little and often is a good guiding principle. If communication channels have been maintained over a period of time, their use is not likely to arouse cynicism and resistance when special situations arise, such as site closures, mergers or difficult negotiations over pay and conditions.

Suppliers and trading partners

Purpose

The purpose of communication with suppliers and other trading partners – whether on the supply side or on the sales and marketing side – has to relate to the objectives determined at the planning stage, and to the translation of these into operational strategies. For instance, the prime concerns of the buying function are concerned with obtaining:

- the right materials
- in the right quantities
- in the right quality
- at the right price
- delivered at the right time.

Procurement goals in relation to suppliers are likely to be focused around these objectives, whether the company is buying textiles manufactured in India, opencast-mined coal from Australia, classed growth claret from Bordeaux, or for that matter services such as investment advice. The key interest of the moment may for example be quality, in which case this is what communications will focus upon, to try to ensure that the overall quality of product or service delivered reaches the quality goals of the company's purchasing function. The purpose of communication is, therefore, to ensure that there is no misunderstanding between the company and its suppliers as to the quality level desired by the purchaser.

In today's world, there is increasing emphasis on partnerships between suppliers and customers, and excellence in communication is essential to success in such relationships.

Content

This book is not the place to describe the nature of procurement systems and procedures, but the point we wish to make here is that amongst the mass of regular communications with suppliers, involving purchase orders, requests for proposals, tender documents, and general correspondence, some parts must deal specifically with the company's over-riding goals in relation both to the suppliers as a group, and to individuals as necessary.

In the totality, therefore, the company must set up a mechanism to convey the four principles, by way of stories, anecdotes, details of recent company actions and trading performance and the like. The objective here is to cultivate excellent relationships with suppliers to maximise value throughout the value chain. Content should therefore include:

- *ethics:* projecting the company's strong ethical beliefs and insisting on the same high standard of behaviour
- *goal:* discussing the company's needs, and agreeing suitable goals
- *organisation:* demonstrating the way it has organised itself to deal very effectively with the purchasing function and relations with suppliers; also, the value chain approach should be remembered and all trading partners should have the same motivation towards improving total effectiveness
- *reporting:* in order for this approach to work, it requires 'partners' in the value chain to know each other and so more detailed information than the day-to-day business between them is required. Attention can also be drawn to the fact that the company is taking pains to open channels of communication with partners, so that the same can be encouraged on their part

Distribution

The channels by which these communications with suppliers are conducted may, in some ways, be more limited than channels to customers, but a company can market to its suppliers as well as its clients.

Example

Marks & Spencer has a unique relationship with its suppliers, owning as it does large parts of the supply chain. On the one hand this means that it can impose its strict quality control standards on the supply companies, but, in order for the system to work, it also looks after them, from very effective and sophisticated EDI (electronic data interchange) based systems to backward marketing and buying loyalty (many now only exist to supply this huge purchaser).

The important point to remember is that the company's image is conveyed both by one-off communications, such as special mailings, but also by the whole raft of day-to-day transactions, such as orders, payments and remittance advice, acknowledgements and every-day correspondence. At Marks & Spencer, although procurement is entirely network computer-based nationwide, personal contact is still very much part of the relationship.

Frequency

There will be frequent, if intermittent, contact between a company and its suppliers, but regular contact is the way to build the best relationship, and the principle of little and often can be well applied in this area too.

Community

Purpose

The strategic plan will have been framed with certain goals in relation to the local communities in which the company is a significant employer. A small employer may regard itself as having a civic duty to contribute to the local community, but in a sense this is a voluntary act. The local well-being is not significantly dependent upon its activities. However, a large employer has clear obligations inasmuch as it holds in its hands the livelihood of its local employees and their families and dependants, but also to an extent the livelihoods of all the local traders whose prosperity is dependent upon that of their employees. We discussed in Chapter 12 the need to arrive at a balanced set of objectives, taking into account the company's ultimate survival and long-term prosperity. This balanced set of objectives will certainly include goals which take into account the best interests of the local communities in which the company does its business, and the purpose of communications with these communities must be to promote the company's good name through actions which reflect this.

Building a good relationship with the local community during benign circumstances may seem a waste of effort, particularly when it appears to attract little local interest or response. However, the commitment will be amply rewarded if circumstances change for the worse and the organisation has to take unpopular steps. The reputation it has painstakingly built will then stand it in good stead.

Content

Local people are primarily interested in local issues, so the communications will focus largely on the way in which the company's business and its prospects are likely to affect the locals. Overall, therefore, we will once again pick up the four elements which we should be projecting to these local communities:

- *ethics:* the core ethical beliefs by which the company is guided
- *goals:* its goals, with particular reference to those relating to the local communities
- *organisation:* the way in which it has structured its organisation to look after the particular interests of the local communities. This would include the procedures it has put in place to demonstrate local accountability and ensure transparency in its dealings with local people
- *reporting:* a local information service and help office may have been set up, and describing the work of this function could be a useful way to convey several of the desired messages. Also, the company may have sponsored local good causes, and stories of this nature will also be welcome news in the local community.

Distribution

The company will certainly make use of the local newspapers to carry its messages. It may also issue its own local newsletter, or distribute a local version of its in-house magazine. It may make use of advertising in all its various forms, together with local mailings for appropriate issues.

Frequency

As long as the content is sensibly controlled, it is difficult to believe that a company can get too much local publicity. Only if it is consistently behaving in a reprehensible way is it likely to wish to shun the daylight and hide itself away. If a well-run and ethical business makes a mistake, the best way to protect its long-term image is to be as frank as possible and admit its error, while taking all possible steps to compensate local society for any damages suffered.

NOTES

[1] Quotation from Barbarians at the Gate, by Bryan Burroughs and John Helyon, Jonathan Cape, 1990.
[2] *Finanzmeister*, Kendall and Sheridan, Pitman Publishing, 1991.

Chapter 15

WHAT DOES BUSINESS THINK?

Introduction *247*

Responses to Hampel *247*

The popular view *248*

Usefulness of the non-executive director (NED) *251*

Corporate governance at its best *252*

Conclusion *253*

'We must not stifle, we must stimulate. Without prospering business we have no corporate governance.'
Sir Ronnie Hampel, 1996

Introduction

Sir Ronnie Hampel seemed to have struck a chord among industrialist discords with his approach to the task of taking the corporate governance debate forward. Most people shudder at the thought of another code to add to their already onerous 'corporate governance requirements'. However, this view is a little melodramatic, as supporters of recent reforms will agree. Good governance has more to offer than accreditation, as hopefully the reader will be aware by this stage in the book. The main concern now is to put an end to the fuss and nonsense surrounding corporate governance and end the negative feelings towards the subject through effective, practical solutions. Certainly Hampel was expected to pour oil on troubled waters, but initial reactions to the Preliminary Report were mixed.

Responses to Hampel

Hampel's views on (and fears of) over-regulation appear to be shared by the majority of companies and professional organisations. In early 1997, a poll of 200 finance directors for *Accountancy Age* (AA) and Reed Accountancy Personnel showed that while 59 per cent approved of the spirit of the Cadbury report, just 7 per cent would have advocated an increase in corporate governance demands. A similar survey by Binder Hamlyn put the figure at 13 per cent, with only 11 per cent believing that the Cadbury Code should be compulsory under the Stock Exchange's listing rules. And it is not just the finance directors, responsible for implementing the Code, who feel that current requirements are enough of a burden. Of all the memoranda received by the Hampel committee, most of them, including the CBI's, seem to have begged Sir Ronnie to do as little as he could decently get away with.

> There is some contradiction, despite claims in the business press of a unanimous call for a back-pedalling on corporate governance. Some think that self-regulation is the way forward; one finance director questioned in the AA/AP survey said: 'I don't believe corporate governance should increase – we have enough to do as it is'. But another said: 'Self-regulation is a non-starter. Legal regulation should be toughened'.

Professional associations have been less dismissive than many finance directors have been. They believe that codes of best practice are essential, but should not be heavy-handed. The Institute of Chartered Accountants for England and Wales (ICAEW) has produced a report backing the reforms and making sound suggestions for going forward. It makes its case that there is no point in constructing complex systems to improve governance if the wrong people are on the board in the first place. 'A company with a properly balanced board and effective independent directors should be left to run its business with the board being accountable for its stewardship', according to Sir Brian Jenkins, chairman of the Institute's corporate governance committee.[1] The National Association of Pension Funds agrees with the ICAEW. John Rogers, investment services director, talking to *Accountancy* magazine, said that the adoption of better corporate governance practice 'is more likely to emerge from an understanding and relevant interpretation of sound underlying principles than as a result of prescription'.[2] This echoes our certainty that incorporating good corporate governance and ethics into the fabric of the company will eliminate the need for specific rules on the subject (see Chapter 2).

What is also true, and explains certain contradictions, is that different people have different views of what corporate governance actually *is*. Some regard it purely as the issue, that is the codes and recommendations, and related procedures – which in our view is missing the point, as we have repeatedly stressed. In some people this causes an aversion to the very subject of corporate governance – that is, an understandable aversion to externally imposed and therefore often cost-ineffective rules. Each company is different and as a number to whom we have spoken declare in no uncertain terms, these rules often appear to serve no one – least of all the shareholders, whom they are particularly meant to be benefiting! On the other hand, some senior managers positively enthuse about the subject, and have allocated significant human as well as financial resources to improve corporate governance, being convinced that there are consequential benefits in improving overall procedures.

The popular view

We believe that, in some respects, everybody is right, but in different ways – because they are looking at the same subject from different angles. To explain: we recently carried out a survey of some of the biggest UK and European companies, in terms of market capitalisation, to ask their current practice and views of corporate governance.

Attitude towards corporate governance

We were able to divide the responses into three main groups – though this entails some generalisation for the sake of simplicity. These groups were:

1. Those companies who think (rightly or wrongly) that they are already responsible and honest and that corporate governance, with its rules and regulations, is an *unnecessary* and *superfluous* addition to existing requirements (the chairman of a financial institution was an example of this response).
2. Those companies who feel they would be responsible and honest without corporate governance, but nevertheless believe it is *good and necessary* (the company secretary of an international fibres company gave this reply).
3. Those for whom corporate governance is a *high priority* and who believe that it has real benefits, from improving the company's image to actual increased value, especially shareholder value (the company secretary of a large transport company gave this enthusiastic response).

Each of these respondents has a valid point to make, as we explain below:

1. **Superfluous imposition:** the belief that corporate governance is about honesty and competence – very true. And if we are already performing well and honestly, why do we need universal rules which do not take our individual characteristics into account?
2. **Good and necessary:** an appreciation of the need for good corporate governance in the modern company and an acknowledgement of the existence of some (modest) benefits; these respondents do not generally spend resources specifically for corporate governance purposes as they consider it to be what they should be (and are) doing anyway.
3. **High priority:** a commitment to improving standards through corporate governance – paying particular attention to Cadbury and Greenbury – often with the goal of being 'best in class'.

Each presents an angle, but none really encompasses the whole picture; the third group probably comes the closest as it represents the most positive attitude, and many in that group actually try to incorporate good corporate governance into strategy as we recommend. It has been encouraging, among some quite negative sentiments, to see companies like our transportation respondent realising that it is not just about complying with codes – as a kind of label for shareholders to see – but that it has some positive, practical applications.

Perception of results of action taken on corporate governance

Most companies these days have a section in their company reports entitled 'corporate governance'. Usually, however, this is no more than a compliance statement by the directors with a certification from the auditors that they do indeed follow Cadbury and Greenbury (often the wording is taken directly from these reports). This is precisely why corporate governance receives negative reactions – because it is so often perceived as simply Cadbury and Greenbury.

In our survey, this was an area which had a fairly poor rating among boards. The general feeling was that most stakeholders, apart, perhaps, from institutional shareholders, have very little or no interest in the subject of governance. When considering the effort that they perceived that they were putting in for the sake of good governance, this contributed to the feeling of resentment that many companies felt towards having to devote such resources to such an unrewarding purpose.

Benefits of a corporate governance programme

If the Cadbury and Greenbury guidelines had been commercially driven, targets would have been drawn up for benefits to be achieved against the budgeted costs. Sadly, as all readers will know, this was not the way the guidelines were planned or introduced. Therefore it is not surprising that there was a largely neutral to negative response to the questions seeking to establish what benefits had been achieved from introducing the new procedures, under the headings of:

- competitive advantage in the marketplace
- improved efficiency/effectiveness
- increased shareholder value
- increased market value.

It is for this reason that we have proposed the redefinition of corporate governance as not just adherence to rules and standards, but as the need to take all stakeholders into account. Once the benefits of this approach become clear, the inclusion of corporate governance into strategy which we have proposed will become a natural action to take.

Usefulness of the non-executive director (NED)

A relatively sensitive issue at present is that of the usefulness of non-executive directors, now that they are a requirement in the Cadbury statements of good practice. The very title implies that they have less responsibility than executive directors, though in law, of course, there is no distinction, and it is undoubtedly the case that some people still regard such appointments as a well-paid sinecure. This role was questioned in Chapter 7 and discussed again in Chapter 13. We have personally found a degree of scepticism regarding the usefulness and cost-effectiveness of NEDs, especially in the smaller companies which have become subject to the three director recommendation.

A memorable comment was made a few years ago by the chief executive of a large public company when he compared non-executive directors to bidets:

'they both add a touch of class, but no-one is sure what to do with them!'

In the press every week there are stories which can be seen to challenge their effectiveness and value. One example (quoted verbatim from *Accountancy Age*) was related against views expressed by Nigel Maw, partner in Rowe & Maw, the City solicitors.

Case study: The role of NED – one journalist's view

HANSEN PROFITS

Nigel Maw, visiting professor of law, corporate governance guru, and the man who put the Maw in Rowe & Maw, is not a happy man. The reason for his malaise? Too many non-executive directors getting bonuses and share options from their companies.

Speaking at a Baker Tilly seminar last week on the role of the NED, Maw said: 'There's nothing wrong with paying non-executives properly for doing a good job,' … but receiving shares or bonuses clouds the judgement, he believes. What then would Professor Maw make of the little bundle of share options Alan Hansen has received?

The former Liverpool star and now Match Of The Day pundit has been granted £100,000 in share options in Soccer Investments, where he is a non-executive director. That's on top of the £15,000 a year he gets for working at SI one day a month, the hundred grand a year he receives as adviser to Singer & Friedlander's £34m Football Fund, and whatever he gets from the BBC ...

Taken from *Accountancy Age* (24/4/97)

Corporate governance at its best

Unipart

Group chief executive John Neill led a management buy-out from Austin Rover in 1987 and has since seen the value of the business rise 460 times. He is an evangelist for the stakeholding culture – an unswerving commitment to customers, staff, suppliers and the communities in which the company is a significant presence. At the time of the management buy-out, he managed to persuade 50 per cent of the employees to take a stake, generating an initial stake for employees and management of 22 per cent.[3] He subsequently devoted massive effort to internal communications, to involve the staff in the facts of ownership of the business, and to train them both to improve their operational performance and to develop them as people. So successful has this been that, at the time of writing, staff own almost half the company.

In regard to relations with suppliers, Unipart treats its suppliers as long-term partners, working together in supply chain management since it sees its success as inextricably tied to the performance of its trading partners. This formula, and John Neill's inspired leadership, has taken the business to a turnover in excess of £1bn.

John Lewis Partnership

The John Lewis Partnership is a highly successful retailing organisation which has consistently had outstanding performance figures. The company not only practises a very open communications policy with regard to its employees, but since 1929, when John Speedon Lewis put the family assets into a trust for the benefit of past, current and future employees, the company has operated as a partnership with its employees. They participate in the affairs of the company through elected councils and also through elected membership of the board. Under the partnership's constitution, five of the 12 directors hold office by annual election of the partnership's central council. Management has great freedom, but is held strictly accountable by the employees (or partners, as they are called). As John Speedon Lewis put it,

> The supreme purpose of the John Lewis Partnership is simply the happiness of its members.[4]

Thus two key stakeholder groups, the owners and the staff, are united in a unique partnership, bound together by what Stuart Hampson, chairman of John Lewis, called[5] the three key elements:

- the sharing of knowledge
- the sharing of power
- the sharing of gain.

The contract with the all-important customers – the third key stakeholder group – goes back to the beginnings of the business, in 1864, with the unique selling proposition: 'never knowingly undersold'.

The result is that the Partnership outstrips its retail competitors in sales per square foot and has had better returns on fixed assets than Marks & Spencer for 20 years.

Conclusion

Talking enthusiastically about dedication to customers, staff, the environment, local communities and others, is one thing. If the company believes wholeheartedly in the stakeholder approach and implements it in a practical way as expressed in this book, the philosophy will permeate every part of the business. This will shine through in the annual report and it will be apparent that this, rather than external regulation is what corporate governance is all about. 'Corporate governance requirements' then become the more attractive proposition of improving every part of the organisation. This is a course of action which will have clear and measurable benefits, and the key is understanding that good corporate governance is all about uniting under the same banner, and in a common cause, all the parties which have an interest in the company.

NOTES

1 Quoted in an article in the *Financial Times*, 9 January 1997.
2 Rogers, in an article in *Accountancy Age* in February 1997, also said that recent legislation would not have stopped Maxwell. Ron Paterson, technical partner at Ernst & Young, was in no doubt: 'If Maxwell were alive today he would have been given a clean bill of health.'
3 Detail drawn from article in *Accountancy Age* 5 June 1997.
4 *Business Performance in the retail sector, the Experience of the John Lewis Partnership*, Keith Bradley and Simon Taylor, Clarendon Press, 1992.
5 Address to the Institute of Directors Annual Convention, 1997.

Part C

CORPORATE GOVERNANCE IN PRACTICE

Two case studies to illustrate corporate governance in practice

Chapter 16

A LARGE INSURER

UNITED FRIENDLY INSURANCE
Merged with Refuge Assurance
in October 1996
to form United Assurance

History of the company *259*

Current goals *262*

Stakeholder analysis *262*

Conclusions regarding corporate governance *272*

'Richard, the British working man is the salt of the earth. To serve him and his family is an honour and a privilege.'

EDWIN RICHARD BALDING,
founder of United Friendly,
to his son, Richard Courtney Balding,
who was later to head the company himself

United Friendly Insurance was selected as a case study in corporate governance as it had a history and tradition which seemed to embody most of the desirable features of good corporate governance, but had merged with another similar sized insurance company, Refuge Assurance, ending up with 52 per cent of the newly formed United Assurance. It seemed to the authors that the effect of this on the traditional values would be interesting to observe, and the case study therefore focused on the United Friendly side of the new business, with the exception of the community aspect, which will be explained below.

History of the company

Edwin Richard Balding came from insurance stock, his grandfather having been one of the founding members of the Royal Liver Friendly Society, and one of the first managers to open up London, selling life assurance to the industrial classes. His father also was an agent, as were several of his relatives, and young Edwin followed in the family footsteps by joining the Royal Liver at the age of 16, and 10 years later held the job of manager, New Cross Division.

In 1908, at the age of 32 years, he founded his own insurance company, which he called United Friendly, with a product designed specially to serve a local need. The man in the street in Southwark at the turn of the century had plenty of work opportunities by the banks of the busy River Thames, but was vulnerable to loss of work, and hence income, through sickness, and to loss of the contents of his dwelling through fire. Insurance was available, but the yearly premium was out of the question to someone with his level of income, living from hand to mouth. It was not unique, but comparatively rare in those days to find a member of a middle class family who had much of a concern for the problems of the working class, but Edwin Balding was such a man. He set up a scheme which provided 'adequate cover' for sickness or accident and threw in fire insurance cover of £100 within the premium of one penny a week.

A true entrepreneur, he had his financial ups and downs, roping in members of the family to help in the early days, and moving the office several times, even to rooms over a pub at one point. But his belief in what he was trying to build never wavered, and the *Agent's Journal* described the company's policies as 'clean, straightforward contracts, couched in simple language and with no objectionable clauses; in fact they may be said to be unconditional'. These weekly policies continued to be issued for many years and premiums were still being collected on some of them in the 1980s.

By 1921, premium income had risen to £103,264, and there were 24 district offices, almost without exception started by a highly dedicated enthusiast on a bicycle, working very long hours and operating from his own home. At that stage, there were no targets for staff, but Edwin Balding fostered the spirit of competition, and awarded the United Friendly Challenge Cup to the manager whose district showed the most progress during the year.

Progress continued rapidly, and in 1931 the *Agent's Journal* and *Official Gazette* reported that the United Friendly had made record progress in the preceding year, increasing premium income to £323,739, and remarking that 'marked progress is being maintained over 1931 ... [which] ... goes to show the value of the stimulus afforded by staff ownership of the shares in the company and a liberal pension fund'. By the advent of World War II, there was an office in nearly every city and major town in England and Wales, and a small number of offices in Scotland and Northern Ireland.

As war ensued, United Friendly's concern with its policyholders' security caused it to introduce a war risks extension to its major policy, at trivial cost, thereby prompting its rivals to predict disaster. In the event, it served the company and its policyholders well, proving the foresight and courage of the directors.

In 1941, Edwin Balding died unexpectedly, to be succeeded by his son, Richard Courtney Balding, then aged 33. To succeed his entrepreneurial and inspirational father in those difficult war-time conditions was a tough task, and raised uncertainty as to whether his father's ideas and ideals would live on. He took over a company with a premium income of £1m a year and was as quiet and introverted as his father had been outgoing and flamboyant. However, he had been brought up in the atmosphere of the business, being taken by his father as a boy to meetings with managers in a local pub on a Sunday morning, and later joining the firm at the age of 19 as an agent. He showed the ability to build the business and in seven years had grown the company by 300 per cent. He appointed a second generation United Friendly man, AY Radford, his right hand man as agency manager, and progressively built a powerful management team. At the same time, during the war years he shared the firewatching duties with his staff and played billiards and darts with them, building a reputation as a friend, as well as an employer.

As with his father, Richard Balding refused to set targets, but he ensured that milestones in progress by individuals were suitably acknowledged. These included a gold watch for managers who achieved a district premium increase, a bonus for agency staff based on the district's progress in the year, and a week's extra salary twice a year as a bonus for head office staff. Interestingly, this acknowledgement of performance became two way, as the staff adopted the practice of making a presentation at divisional dinners to Mr and Mrs Balding. At his retirement presentation party after 50 years, in 1977, he was able to say, in his reply to the toast, that

> When mixing with the chairmen of other companies, I have heard them say, 'You know, Balding, we never hear of one of your staff talking badly about their office. This is unique in our industry!' – that made me extremely proud of my staff.

By this stage the company had a premium income of £60m per annum, and by the time of his death in 1980, it had risen to £110m. His successor as chief executive and later chairman, was John Rampe, a grandson of the founder, who was also held in high regard and great affection throughout the company. He presided over steady growth through the 1980s and the move through a USM quote until the formation of a group holding company, United Friendly Group plc, and a full stock market listing in 1991, by which time premium income had more than doubled to £237m. By 1996, when the move was made to merge with Refuge Assurance, Richard Edwin Balding, also a grandson of the founder of United Friendly, and by this time himself chief executive, presided over a company with over 130 branches throughout the United Kingdom, and group shareholders' funds exceeding £0.5bn. In nearly 90 years, he was only the fourth chief executive.

After the merger with Refuge, the United Assurance combined business was roughly double the size, with shareholders' funds exceeding £1bn, an embedded value of £1.5bn, and market capitalisation slightly higher still, ranking it as Britain's fourth largest home service insurer. Thus in just short of 90 years the business had grown from a start-up to a value in excess of £1.5bn.

The remainder of this case study examines what has happened to corporate governance in United Friendly over this period, and particularly in the light of the dramatic changes in the last few years.

Current goals

A corporate video was made shortly before the merger discussions commenced, in which the directors expressed to employees the following objectives:

- against the background of an increasingly competitive marketplace, the company's objectives, over the next five years, were to be:
  - the leader in its chosen market sector
  - a well-known name in financial services
- these objectives were to be achieved through:
  - a relevant product range
  - an excellent investment performance
  - a service standard second to none
- the market would see:
  - a developing company
  - a company dealing in a highly professional way with individual clients
  - a modern, up-to-date company but a friendly one with a human face.

The view was that the company would be different, but one of which the staff could be proud. The message to the staff was: 'to be the best'.

Stakeholder analysis

To determine the overall picture of corporate governance in action in United Friendly, recognising that it is now part of a larger entity, we interviewed each of the main categories of stakeholder, namely:

- owners
- customers
- employees
- suppliers
- community.

The results of these discussions are summarised below.

Owners

A large institutional shareholder was interviewed. He first expressed his views of corporate governance.

My company always tries to be whiter than white, but the corporate governance industry seems to have gone beyond control. There were some good aspects – abuses needing to be controlled – but it is political correctness gone mad. Worrying more about the chairman than the business. Cadbury produced good guidelines, but the whole business has gone way over the top, and if it continues there will be a reaction against it.

His concern was his responsibility to 'look after other people's money'.

His company's expectations were, he felt, quite 'self-centred', and his view on any particular course of action by the board was governed by the answer to the question: 'Is that action in the shareholders' interests?'.

He did, however, believe that the management needed to take account of the other stakeholder groups, particularly the customers and employees, and of the various groups, he felt that the customer was the most important.

While he suggested in a self-deprecating way that he used 'seat of the pants' judgement, this judgement was clearly based on a lifetime of experience, and his guiding principles were:

- the 'top line' – sales – was of key importance
- his fund looked on itself as a medium/long-term investor
- they would support management as long as they seemed competent.

He had invested in United Friendly at an early stage of their public status, 10 years previously, and had not been aware of any corporate governance issues since that time other than the recognition of the potential difficulty of getting beyond the family business dimension with its blocking shareholding. His initial shareholding had been through a Small Company Fund, and he had added to his holding over the subsequent years, currently owning a little under 2.5 per cent. Representing a fraction of a per cent of his total funds invested, this was clearly a small investment for him, but one which he felt had been well judged.

His contact with management was to meet them over lunch once a year, this being adequate for his needs, and he found them open and informative at these meetings.

Customers

Interviewing a representative sample of the total policyholder body was beyond the scope of this case study, and getting the views of this group was addressed by interviewing the senior manager responsible for marketing, who had conducted recent studies of policyholders, viewing a series of interviews with policyholders and interviewing a typical policyholder of long standing.

The policyholders selected in the film were very similar in background to our interviewee, and, reassuringly, the views they expressed in the film coincided very closely with those of our interviewee.

Our policyholder, Anthony, had taken out his first policy in 1969 when working as a signalman in Scotland. He had moved to the south east in 1973 and remained there ever since, with the same United Friendly agent, Terry, from that time up to the present day.

He had taken out his policy as a result of a family introduction to United Friendly, and in turn had been instrumental in his oldest child taking out a policy with the company. Interestingly, and possibly indicative of the breakdown of tradition, his second child had chosen a different insurer with whom to start a savings scheme.

His relationship with Terry, as the United Friendly representative, had started out as that of agent/client, but had developed over the years into good friendship, and for years they have played golf together. (This friendship, incidentally, was paralleled in the filmed interviews.) He looked to his friend for advice in financial matters and trusted him absolutely. Terry never goaded him into taking out a new policy, but explained everything fully – 'He is that type of person'. And Terry has become friends with the whole family.

Anthony had met one other salesman from United Friendly on a couple of occasions, but essentially, Terry was the only person in United Friendly that he knew, and Terry provided all the contact that he wanted or needed from the company.

He had never had a problem until this week, when an administrative mistake wrongly caused a policy to lapse through non-payment of premium, but this was quickly corrected by the office. He still enjoyed home collection of premiums.

Regarding the merger with Refuge, he knew very little about it. He had had no communication from United Friendly on the subject, but Terry had kept him informed as a friend. He felt that though it probably wouldn't affect him personally, he would have expected to be informed by the company regarding the question: 'would it affect my policy?'. No one had told him what was going to happen: 'the customer's been left in the dark to a certain extent'. His only other concern was that if Terry was made redundant as a result of the merger, and they introduced someone else, this would end the close client/agent relationship he had enjoyed all these years.

His expectations from the company were that he needed an agent to offer him advice in his dealings with United Friendly. It was not personal enough over the telephone – he wanted the human contact. Moreover, he still liked the contact after he had bought a policy. Service was very important; he could go to their office, but preferred a home visit. He drew a comparison with home delivery of milk: the milkman costs more, but people want the convenience.

Having said this, he felt that it would not make much difference to him at his time of life if the agents and home service were discontinued.

Employees

We took a vertical section through the organisation, talking to representatives of top management, middle management, junior management and staff. Their views are summarised below.

a. Top management

We interviewed one of the directors. He regarded himself as having a responsibility to several groups of people, in particular:

- his staff:
  - developing them
  - making sure the company treated them properly
- the clients:
- ensuring that existing clients were properly serviced
- delivering performance
- ensuring that the company was in proper shape to serve clients in the future
- his colleagues:
- delivering the performance that they expected from the function for which he was responsible; mainly a financial target
- shareholders:
- a broad responsibility for delivering his part of the business objectives
- the regulator:
- ensuring the company's compliance with the panoply of regulations governing its activities, though employing stainless steel in procedures rather than gold-plate
- ensuring that the regulator was happy

He saw the board's duties as being:

- to run the company properly ...
- ... through honest endeavour ...
- ... making a profit ...
- ... for the future well-being ...
- ... for all stakeholders ...
- ... concerning themselves with where the business was going.

He believed that they currently were doing this well. They did look after all the stakeholders, and it was rare to find dissatisfied people – at least prior to the strains of the merger.

The vision and mission statement stressed: *client first*, though there was probably still some way to go before this achieved full acceptance from the staff.

Regarding the merger, he felt that the effects on the company were likely to be:

- short-term pain, involving significant staff reductions, for long-term gain
- long-term protection for the stakeholders generally, and particularly the shareholders. In this regard, it is interesting to note that 60 per cent of the staff are shareholders.
- a perception (inevitable?) that the equation had been couched in terms of financial rather than human costs.

In regard to the last point, he drew attention to the traditional paternalism running through the bones of the company, which readers will have noted from History of the company – page 259, and the reverence in which Richard Edwin Balding was held throughout the company. It was likely that the philosophy underlying the merger would be seen in a very different light.

The merging with the traditionalist, and different culture of the Refuge, would also create strains, and he drew attention to the particularly good staff and union relations which United Friendly had enjoyed over the years, approaching personal friendship between the individuals concerned, and hoped the long-standing relationships built up over the years would not be damaged by the process of combining the two companies and taking on board the unfamiliar staff relations of the other workforce.

Regarding corporate governance generally, though United Friendly complied with the Cadbury Code, he felt that they did not really talk about it much: they simply knew what was the right way to behave.

b. Middle management

We interviewed a middle ranking manager, who was part of the team executing the merger programme. Her concerns were, naturally, mainly focused on the merger process, and as a long-standing United Friendly employee, she was sensitive to the culture changes that were under way.

Above all, she believed that they had to take account of the need to change, under market pressures, in a mature industry such as insurance. Hence, when mergers were needed, the company had to take account of the greater good, since everyone was potentially at risk as the environment grew more hostile.

In the present circumstances, Dr George Mack, as the chief executive of the newly created United Assurance, was representing the interests of both constituent organisations – a difficult balance to maintain. In her perception, for his part, representing United Friendly before the merger, Richard Balding had shown great concern about staff, and once convinced about the overall strategic imperative, had ensured a generous package for those who were to leave. Of great concern too was the need to keep staff with skills critical to the success of the merger, felt to include:

- those with the knowledge and experience to make the integration happen
- sufficient strength in numbers to carry through key aspects of best practice from the United Friendly culture and procedures into the newly combined business

and these key staff were rewarded for their loyalty and the disruption to their lives caused by managing the transition projects.

Once the decision had been taken, the merger process had been thoroughly planned by Dr Mack, and a series of workshops had been run for as many middle managers as possible, initially at a high level then at a detailed level. She felt she spoke for all her colleagues when she said that Dr Mack had impressed by his availability and openness, and his willingness to answer every question, however big or small.

Regarding the customers' views, she referred to a special team which had been established to aim at achieving zero client defection. This was naturally a matter of concern to all. The biggest problem area was seen as managing clients through this time, as the organisation was clearly vulnerable to damaging behaviour by any disenchanted staff in the sales and collection forces. This was taxing the minds of the branch managers, particularly in the knowledge of the staff reductions that were known to be coming, and not much mitigated by the belief that 'best of breed will survive'.

She felt that no approach had to her knowledge been made directly to customers, though branch staff had been briefed on questions that might be asked and answers that should be given.

Overall, as leader of one of the key systems integration teams, she saw her role as being to provide a seamless transition for customers, including changes in collectors. She saw this as requiring the full-hearted support of local managers, who must recognise their responsibility in this respect, and in turn be supported by good systems, education and central support.

c. Branch manager and agent

We had an interesting discussion with one of the senior branch managers and one of his most experienced agents. Both had been with United Friendly for 36 years, and both were steeped in the ethics and culture.

Looking back over the years, the manager commented that he 'would have lived and died for United Friendly'. He 'would have done anything for United Friendly and for Richard Balding'. He had known Richard for years, had an excellent personal contact, and that was how he felt. Over the years, he used to trust him completely; the company *was* Richard Balding.

Not unnaturally, perhaps, he could not look forward with the same enthusiasm to his role in the new company, since the merger would change for ever his familiar way of life which had all these caring connotations, both for staff and for customers. Indeed, he had said as much to Richard Balding recently.

His agent colleague had joined United Friendly from school, following in the footsteps of his father who had been with United Friendly in 1936, and rode 600 miles a week on the company's business. He had known Richard Balding's father and his uncle, Noel, and one of the previous chairmen, Peter Williams, had played cricket with his own father.

He appreciated that it was now a big company and he supposed that it couldn't go on like it used to. He stressed the degree of trust inherent in the relationships between company and staff, and between agent and client. 'The agent *was* the company to the client, and the customer had *total trust* in the agent.'

Obviously there had been the occasional bad apple, but it had caused great hurt to the rest of the staff when they heard about it. Now, with legislation doing the job of moral standards it was not the same, and no longer a family business.

One of the greatest sadnesses resulting from the merger was to learn that the company was to leave its traditional home in Southwark and move to Wilmslow, the home of Refuge.

Regarding his clients, he felt let down. His customers were asking: 'What's going to happen, will the agent still call?'; 'Will policies still be honoured?'.

It was felt that only a small proportion of customers knew about the merger even six months after it had happened. Possibly the merger ought to be marked with a distribution, like the mutuals on demutualisation! How would the shareholders react?

He saw a precedent with the Prudential where he felt they were seen as losing personal contact. He felt that the lower echelons were not being adequately served by the insurers, and that home service was still desired. He gave the cry of field staff everywhere that Head Office had not listened enough in the early years to their advice regarding the development of new products, citing child endowments, and right to buy house purchases as opportunities to lead which had been missed through delayed introduction.

Why had the apparently good channels of communication to the board not worked in these cases? It seems that the head office to field hierarchical forces were in these instances strong enough to block the lines which the family culture normally kept open.

Overall, though, he described a culture with immensely strong loyalty, reflected in a lower than average staff turnover rate. Developments over recent years, driven by the needs of the profit and loss account and balance sheet, had threatened the very existence of that loyalty and his earnest wish was to see it become again the thread running through the company.

As senior manager and senior agent, they both saw youngsters driven by a desire to maximise their income, with no loyalty towards the company. None of the new boys would contemplate the 7.00am to 9.00pm day of the traditional agent, or his primary concern for the customer's needs before thinking of his own commission.

d. Staff association

We met one of the union representatives, who was complimentary about management's conduct of the merger, giving it 8–9 out of 10 for the way it had been handled. He saw the merger as an attempt to preserve the home service ethos by creating a competitive company which would be strong enough to continue this business, and was a supporter of the overall process because he recognised the strength of the competitive pressures in the marketplace.

One of his concerns lay in the client trust relationship which was at the centre of the home service business, and whether this might be put at risk by the rationalisation of the two agent networks.

A second concern lay in the changing way in which the 'people at the sharp end' were regarded. Continuity of agent, and investing in the relationship with his clients, was not apparently seen as so crucial any more, and agents were changed without due regard for the effect. More emphasis was needed on motivation. Was it in the best interests of policyholders if sales performance, promotion and career paths had priority over this client relationship? Was this perhaps a reaction to the demands of the stockmarket, and the need to report to shareholders? Was the customer really getting the necessary consideration? Home service depended on this.

Interestingly, he felt that regulation had gone too far, and that regulatory bodies were interfering, having an adverse effect on the whole business. Clients were having to have very full documents filled in which they didn't want. He felt that the continuing pressure would affect the whole industry and the costs of compliance would have to be taken out of the salary bill, and the result would be less time that could be spent with the client, and that regulation could kill the industry.

Suppliers

We talked to two suppliers: one of United Friendly's two IT providers, and its auditor.

a. Unisys

The Financial Sales Director of Unisys was Paul Millard, and his objective in his dealings with his client, United Friendly, was to achieve an open business relationship. By this he meant a relationship in which:

- total trust prevailed
- his client could tell him confidential information
- advice and guidance could be given on the basis of this trust
- his advice to his client would be based on his understanding of the client's mission and strategy.

Equally, Unisys had to be as honest with its client, and admit its own limitations, for instance if it could not supply as requested.

This mutual honesty was the basis for a fruitful ongoing relationship. This relationship was strong enough to survive the occasional hiccup, and with this degree of trust, price rarely became an issue.

To provide the best service, what he needed was knowledge of his 'client's client', and this was the crucial difference between his relationship with United Friendly and that with some of his more old-fashioned customers who preferred to 'squeeze out the last drop of juice'.

Service Level Agreements are the name of the game today, as part of a business partnership relationship. They, at Unisys, saw United Friendly as a model client.

b. Price Waterhouse

The audit partner, Kieran Poynter, did not regard himself as a stakeholder. His expectation of his customer was that it would run the business in such a way as not to damage the reputation of Price Waterhouse, its supplier, and of course that it would pay its bills in accordance with the agreed terms. Price Waterhouse's role as auditor made it different from other suppliers because of its exposure.

In his view United Friendly complied with the spirit as well as the letter of Cadbury.

Community

The impact on the local community in Southwark of the closure of the United Friendly head office is unlikely to be significant in terms of local employment since few of the staff live locally, and there are many other large local employers. Moreover, the loss of local spending by employees during and outside their working hours can have only a relatively modest local impact in Southwark. We considered the situation of Refuge as a relatively large employer in Wilmslow, but discovered that it was a recent arrival, having migrated from central Manchester eight years ago. Hence, though it was a big change for all concerned, the impact on local employment was limited by the fact that they brought most of their staff with them, and these still related to Manchester. Subsequently, they have been seen as seeking to build links with the local community, but frankly, the representatives of the local community didn't express to us any strong desires for additional activity in this direction.

Conclusions regarding corporate governance

How do the interviews described above portray United Friendly against our definition of the wider view of corporate governance? Let us consider them against our Five Golden Rules.

Ethics

There has been a strong core ethic in United Friendly from its inception, to care for the needs of the less advantaged members of society, and to instil in its employees a strong sense of this duty. This still permeates the business, but as the customer base ages the market pressures may take the company into different fields where this approach may not be familiar, or even appropriate. Such a change would require a clear-sighted and clearly expressed view of the appropriate ethical stance. Similarly, the early decision not to target salesmen, but to encourage competition by peer pressure and reward personal progress, has been superseded in modern times by widespread targeting. The effect on personal motivation will emerge as time goes on, but it seems likely that change will occur in the traditional attitude towards the client. The ethical lead will have to come clearly and loudly from the top of the business.

Goals

The goals have been recently expressed in a corporate video, but prior to the recent merger. Compared with the goals of the founder, Edwin Balding, the current objectives, worthy though they are, lack something of the founder's clear focus. The interviews indicate a drive and purpose to succeed at senior levels, but further from head office, and most importantly at customer level, this clarity of goal and common sense of purpose may not yet be coming through.

Strategic management

A strategic management approach to running the business is evident in the company's strategic view of the insurance marketplace, culminating in the decision to seek a merger of equals to sustain United Friendly's continuing presence in the home service market. The planning of the merger has clearly been thought through in detail and is being implemented smoothly, with acceptance from most of the stakeholder groups. There is predictable concern in the most threatened employee areas of duplicated head offices and overlapping sales forces, and the carefully planned briefings appear to have taken the edge off the worst scenarios of potential disaffection. Where planning seems to have struck difficulties, or suffered a blind spot, is in the customer interface, relying on the field sales force – itself a vulnerable element – to cover this exposed flank.

Organisation

The organisational structures set up over the years seem to have handled the needs of each of the main stakeholder groups to their satisfaction. Hence the institutional shareholders appear happy with the structure and behaviour of the board and senior management. Employees have benefited by an enlightened management since the early days, with open channels to the highest levels. Customers seem to have been well served by the home service agency network and branch structure, and an important supplier is pleased with the operational arrangement established between the two organisations. The merger process, with its substantial elimination of administrative and sales posts and the closure of the long established Southwark head office, means that the continuing effectiveness of these arrangements cannot be taken for granted and must be subjected to close review in the coming months and years.

Reporting

Accountability is all about transparency, and this means regular reporting of relevant information in a comprehensible form to all concerned parties. The interviews indicated a long tradition of trust, particularly in regard to staff and customers. The relatively recent transition from a family company into a large quoted business with institutional owners, followed recently by a merger of near equals with another insurer, must have put a strain on this tradition. Particular care would seem to be needed now to address the issue of communication to the three key groups: customers, owners and staff, as the company enters its next stage of development as a Footsie 100 company. Trust takes years to build up, but, like a reputation, is lost very quickly, and transparency is the best safeguard against trouble developing out of sight of one or other of the stakeholders.

Chapter 17

A SMALLER, FAST-GROWTH COMPANY

PHOTOBITION GROUP
A company specialising in graphic display, which floated on the UK Stock Exchange in the Spring of 1995

History of the company *277*

Current goals *278*

Stakeholder analysis *279*

Conclusions regarding corporate governance *282*

'There is no point in wasting shareholders' money on a non-executive chairman who doesn't contribute anything.'

EDDIE MARCHBANKS,
chairman and chief executive

Photobition was selected as a case study as it contains in its recent history the elements of transition from a family business through acquisition of outside shareholders to a full listing. In the process, it has had to face most of the requirements of good practice in corporate governance which thereby arise, and which are addressed in Chapter 5.

History of the company

Photobition was originally set up as a photography business in the early 1960s in south London, by photographer Mick Green. As the business grew, Mick came increasingly into competition with another local photographer, Bob Bushby, who had the edge in business ability. The result was a decision by Mick to offer an equal share in Photobition to Bob and thus absorb the new competitor. Bob, in due course, became chairman and managing director.

The business grew steadily, outgrowing the original premises, and in the early 1970s the major decision was taken to acquire the freehold of a former laundry in Fulham. This provided the space to expand and the company progressively developed a reputation in large-scale photographic display, together with a number of related services including design and printing.

During this phase of expansion, this was a family business, employing Bob's wife and stepson, Phil Parkinson, though an exception was made by granting a stake to a young, energetic and able manager, Eddie Marchbanks.

Following some years of successful growth, the opportunity arrived in the late 1980s to realise the latent capital value, and after discussions with one of the leading marketing services groups, WPP, the company was eventually sold to a smaller company, FKB. The benefits of the deal included an earn-out agreement which valued the business at a potential £12m over the next five years, and which the directors looked set to achieve. The downside was that the assets of the business, which at takeover included nearly £1m of cash on deposit, were pooled in a cross guarantee arrangement with the parent company. The sad consequence was that when FKB went bust some three years later, the earn-out was only half completed, and the guarantee was called by the liquidator, thereby removing a million pounds from the still profitable and expanding subsidiary, Photobition. The directors of Photobition then were faced with the prospect of their company being sold over their heads by the liquidator or making a bid themselves.

In a private agreement, Eddie Marchbanks persuaded his colleagues to make their own bid as the management team. His promise was that if they allowed him an equal 25 per cent stake, and the role of *de facto* managing director, he would generate value equivalent to the £5m lost balance of the earn-out, and realise this for them within five years. Their record as a successful management team won the day in negotiations with the liquidator, and their reputation with the bank enabled them to borrow back the same million pounds that the bank had taken from them in the liquidation, moreover without giving any personal guarantees!

Over the next four years Eddie Marchbanks drove the business very hard, with shrewd backing and support from Bob as chairman, building by a combination of organic growth and bolt-on acquisitions. He also justified the bank's faith in the company by repaying all the original indebtedness, even while growing rapidly and coping with the effects of the early nineties recession.

By 1994 Eddie was exploring the route to a listing, and in February 1995, as chairman and chief executive of the company, he was able to fulfil his promise to his colleagues. Photobition Group raised £8.5m in a flotation, £5.1m of which went to the directors, the remainder being used in the business. The flotation price valued the company at £15.5m, and since then, the company has grown rapidly, the market valuation at the time of writing being £80m.

Current goals

The goal is simply stated as being to grow rapidly, probably using acquisitions, and to build the value of the business aggressively in the process, but not to take excessive risks by moving too far away from the core skills and experience.

Stakeholder analysis

Owners

Eddie Marchbanks still owns 10 per cent of the company and he and his colleagues are still significant shareholders, but we wanted to get the views of an outsider, so we talked to one of the new institutional shareholders which holds about 11 per cent of the equity. The views expressed were as follows:

The stake in Photobition was held within their policy of having stakes of between 0.5–15 per cent in small companies – defined as having turnover less than £300m. They did not require board representation.

Regarding *ethics*, they would always interview management to form a view, and would avoid companies which had teams which had failed in the past. Moreover, they were impressed by Photobition's introduction from a good City broker, Henderson Crossthwaite, whose respectability and reputation were thereby associated with Photobition.

Their *goal* was to achieve what they called 'total return', by which they meant 'income and capital growth'. They tried to be long-term investors, but wouldn't stick with a situation if the reasons for the original attractiveness changed, particularly if this happened within the first six months. Thereafter, there was no particular definition of a natural exit point.

Their preference was for organic growth over acquisition-based growth, and they were wary of new technology that they didn't understand. They looked to being in growth markets and to their investee having a strong competitive position in these markets. They constantly watched risk levels in relation to returns, and were keen to avoid nasty surprises.

Regarding the *organisation* of the company and the way it was run, they looked to a balance on the board, and were mainly concerned about the company's continuing dependence on Eddie, though recognising that he was taking steps to put the necessary structures and systems in place to remedy this. They were not worried about Eddie being both chairman and chief executive; possibly separating the roles could be appropriate at a later date.

In terms of *communication*, they were reassured by the closeness to customer which appeared to be achieved by the route through the sales force direct to Eddie providing a good sensitivity to the market. Equally he seemed to be close to his staff.

In relation to themselves, they reckoned to meet Eddie twice a year and to attend the AGM. They had also been invited to visit sites, and perceived an assiduous will to keep them informed. For instance, when sales one month were below forecast, he had taken the trouble to give them a special briefing to explain why it had happened and what steps were being taken to prevent its recurrence. Eddie 'always answered questions directly', and they felt that if they asked the right questions, they would get the right answers.

Clearly they trusted Eddie.

Customers

We interviewed a customer whose relationship went back 25 years, and which placed nearly £200,000 pa with Photobition.

They took a serious view of *ethical* behaviour, and interpreted this as including:

- social obligations, as in the health and safety of staff, and not dumping chemicals into the drains
- being open and honest, particularly regarding accuracy on invoicing and avoiding 'slippage' between the quote and the ultimate bill.

In their view, Photobition was an ethical company overall, and had dealt promptly with the few incidents when staff had let them down by lapses from the high standard expected.

Their *goal* was to achieve 'a profitable relationship for both of us'. They were using clients' money, so needed to get the best deal for those clients, but they recognised the need for Photobition to be profitable if it was to give them the level of service they needed.

Secondly, they worked on total trust with their own clients, and had back-to-back deadlines between suppliers and clients, so had to have a similar degree of trust with their suppliers.

Organisationally, they admired the strong leadership evident in Photobition, and the only area for concern was the consequential one in relation to Eddie and planning for succession, though this had been dealt with at the contractual level.

There was a good working relationship with open *communication*, and a very professional photographic relationship. Both parties worked at maintaining the openness of communication channels by visiting each other's premises and ensuring that staff knew each other at both senior and junior levels.

Management processes

We interviewed the chairman and chief executive, Eddie Marchbanks.

Eddie's goal for the business is summarised earlier.

His *organisational* approach allowed for non-executive directors, but only ones who pulled their weight. An independent perspective was necessary, but the individual must be constructive. Since floating, he had parted company with one whose main concern appeared to be his remuneration, but another he described as very active, 'an asset ... I would pay double to keep him'. Regarding the Cadbury recommendation to split the roles of chairman and chief executive, he was adamant that there was no point, in his view, in having a non-executive chairman and wasting his shareholders' money on someone who didn't contribute anything.

At present, Eddie effectively runs the business himself, but he is building a management team which he expects to be fully in place in the next 12 months. This is an evolutionary process as he has found some managers couldn't manage the necessary transition from a relatively small business to a relatively large one, and he has been forced to make some changes since flotation. From his own perspective, he felt that good corporate governance in relation to shareholders meant putting shareholder value before personal loyalties. In relation to staff, his approach was exemplified by a young manager to whom he had given divisional profit responsibility, and whose success he had motivated by bonuses and options. This manager had now benefited accordingly over three years by a trebled salary, substantial bonuses and share options which could make him a millionaire in another couple of years.

Regarding customers, he said that consumer sovereignty was still the cornerstone of company philosophy.

Eddie's approach to *communications* was to be open about everything to his stakeholders. He had always maintained this policy of transparency towards his institutional shareholders, giving bad news with good news, and having no 'dark horses'. He believed this policy was positive and earned trust. In his view, many companies complained about having to 'disclose' more than they used to as a result of Cadbury and Greenbury, and would still prefer to keep their secrets. From the perspective of his institutional shareholders, disclosure was not a relevant word; he kept them all informed as a matter of course.

He felt that because of his approach to his stakeholders, that is complete transparency, he was naturally applying good corporate governance to his company to a better extent than many companies that had a non-executive chairman. After all, he said, especially during times of such rapid growth, he was far more committed to the company than a non-executive and could be looked up to by his staff not only as a leadership figure but as an example of what could be achieved through hard work and dedication.

Conclusions regarding corporate governance

Ethics

The views of two of Photobition's significant shareholders and customers describe a company which has been able to adhere to a set of ethical standards through difficult times as well as periods of high growth. These appear to be exemplified by top management's behaviour and to be enforced down the organisation.

Goals

There appears to be good congruence of goals between the company and its key stakeholders. Clearly, doubling or trebling the size of the business over the next few years and perhaps taking it into other parts of the world in global expansion, would require care in maintaining this close relationship, particularly regarding views of risk and reward. At this point, however, the company's expressed and implemented policy implies that such steps would not be undertaken before full consultation with all interested parties.

Organisation

The organisational arrangements made by the company appear to look after the interests of the various stakeholder groups to their satisfaction, at least at the present time. Eddie Marchbanks is perceived as a hard-driving but fair manager whose concern with customers keeps him close to the market. He is in the early days of learning to deal with the City and institutional shareholders, and as long as he delivers results, it is unlikely that anyone will seriously complain about his refusal to accept a non-executive chairman. Should he start to make mistakes, this acquiescence will probably disappear overnight, and the debate should probably be whether he needs a non-executive chairman as a sounding board to keep his judgement honed.

Reporting and communication

The company seems to have adopted a commendable openness in its dealings with its institutional stakeholder group, which is likely to stand it in good stead. Regarding the customers, the nature of its core business demands a high standard of communication, and at its present size a chief executive who is a good manager will be able to keep his finger on the pulse of its employees without too much difficulty. If the company continues to grow successfully, it is likely that attention will have to be devoted to formalising systems of communication with both of these groups as the relationships become more complex.

APPENDIX A

A Stakeholder Model – measuring stakeholder views

Background – a summary of the methodology

This model is designed to enable the user to see at a glance the current views of all the company's stakeholders and set quantifiable goals (normally only achieved in budgeting) for this aspect of the strategy process; it also allows effective monitoring of progress. The model is constructed using information obtained during the internal, external and stakeholder analyses, most importantly stakeholder survey results and profiles of major stakeholders. Since the whole analysis process involves getting to know the company and all its stakeholders inside and out, the stakeholder weighting process described on page 185, which is behind the model, should be fairly straightforward to perform (though the shape of the weighting can only be decided on with experience, and will probably change with time).

Stakeholder weighting shows the amount of power each stakeholder has and how willing or likely each is to act to protect its interests. For ease of reference we reproduce here the sources/indicators of power within and outside a company detailed on page 188.

> **Within** an organisation, the following are the usual **sources** of power:
> - seniority within an hierarchy
> - personal influence
> - personal freedom of decision-making
> - control over key resources within the business
> - key specialist knowledge or skills
> - significant influence over the business environment.
>
> Useful **indicators** of power for internal stakeholders are:
> - status of the individual or group
> - size of their budget
> - representation in powerful positions on boards or committees
> - symbols of power, such as type of company car, size of office.
>
> Regarding **external stakeholders** the usual **sources** of power include:
> - shareholding
> - buyer or seller control over key resources or products
> - involvement through holding a key place in the value chain, like control over distribution
> - key knowledge and skills in relation to the value chain
> - influence through powerful links with key managers.
>
> Useful **indicators** of power for external stakeholders are:
> - large shareholding
> - how their status is perceived by the company's own staff, and how they behave towards them
> - how difficult it is to switch suppliers or replace a lost customer
> - how much at arm's length the other party is treated in any negotiating arrangements.

Analysis of these factors, conducted internally, and results of a survey, including interviews with key stakeholders and larger scale research into the wider stakeholder population – probably conducted by an agency (there should be an independent input to assure neutrality and balance), will be used to form the basis for initial weighting (subject to testing).

Details of the survey are in Chapter 12. It consists of both quantitative research, in the form of a questionnaire, and qualitative research, in the form of focus groups and interviews in which more detailed discussion of the issues is possible. The questionnaire, best conducted through personal interview, aims to find out stakeholders' perceptions of the company's behaviour and performance, and their expectations and hopes for the future. **This will include statements on ethics, goal, organisation and reporting, which respondents will score out of 10.** For those statements referring to their perception of the company, scores will reflect how well they believe the company is performing, represented by the respondent's agreement or not with the statements (1 being totally disagree, 10 being totally agree). As explained on page 182, proxies will need to be used for the four elements when formulating statements, and the wording will need a fair amount of work to ensure that the right information is obtained.

Example

> **Qu. 15** – I would now like you to look at some statements. If the most successful retailers score a full 10 out of 10, how would you rate GCG? If you are unsure, please say don't know. *(Note to interviewer – use number 11 for don't know)*
>
> 1. GCG encourages people like you [ie as customers, employees, etc.] to recycle – eg bottle and clothes banks in the car park ☐
> 5. GCG is never out of stock on the most popular items ☐
> 13. There are ways of expressing my views as a customer/employee/ shareholder, etc ☐
> 19. There is always local community information around the store ☐

The statements refer to 1 – ethics, particularly environmental concern; 5 – organisational considerations, in this case physical environment; 13 – communication, as a proxy for internal organisation; 19 – reporting, of particular information.

The scores for the remaining statements will reflect the stakeholders' expectations, which will be used to calculate the score for goal. This will need an additional process – finding out how close the company's goals are to those of our stakeholders. This is a key part of the model as it represents the company's efforts at achieving congruence of goals. The background to this involves setting down in detail – and in plain English – the company's overall goals and separately, the specific objectives for each stakeholder group. Respondents will then score each of these according to how important the proposed objectives are to them (where 1 is of no importance, and 10 is of great importance). There will then be an opportunity for the respondent to express any other ideas that have not been included (deliberately or by omission) from the list of goals – and to give these a score as well.

In brief, calculating the overall score will be based on a correlation and aggregation of the number and score for each statement – positive for those corporate objectives approved of (represented by a score of, say, 6 out of 10 and above) and negative for the omissions. The overall (average) figure per stakeholder group can then be used to calculate a separate figure for congruence, based on the difference in scores between the five groups. We will therefore have a score representing the difference between expectation and delivery (congruence between the stakeholder and the company) and a score representing the difference between what different groups want (congruence between stakeholder groups).

The scores can then be cross-referred with the other information gathered in the questionnaire, such as geodemographics, to draw up a complete profile of the stakeholders and their interest in and influence over the company. The scores out of 10 themselves will be grouped according to the original research criteria, initially per stakeholder group and then by segmentation criteria. Segmentation will naturally be a matter for individual companies to perform, but examples are geographical area, socio-economic class and/or even business division, etc – that is so that groups contain stakeholders with the most similar characteristics. A further point to make here is that the original five groups will need to be broken down, as for example there are many levels of employees, with different levels of power and interest, and for customers, we need to interview *actual and potential* – logically we need to find out the opinions not only of those who *choose* to use us, but, far more importantly, those who *don't* currently, to find out why and what their needs are, so we can satisfy those needs.

Once all the findings from the research have been collated and put into a logical structure which is not only easy to read but contains the useful cross-references, it is these scores which will be used to construct the main body of the stakeholder model. There are many options to the model, depending on how much or how little information is required – thus a simple, bare bones model can be used for impact, or a more complicated and informative, multi-image one if analysis and troubleshooting is the objective. In any case, the software used to construct the model can be programmed to embed more detailed information within a simple framework. Finally the model uses, amongst other forms of display, circular charts to plot data, so a shape for target values for each area can be mapped against actual values, and combined bar and line charts, for easy and effective comparison and progress monitoring.

Constructing the model

The methodology of this original model contains four main stages, or levels:

I   Collate and mean scores [plot charts – optional]
II   Weight scores [plot charts – optional]
III   Plot charts for weighted scores, per stakeholder group/research element
IV   Produce total unitary models for all stakeholders/all Golden Rules.

I. Collate and mean scores

The questionnaires and interviewing will give an accurate picture of stakeholder opinions. For each response an average score is calculated for each research element per stakeholder. As this means grouping statements together (except for goal), in the event of particularly bad scoring in any area, the original data will obviously need to be consulted for troubleshooting.

Option: These average scores can, if desired, be converted into charts for each stakeholder group. This is optional here since the weighted picture of stakeholder views – which represents the greater influence of key stakeholders in each group – is more relevant to strategy. They are useful for lowest-level diagnostics, though – there may be factors which under normal situations are not significant, but develop underground; these sorts of events will not show up on higher levels because of the weighting process but can still be traced easily if the raw data is presented in visual form.

Example

A group of pensioners, not normally known for activism, are not happy about payment arrangements, which are inconvenient, or certain re-investment plans. Since they usually have very little power their concerns are sometimes sidelined (contrary to our definition of good corporate governance). They decide, therefore, because they live close to each other and can organise themselves, to take action, bringing in the support of some of the younger members of the community working for the company concerned.

This may or may not lead to serious problems, but if there is regular reporting and records are kept up-to-date and checked, this sort of threat can be spotted at this level, and nipped in the bud by quickly introducing corrective measures.

Table A.1 shows the correlation of these scores as averages per research element relating to perception.

Table A.1 Stakeholder group: Customers

	Ethics	Goal	Organisation	Reporting
Sample 1*	5.0	6.0	6.1	5.5
Sample 2	5.8	5.5	5.7	5.5
Sample 3	6.1	6.0	6.0	6.0
Sample 4	6.2	4.5	5.7	5.5
Sample 5	6.9	6.0	8.5	6.5
Total	30	28	32	29
Average	6	5.6	6.4	5.8

* Samples may represent individuals or groups and may represent regions, divisions, etc

These scores effectively represent compliance with the four corresponding Golden Rules of good corporate governance. Since all four relate back to the strategy process ('everything starts and finishes with the strategy process' –

Chapter 9), this means that if an effective strategic management process is in place which takes them into account, the company should automatically score well on these four. Thus a good overall score for all four elements might be considered as representing compliance with the remaining Golden Rule.

Further, the intermediary stage between the position analysis and formulation of strategy (see Figure 12.1 on page 158 and the description on page 193) of confirming or changing the goal, will run parallel and in conjunction with this process, as it involves summing up all the findings from the research. Evaluation of the results emerging in the model will be a guide to the acceptability of the corporate objectives.

Table A.1 shows what appear to be fairly normal variances in scores that are affecting the averages. But what is important here is that the differences in scores should not necessarily affect the average score – because of the weighting. To demonstrate, let us assume that Sample 1 represents an important customer who will probably be placed in the A1 weighting category; let us also assume that the customers in Samples 4 and 5 are fairly small ones, of, say, category B3. We see then, that while those in Sample 4 clearly have quite different objectives to those represented by the company's goal, this may well be simply because of lack of frequent contact due to low purchase levels. In reality, the customer has no major significance in the company: while this issue needs to be addressed (good governance is about treating *all* stakeholders fairly), and the score demonstrates the diagnostic role of this level, it should not affect the overall average so much. This is clearly because it is far more serious if a major client like the customer in Sample 1 is dissatisfied – the score of 5.0 for ethics is far more cause for concern, as much more is at stake. Similarly, the little customer in Sample 5's enthusiastic 8.5 score for organisation brings up the average score to an unreal level – perhaps because he gets on well with the staff. All this demonstrates the need for the next stage of the model.

II. Weight scores

The weighting process has been described in detail above and in Chapter 12. For each group, all stakeholders must be placed in one of the nine categories: on the next page are the suggested values put forward in that chapter, which represent a redistribution of the total score for the stakeholder group.

In other words, it is as if there were 30 times more A1 stakeholders than C3s.

Let us take customers again to demonstrate this stage. After constructing the first level of the model, ie collating the average scores, a table for each of the four elements (which we will revert to calling Golden Rules) must be drawn showing the nine categories A1–C3 and, having placed each customer in one of these (noting who is in each one), the scores are added up for each category and the average score entered in the table, as in the example below. The scores of all categories are then added together using the percentage weighting shown above, ie

APPENDIX A

Fig A.1 Percentage weightings

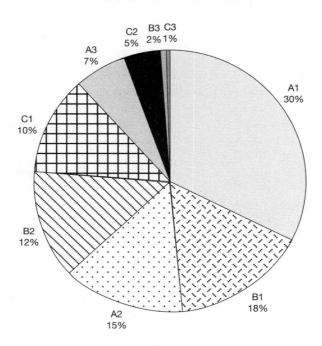

each score is multiplied by its weight figure, 30 in the case of A1, 1 in the case of C3, etc., and the total is divided by 100. Thus the average score is adjusted to better reflect the importance of each stakeholder.

Stakeholder group: Customers
Golden Rule: Ethics

		Hi	Propensity to act	Lo
		will act	**might act**	**unlikely to act**
Hi				
	has power	A1 [30] 6.5	A2 [15] 7.0	A3 [7] 6.0
Ability to influence	**could get power**	B1 [18] 5.5	B2 [12] 6.2	B3 [2] 5.3
	can't get power	C1 [10] 5.0	C2 [5] 6.0	C3 [1] 4.1
Lo				

291

APPENDIX A

Total = 51.6
Average = 5.7
Weighted total = 610(.1)
Weighted average = 6.1

Further, any change in A1's score will cause a much greater fluctuation in the average score than a similar change in C3's, as demonstrated below.

		Hi will act	Propensity to act might act	Lo unlikely to act
Hi	has power	A1 [30] 8*	A2 [15] 8*	A3 [7] 6.0
Ability to influence	could get power	B1 [18] 7*	B2 [12] 6.2	B3 [2] 5.3
Lo	can't get power	C1 [10] 6*	C2 [5] 6.0	C3 [1] 4.1

(* figures changed)

Total increase in score = 5
Original weighted average = 6.1
New weighted average = 5.7
% change in average = 14.1

		Hi will act	Propensity to act might act	Lo unlikely to act
Hi	has power	A1 [30] 6.5	A2 [15] 7.0	A3 [7] 7*
Ability to influence	could get power	B1 [18] 5.5	B2 [12] 6.2	B3 [2] 7*
Lo	can't get power	C1 [10] 5.0	C2 [5] 7*	C3 [1] 6*

(* figures changed)

Total increase in score = 5.6
Original weighted average = 6.1
New weighted average = 6.3
% change in average = 3.2

Option: Before moving on to the next stage, it is an idea, for diagnostic purposes, to plot charts for each category, to show each group's views on the Golden Rules, particularly those of key stakeholders. Once again, this option serves to allow the user to look at the data from another angle – the more directions one looks from, the easier it becomes to find and diagnose problems and address imbalances. At this level, especially, reactions can be measured of particular stakeholder groups towards new policies and strategies. The importance here is the weighting – the lower level just showed all customers, for example, whereas here we can see who are the key ones. Indeed as an additional exercise, customer records could be kept with such charts to help predict movements in the scoring (see also *Using the model to predict strategies*, below).

III. Plot charts for weighted scores, per stakeholder group/Golden Rule

We now have weighted average scores representing all five stakeholder groups' views on each of the four applicable Golden Rules. These can now be picked up easily and plotted into circular charts, as in the example below (which is representative, not accurate) to show visually and instantly to the observer how all parties which have an interest in the company are feeling.

At this stage we will keep the sub-groups separate, thus the chart below is for actual customers – the other sub-group would be the random sample interviewed.

Fig A.2 Weighted average scores

Stakeholder group: actual customers

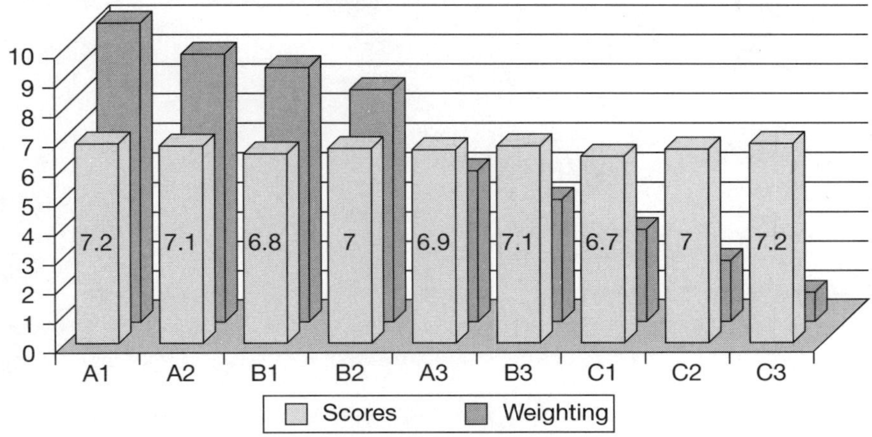

	A1	A2	B1	B2	A3	B3	C1	C2	C3
Scores	7.2	7.1	6.8	7	6.9	7.1	6.7	7	7.2

☐ Scores ■ Weighting

APPENDIX A

IV. Plot total unitary models

An interesting option here is a unitary circular chart, which we call the Kiwi Chart, an example of which is shown below. This shows the overall performance of the company – all stakeholders, all Rules. Since all the Rules are of equal importance, there is no weighting here.

We can then produce two unitary charts:
- one showing the score per stakeholder group, combining all four Rules
- one showing the score per Golden Rule, combining all stakeholder groups.

This can be shown as a progression over time, with a line connecting the groups of bars to show the overall average: that is, all stakeholder groups and all Rules. Finally, this figure – which we call the Corporate Governance Index – can be shown as a separate line chart.

Fig A.3 The Kiwi Chart

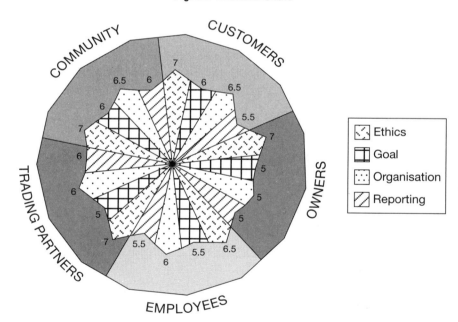

APPENDIX A

Using the model to predict strategies

This model alone will obviously not predict by itself. It needs the input of all other information – the crucial knowledge (or well-informed speculation) gained as a result of the analyses. Armed with this knowledge of stakeholder behaviour, the model can be used to predict reaction to certain strategies – to the extent of displaying physically, via the circular (or Kiwi) charts, the shape of stakeholder rating after particular actions. Choice of strategy is then aided by a clearer perception of consequences: the adjusted shape which best fits the target shape (which will reflect balance, overall survival of the company and the agreed goal) will probably be the best strategic option.

APPENDIX B

Extract from the Preliminary Report from the Committee on Corporate Governance (the Hampel Committee)

2 **Principles of Corporate Governance.**

2.1 We draw a distinction between principles of corporate governance and more detailed guidelines like the Cadbury and Greenbury codes. With guidelines, one asks 'How far are they <u>complied with?</u>'; with principles, the right question is 'How are they <u>applied</u> in practice?'. We recommend that companies should include in their annual report and accounts a narrative statement of how they apply the relevant principles to their particular circumstances. This should not be an additional regulatory requirement, nor do we prescribe the statement's content. But it could conveniently be linked with the compliance statement required by the Listing Rules. Given that the responsibility for good corporate governance rests with the board of directors, the written description of the way in which the board has applied the principles of corporate governance represents a key part of the process.

2.2 Against this background, we believe that the following principles can contribute to good corporate governance. They are developed further in later chapters.

A Directors.

I <u>The Board.</u> **Every listed company should be headed by an effective board which should lead and control the company.**

2.3 This follows Cadbury (report, paragraph 4.1). It stresses the dual role of the board – leadership and control – and the need to be effective in both. It assumes the unitary board almost universal in UK companies.

II <u>Chairman and CEO.</u> **There are two key tasks at the top of every public company – the running of the board and the executive responsibility for the running of the company's business. How these tasks are carried out in each company should be publicly explained.**

2.4 This makes clear that there are two distinct jobs, that of the chairman of the board and that of the chief executive officer. The wording leaves open whether the holders of the two posts need be different people, or whether one person can do both jobs. This is discussed below (3.17–3.19).

III Board balance. The board should include a balance of executive directors and non-executive directors (including independent non-executives) such that no individual or small group of individuals can dominate the board's decision taking.

2.5 Cadbury highlights the need to avoid the board being dominated by one individual (code 1.2). This risk is greatest where the roles of chairman and CEO are combined, though there may be cases where there are important offsetting advantages in combining the roles. But whether or not the two roles are separated, it is important that there should be a sufficient number of non-executive directors, a majority of them independent; and that these individuals should be able both to work co-operatively with their executive colleagues and to demonstrate robust independence of judgement and objectivity when necessary.

IV Supply of Information. The board should be supplied in a timely fashion with information in a form and of a quality appropriate to enable it to discharge its duties.

2.6 We endorse the view of the Cadbury committee (report, 4.14) that the effectiveness of non-executive directors (indeed, of all directors) turns to a considerable extent on the quality of the information they receive.

V Appointments to the Board. There should be a formal and transparent procedure for the appointment of new directors to the board.

2.7 The Cadbury committee commended the establishment of nomination committees but did not include them in the Code of Practice. In our view adoption of a formal procedure for appointments to the board, with a nomination committee making recommendations to the full board, should be recognised as good practice.

VI Re-election. All directors should be required to submit themselves for re-election at regular intervals and at least every three years.

2.8 We endorse the view that it is the board's responsibility to appoint new directors and the shareholders' responsibility to re-elect them. The 'insulation' of directors from re-election is dying out and we consider that it should now cease. This will promote effective boards and recognise shareholders' inherent rights.

B   Directors' Remuneration.

2.9   Directors' remuneration should be embraced in the corporate governance process; the way in which directors' remuneration is handled can have a damaging effect on a company's public reputation, and on morale within the company. We suggest the following broad principles.

I   **The Level and Make-up of Remuneration. Levels of remuneration should be sufficient to attract and retain the directors needed to run the company successfully. The component parts of remuneration should be structured so as to link rewards to corporate and individual performance.**

2.10   This wording makes clear that those responsible should consider the remuneration of each director individually, and should do so against the needs of the particular company for talent at board level at the particular time. The remuneration of executive directors should be linked to performance.

II   **Procedure. Companies should establish a formal and transparent procedure for developing policy on executive remuneration and for fixing the remuneration packages of individual directors. No director should be involved in fixing his or her own remuneration.**

2.11   Cadbury and Greenbury both favoured the establishment of remuneration committees, and made recommendations on their composition and on the scope of their remit. Like Cadbury, we think that the remuneration committee should operate by making recommendations to the board, rather than by discharging functions on behalf of the board. But we would expect the board to reject the committee's recommendations only very rarely.

III   **Disclosure. The company's annual report should contain a statement of remuneration policy and details of the remuneration of each director.**

2.12   This follows Greenbury (code, B.1) except that we do not specify that the statement should be in the name of the remuneration committee. This is in line with our view of the status of the committee.

APPENDIX B

C   Shareholders.

2.13   This section includes principles for application both by listed companies and by shareholders.

I   <u>Shareholder Voting.</u> **Institutional shareholders should adopt a considered policy on voting the shares which they control.**

2.14   Institutional shareholders include internally managed pension funds, insurance companies and professional fund managers. The wording does not make voting mandatory, i.e. abstention remains an option; but these shareholders must consider the merits of an active voting policy.

II   <u>Dialogue between companies and investors.</u> **Companies and institutional shareholders should each be ready, where practicable, to enter into a dialogue based on the mutual understanding of objectives.**

2.15   This gives general endorsement to the idea of dialogue between companies and major investors. In practice, both companies and institutions can only participate in a limited number of one-to-one dialogues.

III   <u>Evaluation of Governance Disclosures.</u> **When evaluating companies' governance arrangements, particularly those relating to board structure and composition, institutional investors and their advisers should give due weight to all relevant factors drawn to their attention.**

2.16   This follows from the discussion in Chapter I, paragraphs 1.11–1.14 on the importance of considering disclosures on their individual merits, as opposed to 'box ticking'.

IV   <u>The AGM.</u> **Companies should use the AGM to communicate with private investors and encourage their participation.**

2.17   Private investors hold about 20% of the shares in listed companies, but are able to make little contribution to corporate governance. The main way of achieving greater participation is through improved use of the AGM. We discuss a number of suggestions for this purpose later.

D   Accountability and Audit.

2.18   This section includes principles for application both by listed companies and by auditors.

I   <u>Financial Reporting.</u> **The board should present a balanced and understandable assessment of the company's position and prospects.**

2.19   This follows the Cadbury code (4.1). It is not limited to the statutory obligation to produce financial statements. The wording refers mainly to the annual report to shareholders, but the principle also covers interim and other price sensitive public reports and reports to regulators.

II **Internal Control.** **The board should maintain a sound system of internal control to safeguard shareholders investment and the company's assets.**

2.20 This covers not only financial controls but operational and compliance controls, and risk management, since there are potential threats to shareholders' investment in each of these areas.

III **Relationship with the Auditors.** **The board should establish formal and transparent arrangements for maintaining an appropriate relationship with the company's auditors.**

2.21 We support the Cadbury recommendation (report, 4.35(a)) that all listed companies should establish an audit committee, composed of non-executive directors, as a committee of, and responsible to, the board. The duties of the audit committee include keeping under review the scope and results of the audit and its cost effectiveness, and the independence and objectivity of the auditors.

IV **External Auditors.** **The external auditors should independently report to shareholders in accordance with statutory and professional requirements and independently assure the board on the discharge of their responsibilities under D.I and D.II above in accordance with professional guidance.**

2.22 This points up the dual responsibility of the auditors – the public report to shareholders on the statutory financial statements and on other matters as required by the Stock Exchange Listing Rules; and additional private reporting to directors on operational and other matters.

INDEX

10:3:1 rule, the, 104–5

Aerospatiale, 45
Ansoff, 197
AT&T, 43, 44
Avis, 197

Belgium, 40
Body Shop, the, 117
Boeing, 44, 45
British Aerospace (BAe), 45
British Gas, 8
BT, 44

Cadbury, 6, 7, 19, 20, 23, 26, 29, 31, 48, 92, 128, 218, 229, 235, 247, 249, 250, 263, 266, 271, 281
report, May 1992, 22
CalPERS (California Public Employees Retirement System), 10, 62, 116
CBI, the, 24, 25, 247
Coats Viyella, 39
company law, British, 16–17, 21, 24, 26–9
competition and competitive advantage, 160, 162, 163, 165, 168, 169, 170, 171, 172, 175–9, 180, 192, 196–7, 201, 202, 208, 270
Concert (telecoms alliance), 44

Dearden Farrow, 200–2
Deutsche Bank, 40, 54–5, 56
Deutsche Telecom, 43–4
direction matrix, 198
Directional policy matrix, 192
directors
duties/roles, 28–9, 105–6, 108, 218–9

remuneration, 5, 6, 9, 114, 129, 221, 229–30, 281
training, 9–10, 223–4
appointment and removal, 221–3

employees
loyalty, 39–41, 55, 80, 126, 139, 194, 238–9, 260–1, 268, 269
representation, 20, 40, 53–4, 60, 63–4, 65, 96, 107, 252–3
Endesa, 43–4
ethical marketing, 138, 140

Financial Services Act 1986, the, 7, 32, 114
five forces analysis, 175–7
France Telecom, 43–4
France, 40, 45, 56–9, 64, 118

Gates, Bill, 44
Germany, 20, 38, 40, 52–6, 64, 65, 66
Global One (telecom alliance), 43
goals, congruence of?, 115, 131, 133
Greenbury, 22–3, 26, 29, 31, 129, 229–30, 235, 249, 250, 281
Guinness affair, the, 7

Hampel, 23–4, 25, 247–9
Hermes, 36–7
Hewlett-Packard (HP), 41, 124, 125–6
Hoescht, 56
ICAEW, 248
Institute of Directors, the, 9, 24–5
Italy, 45

Japan, 20, 38, 43, 44, 59–61, 65, 66
John Lewis Partnership, 41, 238, 252–3

Kairetsu, 60

301

APPENDIX B

Krupp-Thyssen, 38, 40, 54–5

legislation, dangers of, 10–11, 23–4, 31–2, 130, 245, 270

Marks & Spencer, 43, 241, 253
military analogy, the, 104–5, 109, 163
morality and the corporation, 17–18, 118, 119, 128, 139

NAPF, 248
NED (*see* Non-Executive Directors)
Netherlands, The, 40, 64
Non-Executive Directors (NEDs), 9, 36, 52, 60, 62, 73, 102, 108, 148, 219, 221, 222, 223, 251, 281
   role of, 106–8, 251–2

Ost, Michael, 39
ownership and control, separation of, 13, 16, 20

PA Charter, the, 41, 126–7
PIRC (Pensions & Investment Research Consultants), 10, 36, 46, 47, 116–7, 235
planning
   resources, 203–4
   organisational change, 204–5
Porter, Michael, 163, 175, 176, 196, 201
power/interest matrix, 186–9
pressures on a company, 130
privatisation, effect of, 6
Project Management, 205–7
PRONED, 9
Proshare, 23

Renault, 43, 44

Sainsbury, 196
shareholders
   activism, 35, 36–7, 59, 61, 62–3, 116–7
   responsibility, 15, 35–39, 142, 237
   voting restrictions, 53, 57
Shell, 45, 46–7, 118, 140
Spain, 43–4, 119
stakeholder
   perceptions, 139, 142, 143, 159, 181, 183, 184, 185, 207
   expectations, 125, 131, 147, 150, 157, 159, 162, 166, 167, 168, 170, 174, 175, 182, 184, 185, 186, 188, 189, 190, 191, 192, 198, 199, 201, 202, 213, 216, 221, 231
Stock Exchange, the, 22, 37, 114–6, 235, 247
strategy
   direction and methods of development, 197–8
   evaluation and selection of, 198–202
   long-term evaluation of, 208
   Porter's generic strategies, 196–7
strengths/attractiveness matrix, 192

Telefónica, 44
Tesco, 196

Unipart, 238, 239, 252
Unisource (telecoms alliance), 44
Unisys, 270–1
Utilities, 6

Weighting (of stakeholders), 127, 129, 131, 136, 141, 147, 150, 153, 181, 185–9, 204